The Guardians of Art

Conversations with Major Collectors

LA FABRICA

Dani Levinas

To Pelu
À toi ma vie

Introduction

Down through the ages, the world has always been rocked by changes. Yet, in our time, turmoil and unforeseen, transformative events seem to be ever more frequent and their consequences more far-reaching and unpredictable. Our everyday lives are touched by pandemics, wars, climate disasters, new technology, promising and menacing in equal measure, fragile economies mired in misery and inequality, and political regimes sustained on repression and lack of freedom. Experts are just as puzzled as ordinary citizens in the face of the multitude of different revolutions that jolt our existence.

The art world is not immune from what's happening. It is undergoing profound and often incomprehensible mutations that change production, techniques, materials, technology, the offer of artworks and their new distribution channels. And all this coincides with a boom in demand driven by a growth in new markets, museums, collections and sources of funding, and by the appearance of millions or individuals and families all over the world who, for the first time, are beginning to buy art.

How can we understand what is going on? How reliable are the predictions of critics, gallerists and auction houses? There is no easy answer. What we do know are the decisions to buy and sell of major collectors, and these are what are shaping today's artworld. Big collectors are not interesting for what they say—and many of them prefer to say little and avoid interviews—but for what they do.

In his poem *Las dos linternas*, from 1846, the Spanish poet Ramón de Campoamor wrote: '*De Diogenes compré un día / la linterna a un mercader / Distan la suya y la mía / cuanto hay de ser a no ser / Blanca la mía parece / La suya parece negra / La de* él *todo lo entristece / La mía todo lo alegra / Y es que en el mundo traidor / Nada hay verdad ni mentira / Todo es según el color / del cristal con que se mira.*'[1]

Campoamor could hardly have imagined the reach and varied uses to which these last two lines would be put, right up to the present day. It sprung to mind when I started to think about writing this foreword, along with a reflection by Robert Therrien, the great US sculptor who once said, 'there is a diversity in the way people see. Some always see flat. Others always in perspective.'

Despite their different centuries, circumstances and nationalities, yet secretly united by a shared spirit, Campoamor and Therrien knew well what they were talking about. And I was able to see it for myself when conducting each one of the interviews compiled in this book, a reflection of the essence of the dozens of men and women from around the world who feature in it. I admired them all beforehand, and much more now after having gotten to know them in greater depth.

What was it that I wanted to find out when approaching these fascinating elite art collectors, often reluctant to shed their low profiles? Several things. I wanted to know why they collect, what was their original motivation and what keeps them motivated. How they do what they do, and what has allowed them to get as far as they have. Why do they so stubbornly wish to share their passion with the wider public and bring art to the greatest number of people possible, even when this effort can be economically draining. And what drives them in that rare form of generosity we call philanthropy.

I also wanted to know how good collections help artists, why the most notable ones end up in museums, how the task they have undertaken helps to tighten the bonds between society and age-old humanist values and why, in an apparently soulless world, so many of them collect without any interest other than the purely artistic. Finally, I wanted to show that anyone can start to collect, though it is not always an easy road.

I spoke to them all from my own personal experience, with the greatest humility, respect and admiration possible. I am immensely grateful that all of them invited me into their homes and answered my questions so frankly and warmly.

Whether their thing is conceptual contemporary art, Rembrandt or Rothko, what distinguishes these men and women is a particular way of seeing the world. A way and, once again, a color: the color of the glass through which they look. Which, in their case, is beautiful and astoundingly original.

Dani Levinas

---

1. 'One day from a merchant / I bought Diogenes's lantern / His and mine are as far apart / as being and non-being / White mine seems / His black / His, everything saddens / Mine, everything gladdens / For in this treacherous world / There is no truth nor lie / It all depends on the color / of the glass you look through.'

Alain Dominique Perrin

‘Contemporary art is freedom’

Daniel Boudinet, *Parc de la Fondation Cartier à Jouy-en-Josas*, 1988

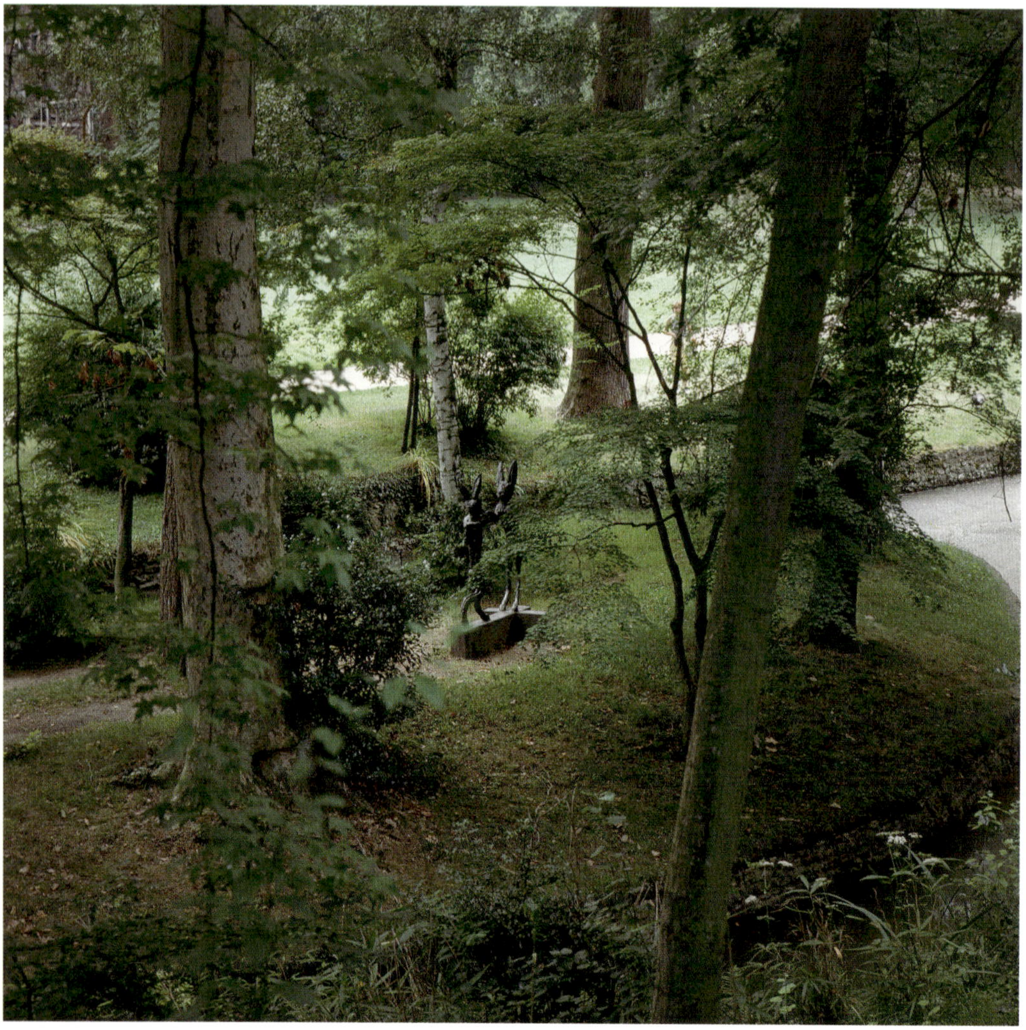

At 75, Alain Dominique Perrin (Nantes, 1942) has never lost his good habits. This French executive, art collector and creator of the Cartier Foundation, has always managed to be at the forefront of whatever field he sets his sights on. And that's not likely to change at this point. Some people show the way, others help mark it, and many others walk it. And Perrin never seems to tire of pointing out new avenues. Made boss of Cartier in 1975, from that position he expanded the luxury industry. And among his decisions, the most audacious was to create, in 1984, a foundation for contemporary art. One that lights up Montparnasse today. It is not only what the foundation has done, but the way in which, a long time later, initiatives from other leading companies in the luxury industry have copied those ideas. Today they are the norm, part of a reality that is funded more from the private sector than from the public.

That strange impulse owed a lot to the political context of France in the mid-1980s. Perrin says, with that characteristic tone of his that some might take for pedantic but actually hides a confidence in his own ideas, that it was an arduous task. 'After Mitterrand was elected [as president of France], the Socialists became fashionable and we were faced with the need to transform ourselves into key players not only in our sector, but in society. So even though Cartier was already a world-renowned brand, we decided to focus on business and patronage. To that end, we created the foundation, with the idea of helping contemporary artists to find subsidies and money from the private sector to give them the economic freedom with which to create. This was an uphill task, because contemporary art did not exist as such.'

The sculptor César Baldaccini, godfather of the foundation, was key from the beginning. He chose the right emplacement and helped Perrin materialize the extravagant idea decades before one could imagine today's craze for contemporary art, with its fairs, galleries, bank collections, museums and individuals. Romantic as it may sound, this wasn't just a corporate expansion strategy. It was also philanthropy in the best sense. Beyond its usefulness for deducting taxes, it enriches the society these initiatives are aimed at.

After Jacques Chirac was elected President and François Léotard was appointed Minister of Culture, Perrin played a key role in what later became a pioneering patronage law, which allowed for corporate deductions to encourage the acquisition of contemporary art.

'At least, I opened a door, starting from a very simple argument: Why the hell can I deduct taxes for my investment in football, but not in art? Isn't this a civilized country? The important thing, then, was to choose: Where do you want to help? Art, soccer or medical research?' he recalls. And, dryly, he adds: 'This is very French, but when I opened the foundation, the project was unique in Europe and everyone was waiting for it to fail. But they were disappointed: it turned out to be a great success and everyone reacted accordingly. And so, thirty years later, Bernard Arnault chose to open the Louis Vuitton Foundation on the same day that we were celebrating our thirtieth anniversary. He was surrounded by [President François] Hollande and celebrities, but the great artists were with us.'

Perrin highlights the way the foundation is funded: 90% by Cartier and 10% by suppliers who work with the brand and, of course, by individuals. Buying work, mounting and holding exhibitions and maintaining the spectacular building that Jean Nouvel gave birth to in 1994, costs over ten million euros per year. About two million are recovered through the sale of books, catalogs and tickets. 'After all this time, we have a true family of artists, who are our friends that understand and share the identity of the foundation, like Guillermo Kuitca and David Lynch.'

When I ask him about the rules governing this closed world, he explains: 'Hervé Chandès is the director and, although I have the right to veto, I have only exercised it twice in thirty-three years, like when I refused to do an exhibition by the photographer David Hamilton. Essentially, he is the boss.' After that clarification, he responds with the determination of someone who has taken decisions—whether as a student, a manager, a businessman or collector—without being racked by doubt: 'The budget, the accounting and planning of the exhibitions is the responsibility of the Executive Committee of the foundation, where around forty people work, five of whom are curators. But the rules have always been clear: to hold an annual thematic exhibition completely open to the public and not to mix Cartier with the foundation, so that artists do not work with the company and we are not suspected of favoritism. That means we can help them promote their work without asking for anything in return. This is extremely rare and, although our style has been copied, putting together thematic exhibitions with such coherence and depth, like the ones we have dedicated to Ferrari, rock and roll, mathematics, or the 60s, is not something the competition has been able to replicate,' he claims.

Poisoned darts fired toward the tail end of the conversation with Perrin as night falls and electric light floods the top floor of Fondation Cartier with the arrogance and elegance only Paris is capable of. But there is more to come from this Commander of the Legion of Honor. 'The luxury industry has put its money behind contemporary art, although I fear that this might lead to it being excessively fashionable and becoming too expensive and exclusive.' And he concludes: 'Although what people like François Pinault have done is admirable, we must be careful not to go too far or lose sight of the fact that, basically, contemporary art is freedom.'

With the hope that Fondation Cartier will become a permanent part of the DNA of the French brand, the conversation draws to an end. Centuries of wisdom hanging over the late evening in Paris seem to repeat, like the general and politician José de San Martín: 'You will be what you must be, or else you will be nothing.' A quote we could well attribute to Perrin.

Guillermo Kuitca, *Untitled (Peep Show and Video Booths)*, 1999

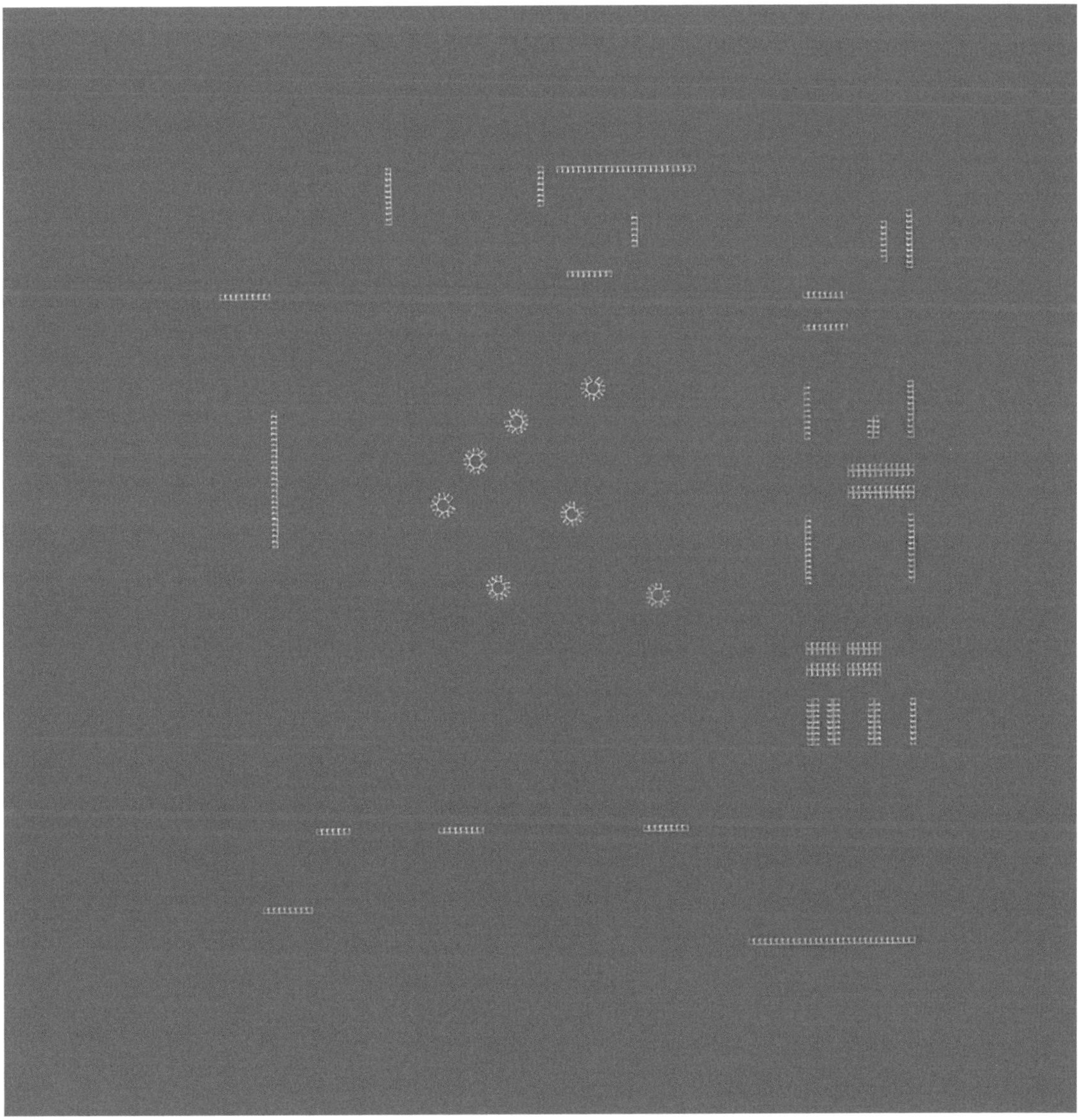

Rosa de la Cruz

‘In a collection, the word “logic” is more important than the word “love”’

Ana Mendieta, *Untitled*, 1985

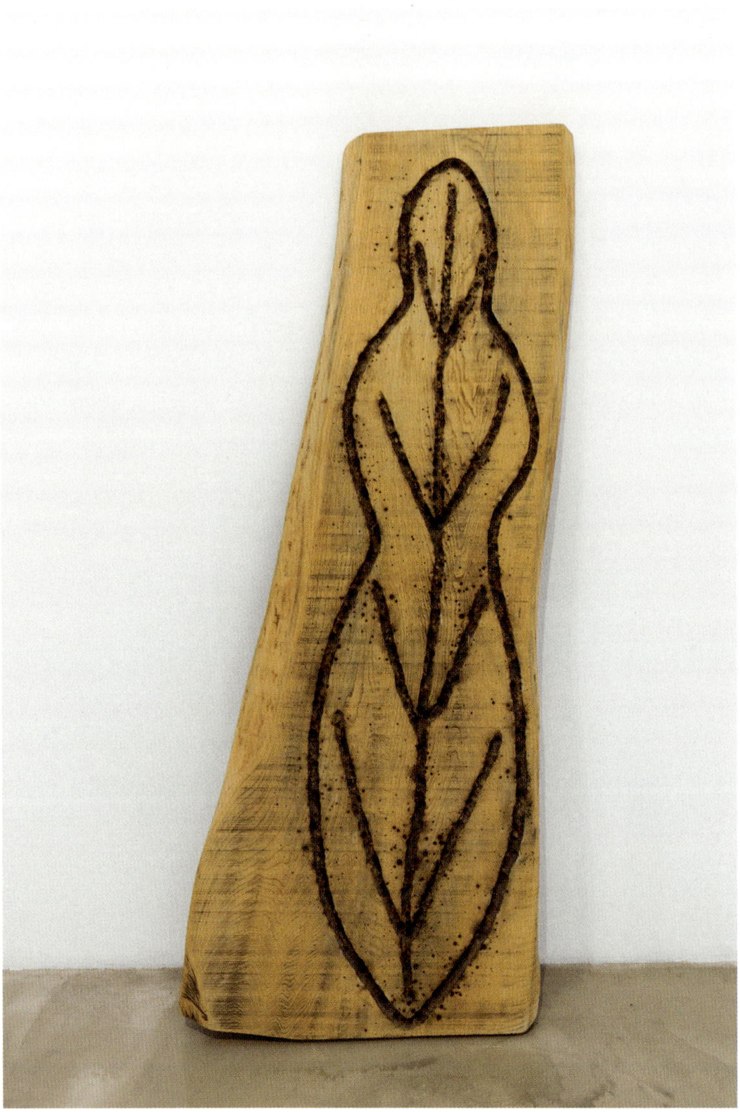

In the 1950s, a woman called Dolores Suero Falla commissioned Salvador Dali to paint her portrait. Years later, her daughter-in-law, Rosa de la Cruz, continues to honor that early vocation as a patron of the arts in a very personal way. Based in Miami, de la Cruz and her husband Carlos are the owners of one of the most important collections of contemporary art in the world. And her triumph, beyond the list of virtues one supposes inherent to all collectors, is above all a triumph of the will.

One can immediately detect the determination in Rosa's gaze, the same unique eye that has allowed her to bring together so many exceptional artworks. In her home, and even more in her museum, open and free to the public since 2009 in the Design District in Miami, there is room for such diverse names as Dan Colen, Kathryn Andrews, Jim Hodges, Martin Kippenberger or Sterling Ruby.

Faced with the old prejudice that presupposes foundations to be mere facades for lobbying, vanity or tax exemptions, de la Cruz, whose frankness sets her apart in a world where pretense is often confused with diplomacy, proposed an alternative model. Because, in fact, her collection is not a foundation and does not receive state funding of any description, a decision taken deliberately by the couple. 'I don't remember how we got started, because we were always interested in art, but the collection, which dates to around thirty years ago, is really Carlos's and mine, and even though everyone asks how we manage to agree, the truth is that we always get there,' Rosa says before going on to clarify that 'before and after creating the museum, our home has always been open to anyone who wants to see the collection.'

What is the secret to putting together a set of recognizable works with an identity and an esthetic sense that furthermore is not anachronistic in any way? 'Knowing that collecting art is not just accumulating works that are the result of random impulses,' she responds.

'Even if we can afford it, we don't buy everything we like. Instead, we evaluate whether there is room for the work in the collection and whether it can be integrated coherently. And it's not something you can do from one day to the next. In a collection, the word "logic" is more important than the word "love", and we believe that in order to acquire new work we must adhere to strict discipline in order to avoid having a mere assortment and losing focus. This way, when we think an artist fits in, we acquire a group of works large enough to produce an exhibition. When I buy an artwork, I always think of exhibiting it so the public can enjoy it. If I can't show it, what's the point? I'm not interested in warehousing,' explains de la Cruz, who started buying works by artists such as Mark Bradford, Ana Mendieta and Felix Gonzalez-Torres long before they hit the limelight.

Rosa de la Cruz does not believe that her vision of contemporary art is more audacious today than in the beginning. 'At first, we focused on Latin-American art that was more classical, less daring. But at some point, we realized that those works had to be purchased at auction or at exorbitant prices if we expected to maintain the high quality. And that is when we transitioned to contemporary art, which is a way of understanding what is happening right now instead of exploring what has already transpired.'

Referring to the boom in the arts in Miami, she believes that 'Art Basel has helped, but even if the city has improved thanks to museums and collections dedicated to contemporary art, it still has a serious problem, and that is the lack of a network of top-end galleries.'

De la Cruz is also concerned about inequality. The couple fund educational projects for underprivileged children through leading institutions in Florida, though this is not something they care to publicize because philanthropy has a definite and nonnegotiable essence that does not seek publicity. It is what exemplifies the de la Cruzes and what has made Rosa such a very special woman in the artworld. 'What is ours, from the electricity to the works in the museum, is paid by us and should not be deductible,' she claims.

She concludes, 'when we are no longer here, I don't know what will happen to the museum because our children, even though they are interested in art, don't live here. We wouldn't want to leave them with a burden or an obligation to have to continue.'

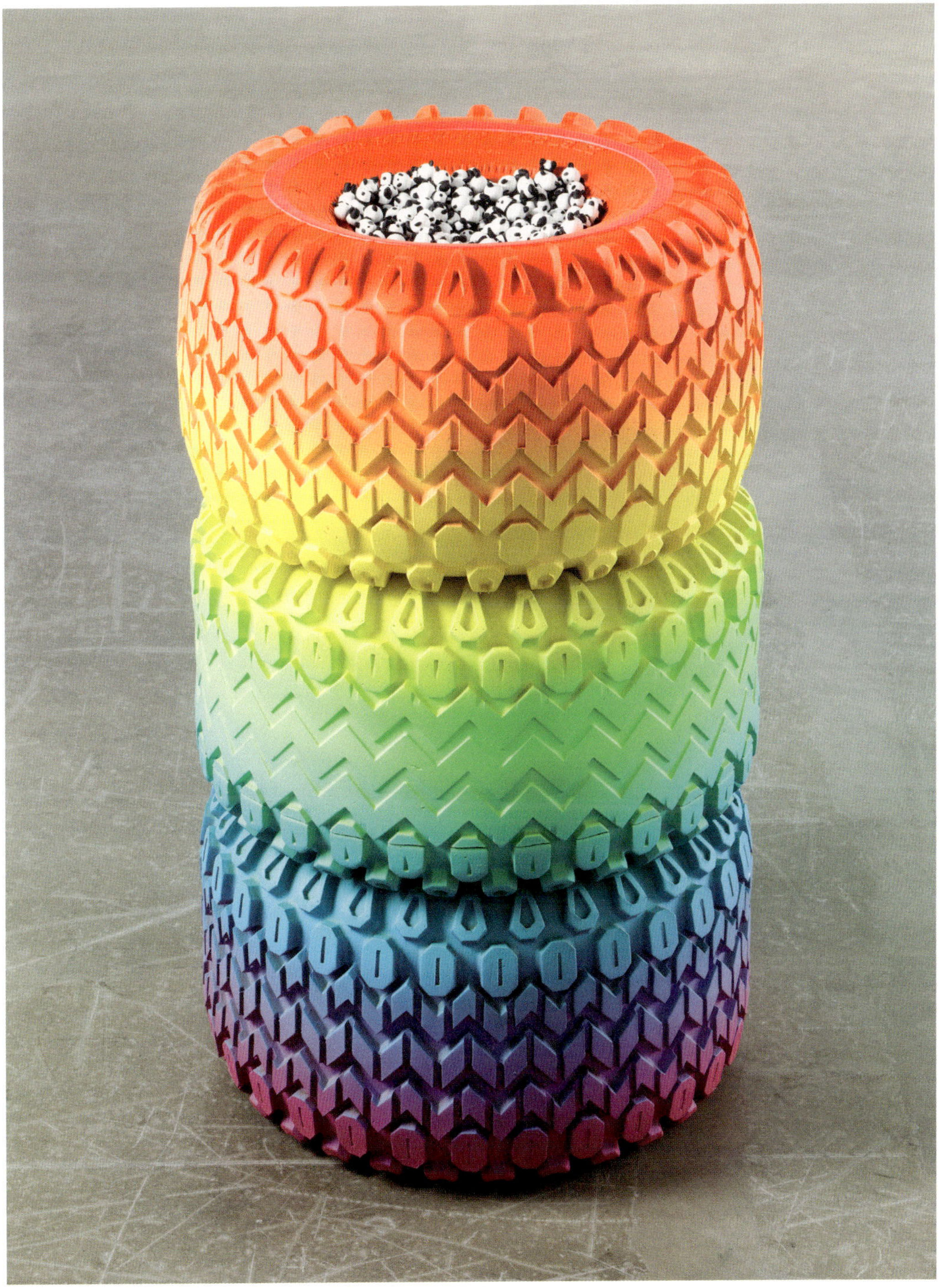

Rob Pruitt, *Panda Erasers (Spectrum)*, 2012

Helga de Alvear

'Art should be free'

Rachel Whiteread, *Drill*, 2008

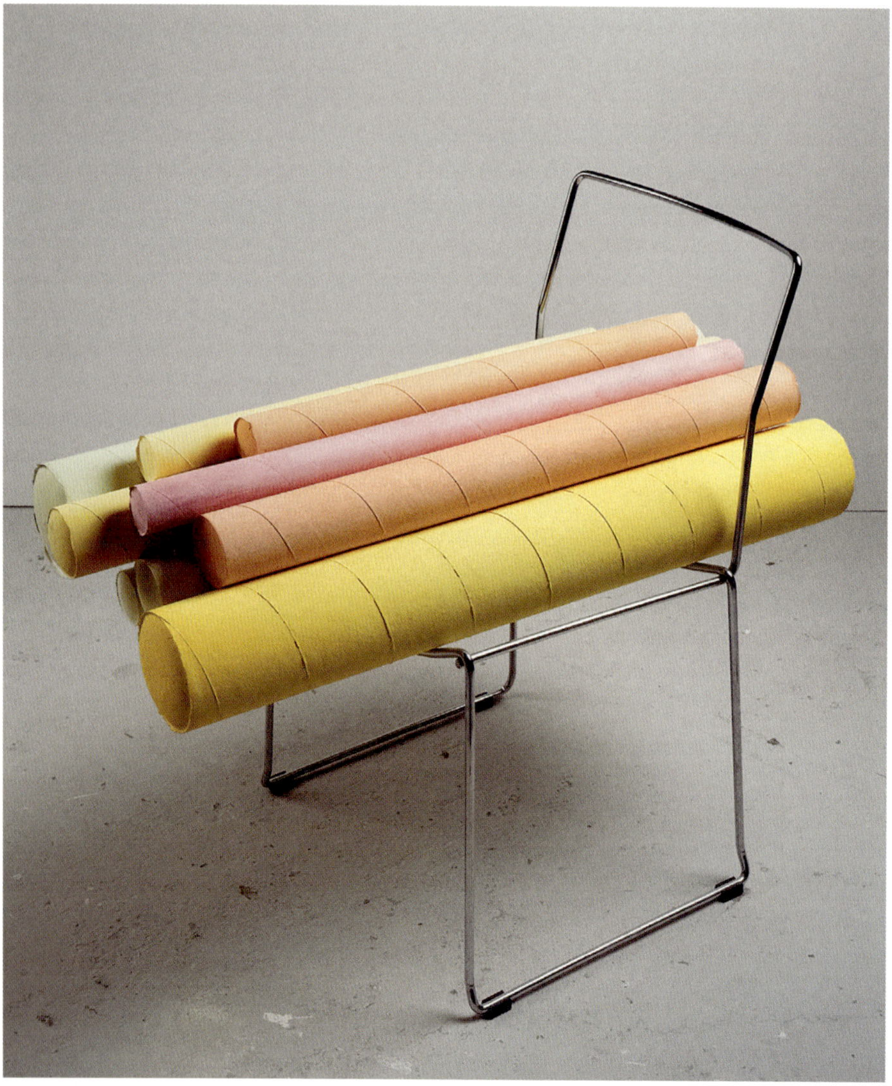

There's a woman in the art world who doesn't give a fig about what you think. And that is largely the key to her success. Helga de Alvear (Kira, Germany,1936), a collector and gallerist settled in Spain for decades now, has reaped success precisely because she is not overly concerned with what others think and relies on an unerring taste that is not swayed by the pantheon of demigods adored at the altar of changing fads. This is the spirit that presides over the work at her gallery in Madrid as well as at the Visual Arts Center bearing her name in Caceres.

Helga's romance with art started a little over half a century ago. Since that early first purchase—a work by Fernando Zobel—a long and valuable time has passed, which this intuitive German-born woman, for whom academic formality is completely alien, has worked to her advantage. 'Paint your village and you will paint the world,' goes the refrain. And that is what Helga de Alvear does when purchasing following her heart, putting together a set of works that narrate her life and her surrounding world; a mosaic with no meaning outside itself, but with a profound, modern and beautiful significance within its context, giving rise to one of the best European collections of contemporary art.

My meeting with de Alvear was as authentic, unaffected and cheerful as she is herself. It happened shortly before her name would hit the headlines with her decision to remove Santiago Sierra's work *Political Prisoners in Contemporary Spain* from her gallery's space at the ARCO fair, igniting a debate over freedom of expression.

Helga started out collecting stones when she was very young, a time she remembers with a weight that her country's history has imprinted on her expression. Much later would come her encounter with the gallerist Juana Mordó, which would change her life forever. A life which could well borrow the title of Michael Haneke's film *71 Fragments of a Chronology of Chance*.

Her encounter with Juana Mordó and the reason why she stayed in Spain were pure chance. She had come to learn Spanish and met the architect Jaime de Alvear. What follows is a success story to which her 9000 square feet gallery pays good testimony. Neighboring the Reina Sofia Museum, it focuses on bold and provocative works of contemporary art, with an emphasis on video, installation and photography. Helga has been honored with several distinctions, such as the Medal of Honor for Merit in the Fine Arts. And from there, she has become something like the Johan Cruyff of contemporary collecting.

How does Helga de Alvear find what she buys, for example the Tàpies which hangs in front of us during our conversation? 'I saw this painting and I fell

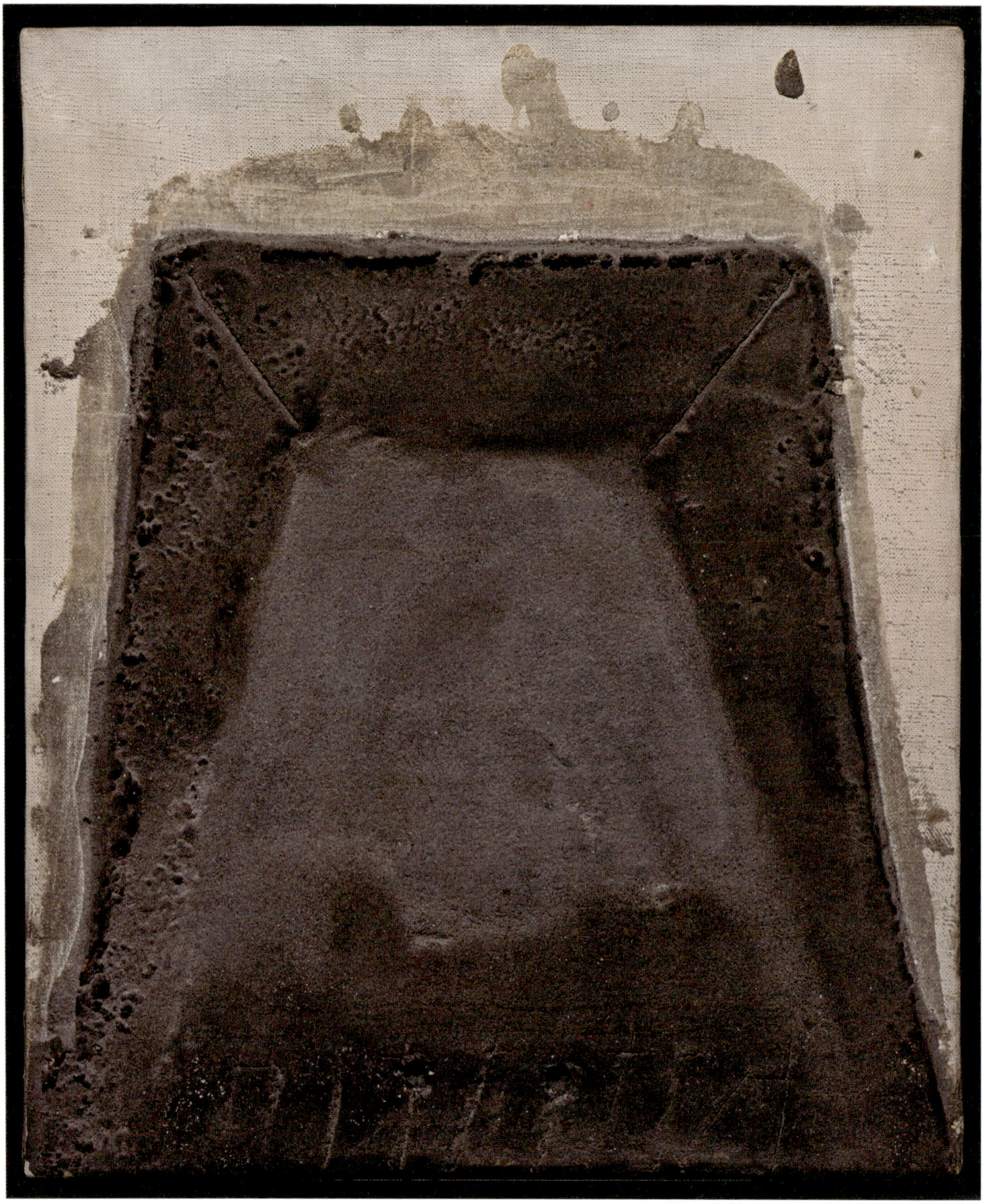

Antoni Tàpies, *Trapecio*, 1964

in love. I don't look for anything. I buy at fairs from my colleagues and other gallerists, and I pay for everything properly, as it should be, because I'm creating culture, do you understand? I fall in love with very different things, and that's why the artists from the collection as well as the artists on the gallery roster form a very eclectic grouping,' she points out when asked about the criteria by which she chooses, and immediately fires one of her darts: 'I believe that, because of its social function, art should be free but, of course, artists need to earn a living.'

With the same openness she tells us that beyond the continuity of her foundation in Caceres, her historical gallery in Madrid will not outlive her. Refusing to succumb to melancholic thoughts, Helga returns to her enthusiastic tone. 'The truth is that I wanted to be a pianist and my father, who started out from nothing and rose to become a prominent industrialist, wouldn't let me because he didn't want my brother or me to go to the university. So, I said to myself, "then it will be languages." So I went to Switzerland, then to England and finally I came to Madrid to study Spanish. I fell in love and I stayed. It was the only time I saw my father cry. Don't get me wrong, my father was very fond of my husband who was very engaging and built social housing because he was not interested in being an elite architect. I suppose that's where I get this thing about sharing and not holding on to things.'

Something for which it's difficult not to admire her, even when, in a typical demonstration of character, Helga declared publicly a few days after this interview and the scandalous censorship of a work by Santiago Sierra about alleged political prisoners in her stand at the ARCO fair: 'IFEMA is the host and if the host asks me to take down a work, I take it down. Yet, as my artist, I am completely behind Santiago, I give him whatever he wants and I defend him, whether people like it or not.'

Irrespective of whether you agree with her or not, who could deny her loyalty to her own principles?

Aaron and Barbara Levine

'Many people buy fashionable art as though they were bonds. Besides being harmful, that bubble is not sustainable'

Juan Muñoz, *Stuttering Piece*, 2009

The fashionable eyeglasses Barbara and Aaron Levine wear, which give the finishing touch to their personal image, are not a sign of superficiality, but rather just the first hint of eccentricity that hits you when you meet these two major players in the contemporary art world, whose passion for collecting has not diminished with the passing of time. And when passion dictates, trips to Europe, discreet searches and unplanned purchases are at the order of the day.

The Levines have been widely recognized for the coherence and zeal with which they have channeled their curiosity for contemporary art, understood chronologically and conceptually, and therefore often hard to absorb at first sight. They respond graciously and don't deny what it is that has made them unique. 'We tend to lean toward the conceptual, the idea over the object, and what we consider thought out, following Marcel Duchamp's principle that says that the artist goes halfway, and the observer must do the rest to complete the piece. The intellectual challenge that is behind each artwork: that is what really excites us,' Aaron explains with his venerable voice, assertive tone and kindly manner.

With a fragility that is only apparent and with a more nuanced diction, Barbara interrupts to correct him. 'Not everything you see here is conceptual, as you can appreciate in the work of artists such as William Kentridge. What we mostly rely on is on what inspires us. That is why sometimes we buy thoughtlessly: over and above whether the artist is known or unknown, we simply love it. And, you know? It's funny, but when you get home, you hang a new artwork on the wall and it starts to speak with the piece next to it, and it in turn starts telling you things it hadn't revealed before. There is something, though, in which both Aaron and I agree, and that is that many collectors buy what is theoretically better, without making mistakes and with a coolheaded approach. Whereas we are far less influenced by the market value than by the authentic passion we feel for art.' It is not surprising that David Hume stipulated that 'reason is, and should only be, a slave of the passions, and cannot expect to do anything other than to serve and obey them,' a maxim that these elite collectors—continually at the top end of art world rankings—always bear in mind.

'It is best to be excessively passionate than cold and, if you make a mistake, so be it' Barbara says, as she explains the strange metamorphosis that she and Aaron made from German Expressionism and Minimalism *tout court* to Conceptual Art. A style, she adds, in which the addition of an old masterwork by Raphael Soyer would not only not be out of place, but would enrich it. As they know well, art of a certain level never goes out of fashion.

How did these pacesetters of art collecting become enraptured by Duchamp? 'Very simple: after acquiring our first piece, about fifteen years ago, I became

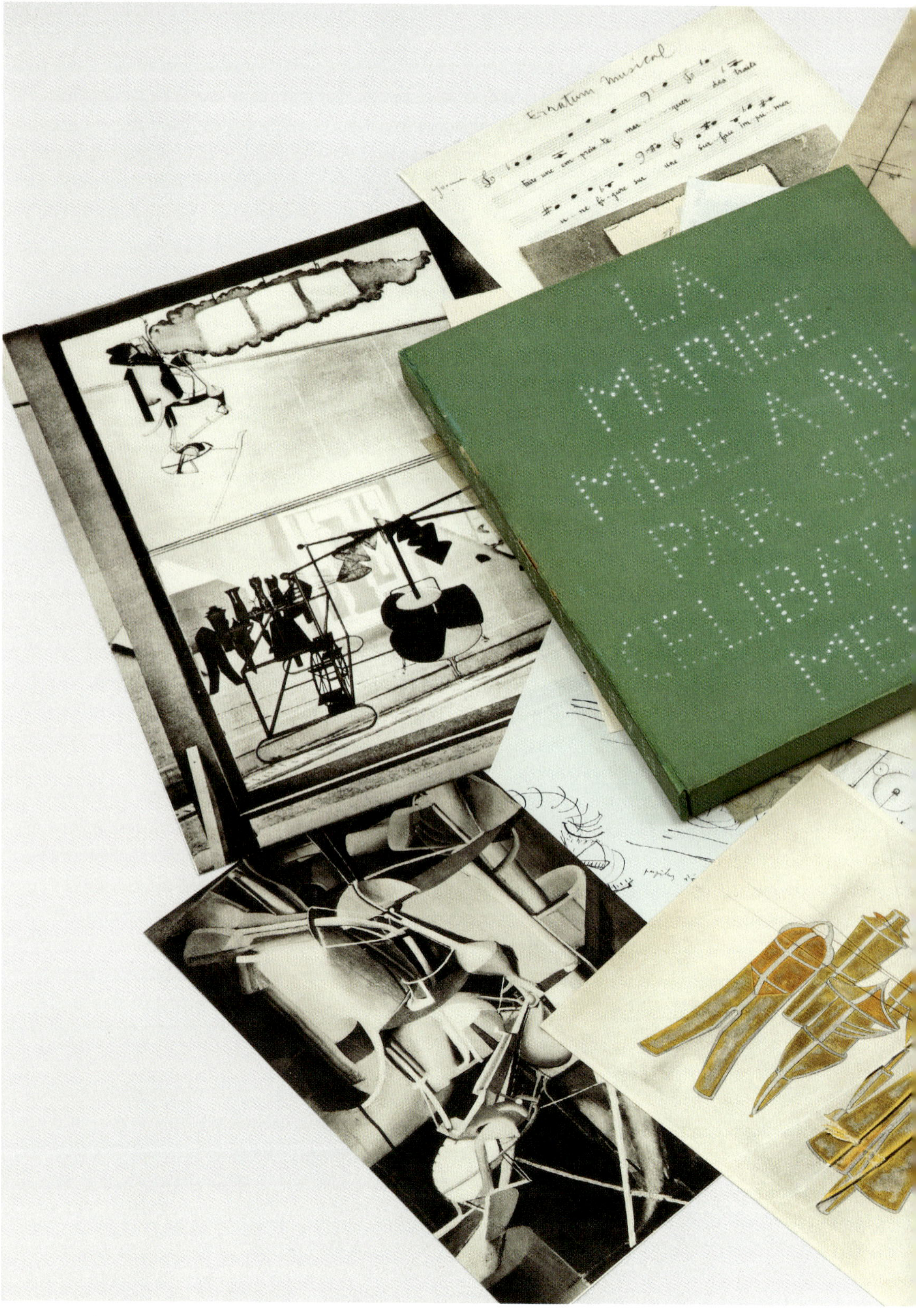

Marcel Duchamp, *La boîte verte*, 1934

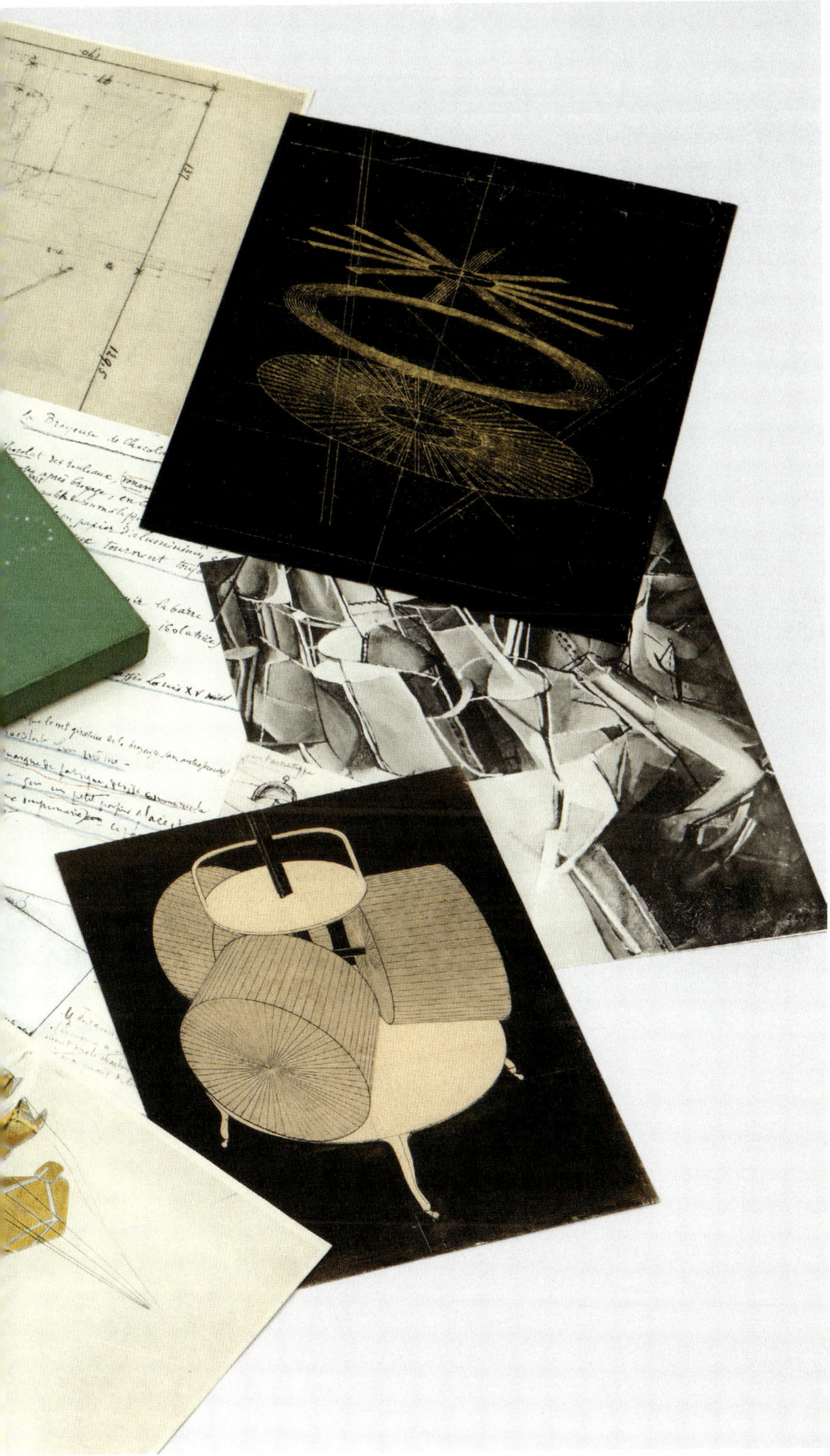

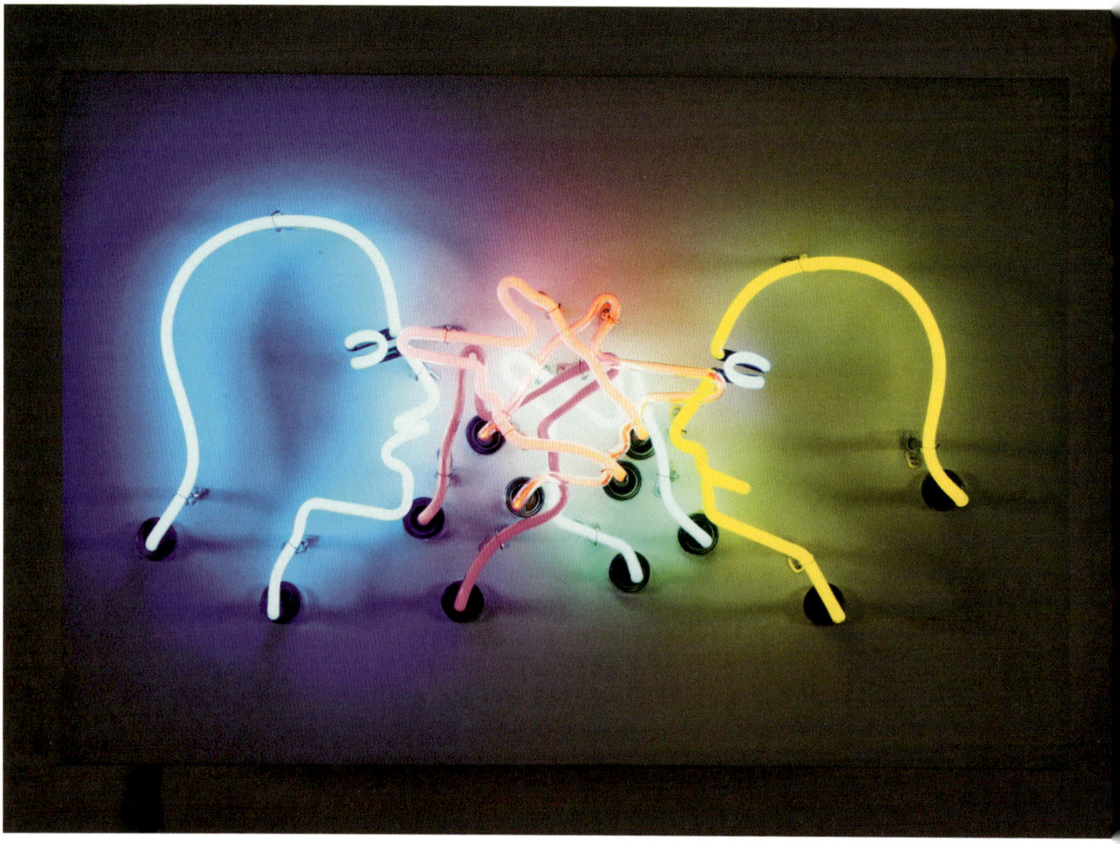

Bruce Nauman, *Double Poke in the Eye*, 1985

obsessed and didn't stop buying,' Aaron confesses laughing. And he further explains: 'Art, like music, but differently from language, can move you profoundly and act upon you in every sense. And the idea that Duchamp truly grasped the artistic universe, that he was the most revolutionary thing since the Renaissance, and that he even revealed the irrelevance of painting, it all cast a spell on me.' Wow! Would Duchamp say that painting is dead today? 'I think that the man who was capable of taking objects from our everyday lives, such as a urinal, and proclaiming them as works of art, would answer yes, that it is dead without a doubt. The idea of beauty, as it existed in the nineteenth century, has evaporated. At the end of the day, what matters more than art is the artist.'

The conversation continues apace for quite a while amid serious debate and pleasantries. At some point, Aaron, who admires and collects Warhol and On Kawara but adores Duchamp to the point of considering him part of his family, will concede: 'Ok, I won't say that Matisse is not art, but he has aged.' As one can readily acknowledge, the Levines epitomize humor and friendliness with the plainest of political incorrectness. All that remains to know from these globetrotters is how their last trip went, a trip undertaken to expand their particular and cultured vision that has so enriched the universe of collectors. 'We bought a gigantic painting by a Chinese artist who has us captivated.'

The Levines are unlikely admirers of the monk, poet and theologian Dom Sylvester Houedard as well of the curator and former director of SFMOMA Neal Benezra. They are voracious readers and pepper their collecting and philanthropy—such as the recent donation of a large part of their library to the Art Institute of Chicago, as well as the future donation of all their Duchamps to the Hirshhorn Museum in Washington DC—with magnetic words.

To end, let's take this one from Barbara: 'In the end, what is happening today in the world with records at auctions and resounding successes will be the death of artists, especially if they are young. That rhythm and pressure is not normal. Let's not forget that many people buy fashionable art as though they were bonds, and then bail out. Besides being harmful, in the long run that bubble is not sustainable.'

Did I say to end? I should have written almost. Because the last word is for Aaron who illustrates that to be bold one does not always need to be complicated: 'For us, first and foremost, collecting is a passion.'

* Aaron Levine passed away on 3 January 2023
in Washington at the age of 88.

Thomas Kaplan

‘Rembrandt transcended the classical concept of beauty’

Rembrandt van Rijn, *Self-Portrait with Shaded Eyes*, 1634

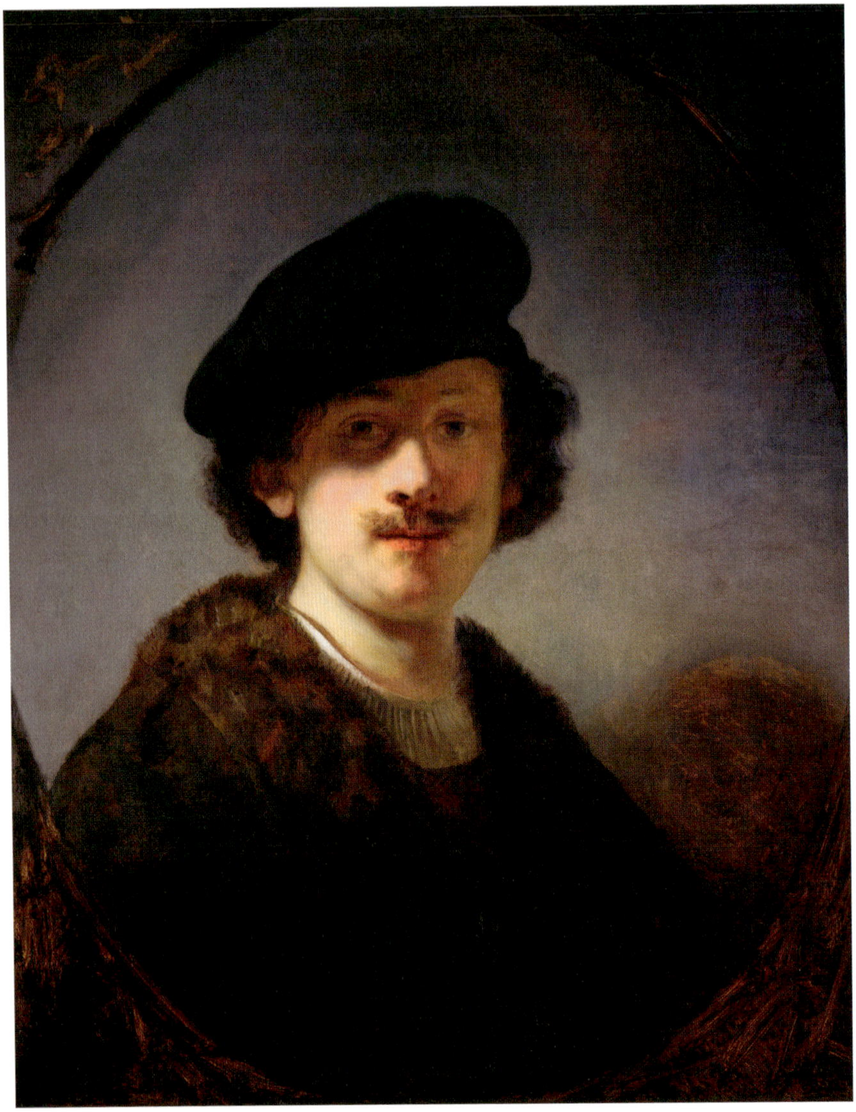

The Leiden Collection, which Thomas Scott Kaplan (New York, 1962) shares with his wife, Daphne Recanati Kaplan, boasts one of the most important groups of Flemish art in history. Are you imagining a solemn, older man? Imagine again, because this 60-year-old American is a real bundle of energy who brings his vitality, intelligence and sensibility of the collection he steers, a true treasure trove where we can find major works by Rubens, Brueghel the Younger, Vermeer and Rembrandt.

An investor and philanthropist, businessman and collector, Kaplan inherited from his father, Jason Kaplan, and from his mother, Lillian Jean Berger, a love of culture and knowledge and an intellectual curiosity, to which he has given his own personal stamp.

In the middle of an agenda demanding the attention of his many facets, this New Yorker of Jewish origin, makes time for the interview. He is not however in New York but rather in his home in the south of France, escaping the pandemic.

The conversation is by Zoom, but no less passionate or absorbing for all that. It couldn't be otherwise, because Kaplan couples the singularity of vision he has dedicated to his passions with a natural informal charm. And he does so with a polite but unconcealed self-assurance, from the beginning to the end of the conversation, in which he explains with absolute clarity the origin of his passion—or at least one of his passions, as the protection of thousands of wild cats on the verge of extinction, through the Panthera organization, is another.

'I was born in New York, and when I was eight in 1969, we moved to Florida, at a time when it was starting to flourish. It was then I discovered my passion for wildlife, although in New York I had already discovered what turned out to be another great love of my life: Rembrandt. I even remember a visit to MoMA when I was six, where my mother, in an effort to get me interested in other types of art, showed me a work of a white canvas with a single line, and apparently I told her: 'Not this! Let's go back to Rembrandt!' That infatuation has stayed with me my whole life even though I didn't start collecting until I was 42,' explains this man whose interest in History led him to study it in depth at Oxford, one of his most fondly remembered times, alongside a business trip to Israel, the Promised Land, where he met his future wife and mother of his children.

'I've always had a lot of luck, but never too much ego,' he claims as he talks about a career in which he was mentored by such giants as George Soros, and which started to take off in Bolivia thanks to Apex Silver Mines, before shifting his focus from mining to the energy industry and to the business of gold and silver. 'I was and still am passionate about things, so when I get involved in something, whether it is in my professional or personal life, I go all in,' Kaplan admits.

'Although we now buy between three to five works a year, in the early years of our collecting, we were buying, on average, one work per week,' he adds, as though he needed to apologize for spending his boundless talent in other endeavors. And to give us a better idea of the sheer scope of his collection he says: 'There are thirty-five to forty Rembrandts in private hands, and we have fourteen of them. The next largest collection is in The Netherlands, and it has two works, and after that come others such as the Rothschilds who had two but sold them to the Louvre and the Rijksmuseum.'

With a photograph of mysterious, majestic and intimidating tigers as a backdrop, the conversation with Kaplan continues apace, openly and generously. He tells us acquiring works by Rembrandt is difficult not just because of the lack of availability but also because export licenses are hard to come by. And this came in the middle of an unexpected explanation: 'During our first fifteen years collecting, my wife and I were completely unknown. If you searched on Google, you would find me for my business activities and for being "the king of cats!" We were very happy to keep a low profile. It all changed when we started to have the largest collection of Flemish masters in private hands, from Rembrandt to Vermeer, Gabriel Metsu and Frans van Mieris the Elder. At that point we agreed to relinquish our anonymity and show the full breadth of our collection, knowing full well that many would ask "Who are these people?" This new phase started with the exhibition at the Louvre in 2018 and with the publication of a large scholarly digital catalogue.'

What was that experience like? 'The Louvre can be a very difficult place to work,' Kaplan confesses openly, before qualifying 'yet it was incredibly interesting, it was very well received in the press and the public and it was well worth it. Rembrandt is the most important painter in history, not only because I love his work, which is irrelevant, rather because he transcended the classical concept of beauty and was able to define it in his own terms, preparing the ground for others who would not have existed without him and who truly idolized him, such as Goya, Delacroix, Turner, Van Gogh, Picasso, Francis Bacon and Lucien Freud. The way an artist can express himself and be accepted changed thanks to him.' For Kaplan, tolerance and humanism are part of a whole in which art is obviously also included.

'To have been instrumental in giving China a chance to appreciate Rembrandt as a universal artist more than a niche painter is another achievement we are extremely proud of,' he assures us, as he recaps the success reaped in other prestigious museums in countries as diverse as Abu Dhabi and Russia.

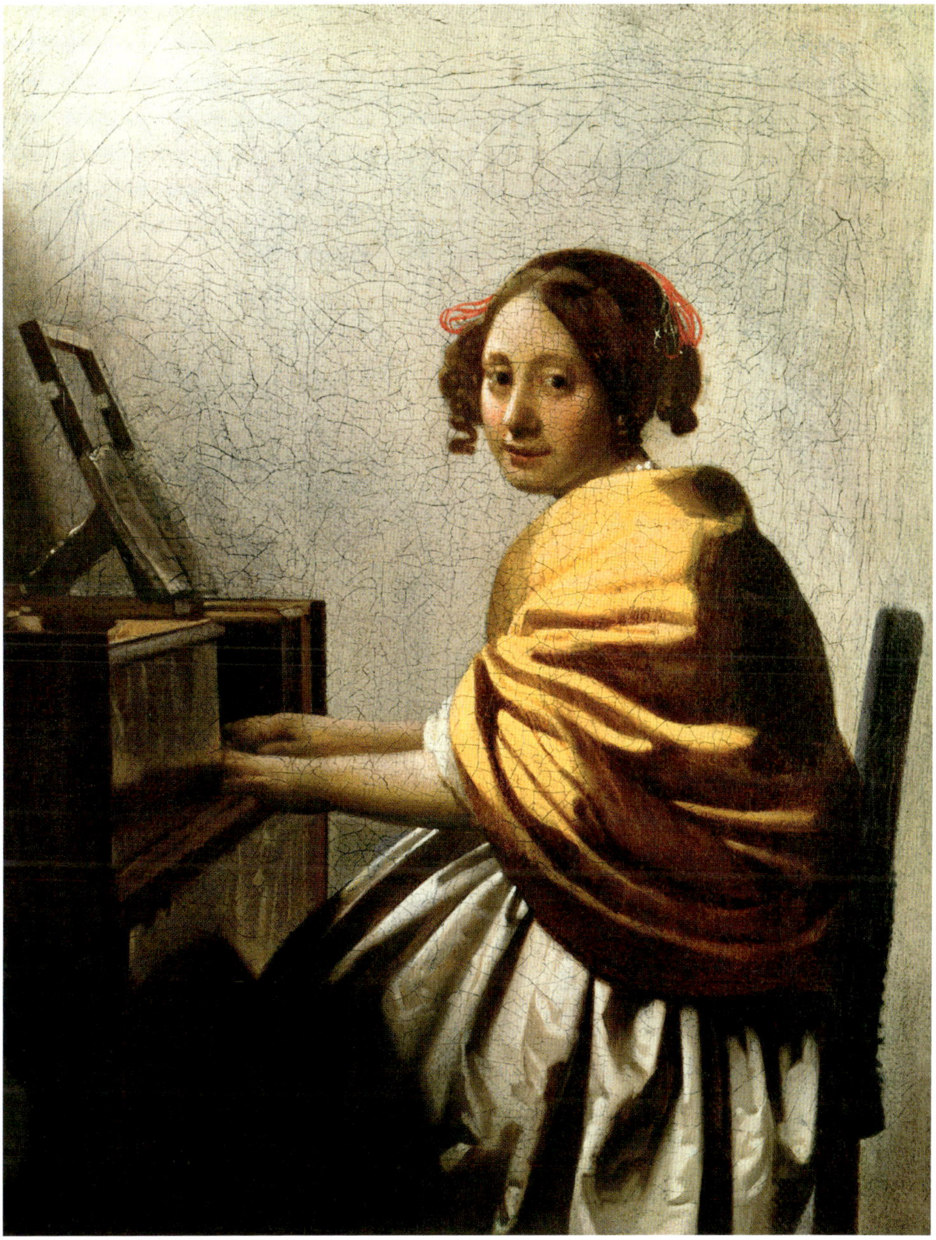

Johannes Vermeer, *Young Woman Seated at a Virginal*, ca. 1670–72

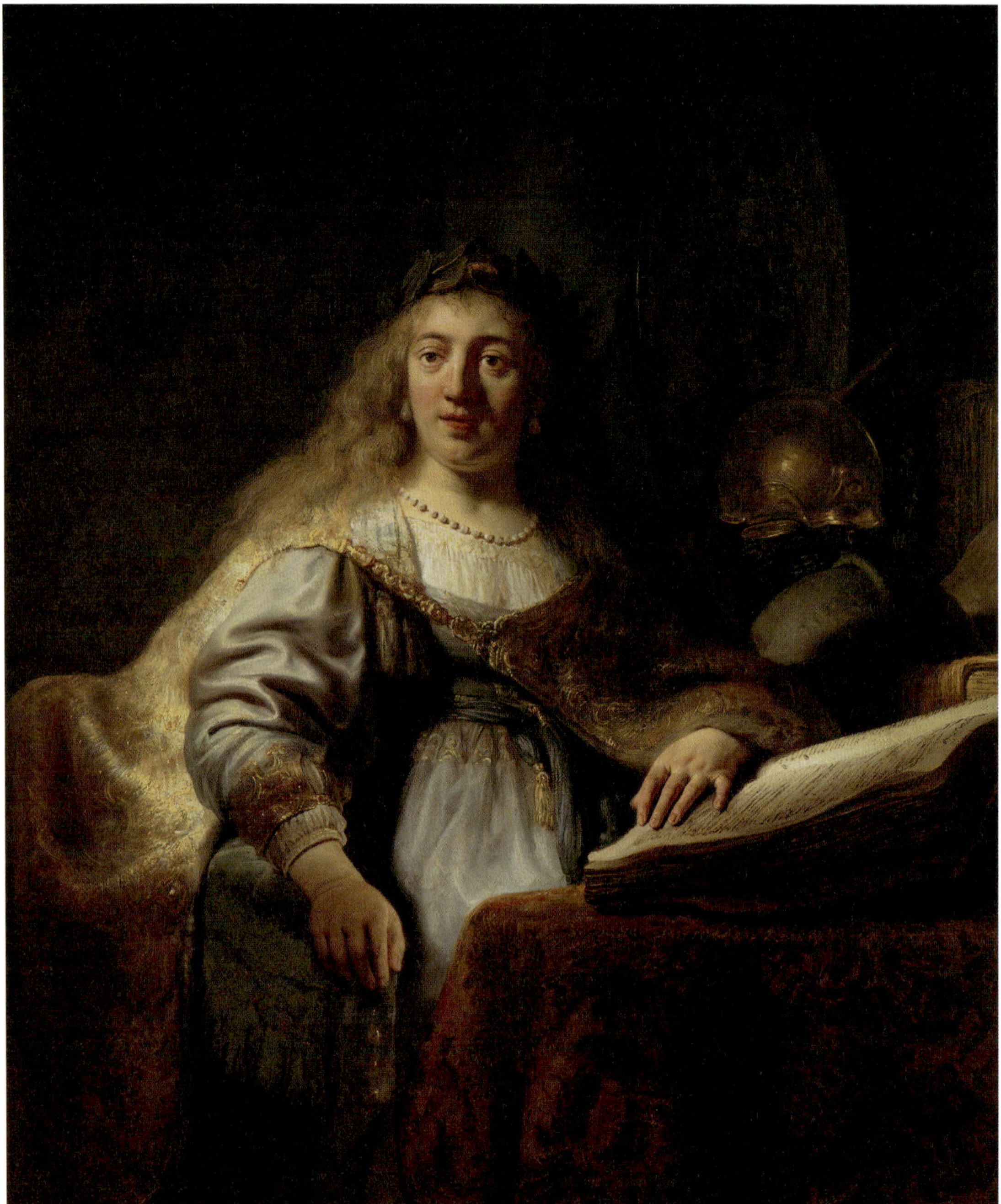

Rembrandt van Rijn, *Minerva in Her Study*, 1635

This true evangelist who travels the world preaching the virtues of painting, publishing elite catalogs that have become bestsellers, but also making this artistic wealth accessible on the internet, there is still time for another essential topic. 'Before I began collecting I had no idea that it could be feasible to acquire works by great masters, and I never imagined that I would become a collector. So self-awareness may not be my strongpoint,' he contends with a smile on his face, a surprising confession from someone who has toured the museums of Europe—including of course his beloved Amsterdam—since early childhood, and who only started to take collecting seriously after a trip to Croatia in 2003 which completely changed his perspective.

As our chat winds up, he confesses that he does not know the ultimate fate of his collection when he is longer with us, he talks about his unexpected approval of the work of Damien Hirst and Jenny Saville, of his wife's grounding in the arts and her keen eye, and also of the close relationship between Rembrandt and the Jewish world. He concludes with one of the golden rules he applies to the art market: 'From the very outset, I made it clear to dealers that they would have to be absolutely transparent, that they would never get a second chance if they did not tell me the truth, but that if they did, and I liked it, I would purchase what they had to offer me at a fair price and after negotiating for a couple of minutes. And if they didn't get the fair price they wanted, they would still be satisfied in terms of volume, because I don't know any other collector capable of buying one painting in the morning and two in the afternoon. I have come across many con artists, but also individuals who have become dear friends and professionals with exceptional ethics, like Johnny Van Haeften, the British dealer of Dutch descent. It makes me a very unusual person for auction houses, and especially for many dealers.'

Unusual, indeed, but also fascinating and fondly admired.

Giorgio Spanu

'More than a collector, I see myself as a sort of temporary custodian of what I own'

Michelangelo Pistoletto, *Adamo ed Eva*, 1962

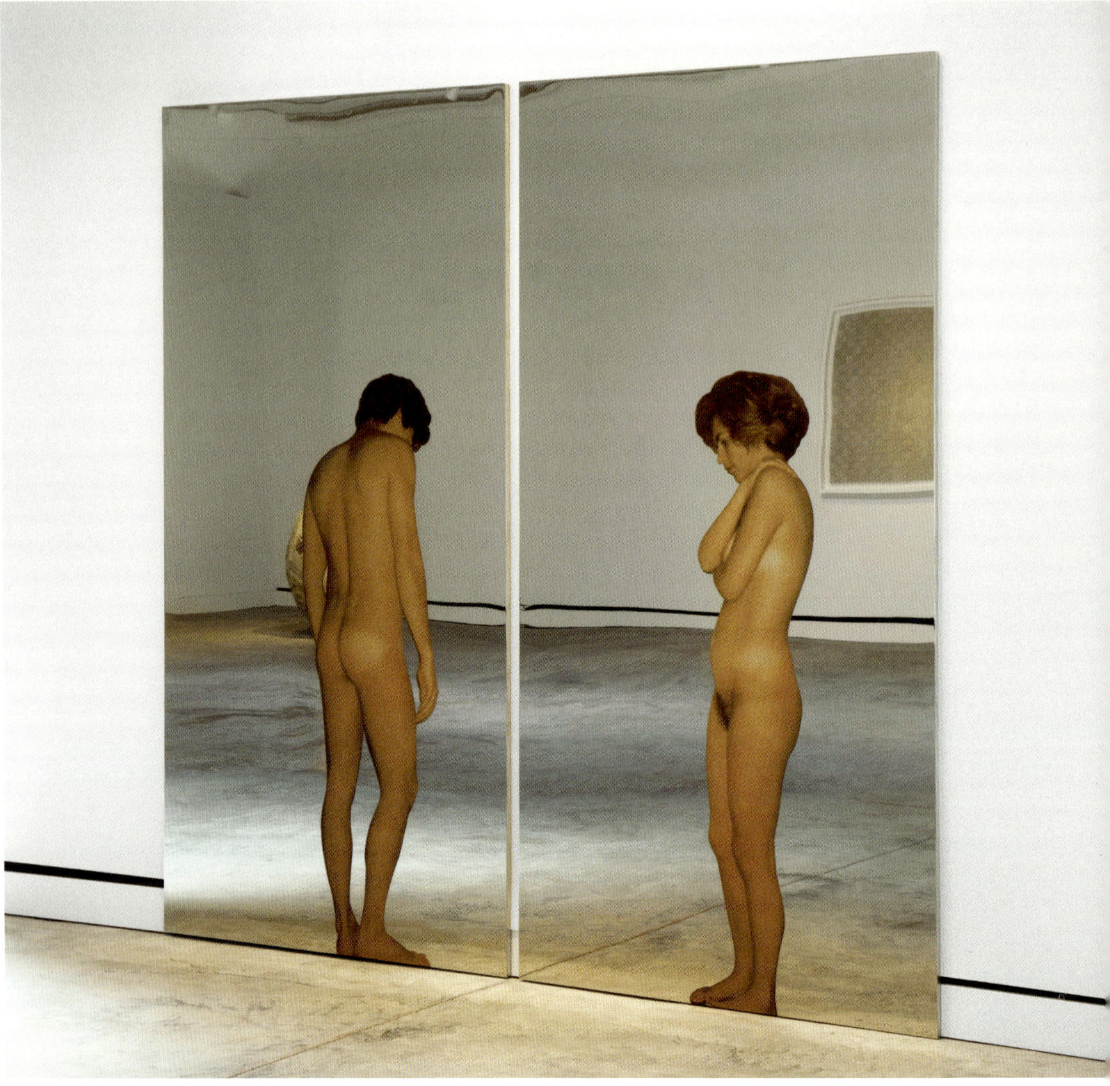

When he started buying Murano glass, it never occurred to him that the conjugation of the verb "collect" would become a constant in his life. Today, Giorgio Spanu owns Magazzino, an extraordinary museum of Italian art in Hudson River Valley, just over an hour from New York City. With the aesthetics and functionality of concrete, it is built on the rubble of an old computer factory, following the vision of the Spanish architect Miguel Quismondo. The wealth of the collection he has built in parallel to his work as an entrepreneur and real estate developer is quite unique.

Mainly because of his obsession and the specificity of his passion: Italian postwar art, especially *arte povera*. And also because nothing Spanu has achieved can be conceived without the driving force of his wife, Nancy Olnick.

With his usual low profile and a warmth of narration that conveys an inexplicable sense of familiarity, even when meeting for the first time, Giorgio speaks long and in depth. 'I do everything as a team with my wife, you know,' he clarifies with expansive enthusiasm and innate calm.

Spanu reminiscences back to his origins, at first on his own, conditioned by his love of modern art and then, from 1989 onward, together with Nancy, under a spell cast by Murano glass, the discovery of architecture as a major artistic discipline, mentoring by the great Massimo Vignelli and later by Margherita Stein, then the acquisition of about 2000 works that speak of postwar Italy as much as of the world and its spirit, and finally, numerous projects with contemporary artists like Vik Muñiz.

As he walks us through the large warehouse that is Magazzino, taking us on a tour that is more conceptual than chronological, Spanu tells his story with the same ease that John Ford used to build myths. Despite the humbleness of the elements used to produce them, the *arte povera* works shine forth in all their grandeur, thanks to the force of Michelangelo Pistoletto, Giulio Paolini, Jannis Kounellis and Mario Merz.

Thematic concerns are just as important as aesthetic ones, and it is clear that even more than a successful businessman and collector, Spanu is a true humanist. His wife—a New Yorker without whom he says 'he wouldn't have a life'—puts it a little more expressively. 'When we started out, we never even imagined we would be setting up a foundation, as will be happening soon. Truth be told, we are delighted. It is beyond our wildest dreams because, in less than one year, 25,000 visitors have come to the museum, which is not exactly located in the heart of Manhattan,' she explained.

Spanu's path is unorthodox for various reasons, and not only for the atypical partnership with his wife. He is perfectly aware of it. But he notes that

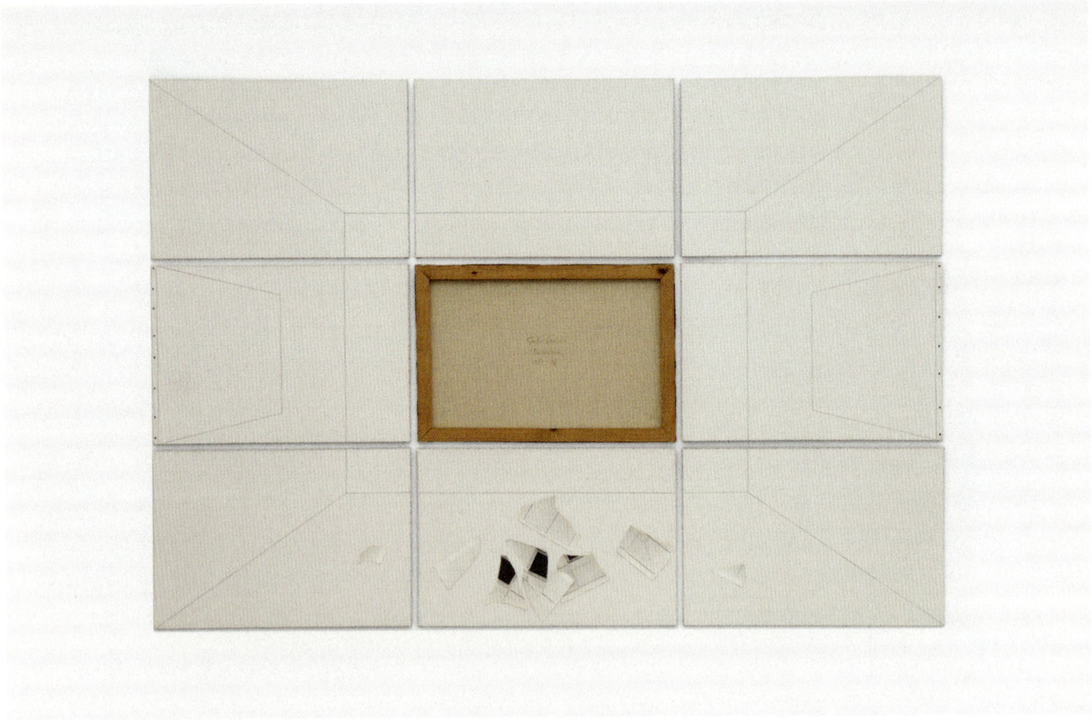

Giulio Paolini, *De Pictura*, 1977

his journey would not have been the same without the substantial contribution of the book *Museology* by Georges-Henri Rivière. And he adds, 'for me, the word "collect" has a negative connotation. More than a collector, I see myself as a sort of temporary custodian of what I own. I feel a strong sense of accountability in having the privilege of being able to purchase works of art. For this reason, I accept the responsibility of protecting them and making sure they are available for everyone to enjoy, not just now but for generations to come.'

A proud Italian and, as such, passionate about history and aesthetics, Spanu sees more advantages than disadvantages in the always ebullient and surprising world of contemporary art that is back on the front pages thanks to new records, like the one just set by the British artist David Hockney.

'One of the most notable aspects of the art world today is the global attention it attracts and the consequent greater appreciation of it. The number of art fairs dotted around the globe allows millions of people to get to know the art world without feeling intimidated,' he contends, before qualifying 'I think the problem lies in the fact that the scene is dominated more by economic incentives, rather than by pure passion.'

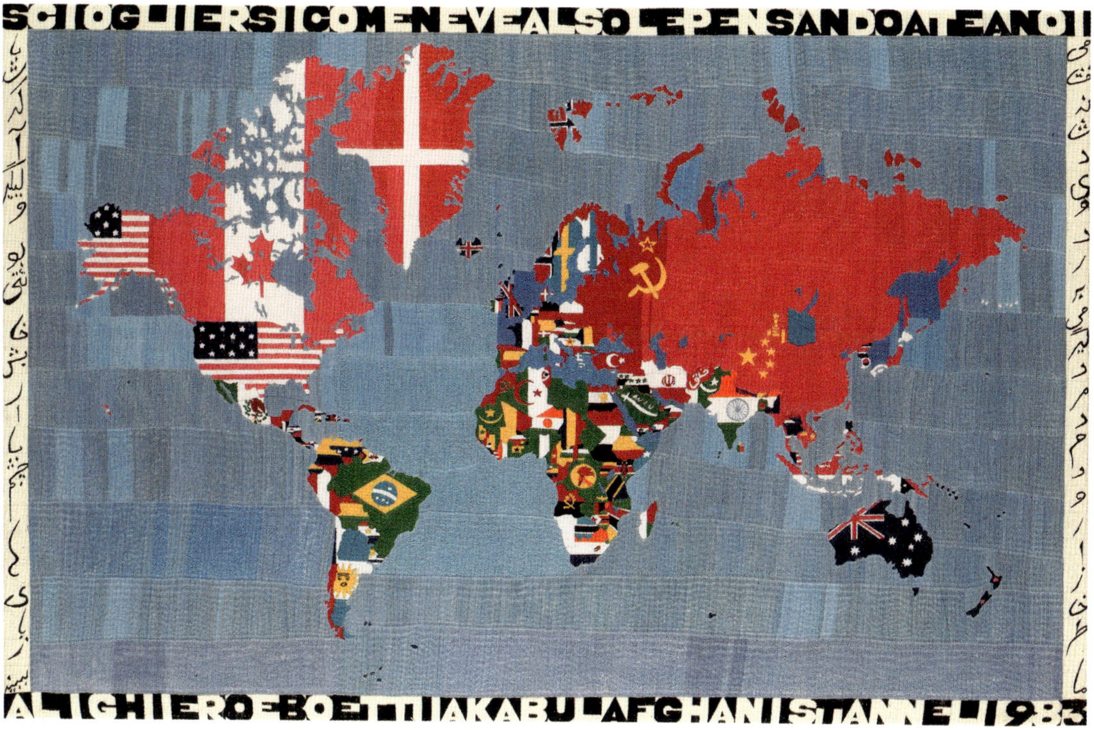

Alighiero Boetti, *Mappa*, 1983

On our walk around the museum, with his memorable stories and deep and emotive quotes, and even as the ghost of George Orwell haunts the room, there is still time for one last question. A simple one, but no less important.

—What does art mean for you?

'At first glance, art can seem unfathomable, and to many people it will always remain a true philosophical mystery. At any rate, I consider art to be truth, and as truth doesn't recognize frontiers, it is universal. Besides, art reminds me of who I am. And I think that, as a discipline, it must find its roots in popular tradition, which helps it to transmit a strong message, both political and social. Furthermore, art should also have the ability to inspire and provoke. Above all else, art is a personal experience. Or, "what sustains the artist is the look of love in the eyes of the beholder," as Henry Miller once said.'

Jan Mulder

'There has been a boom in photography as a language to collect and as a means of expression'

Javier Silva, *Rostro con peces, Iquitos*, 1996

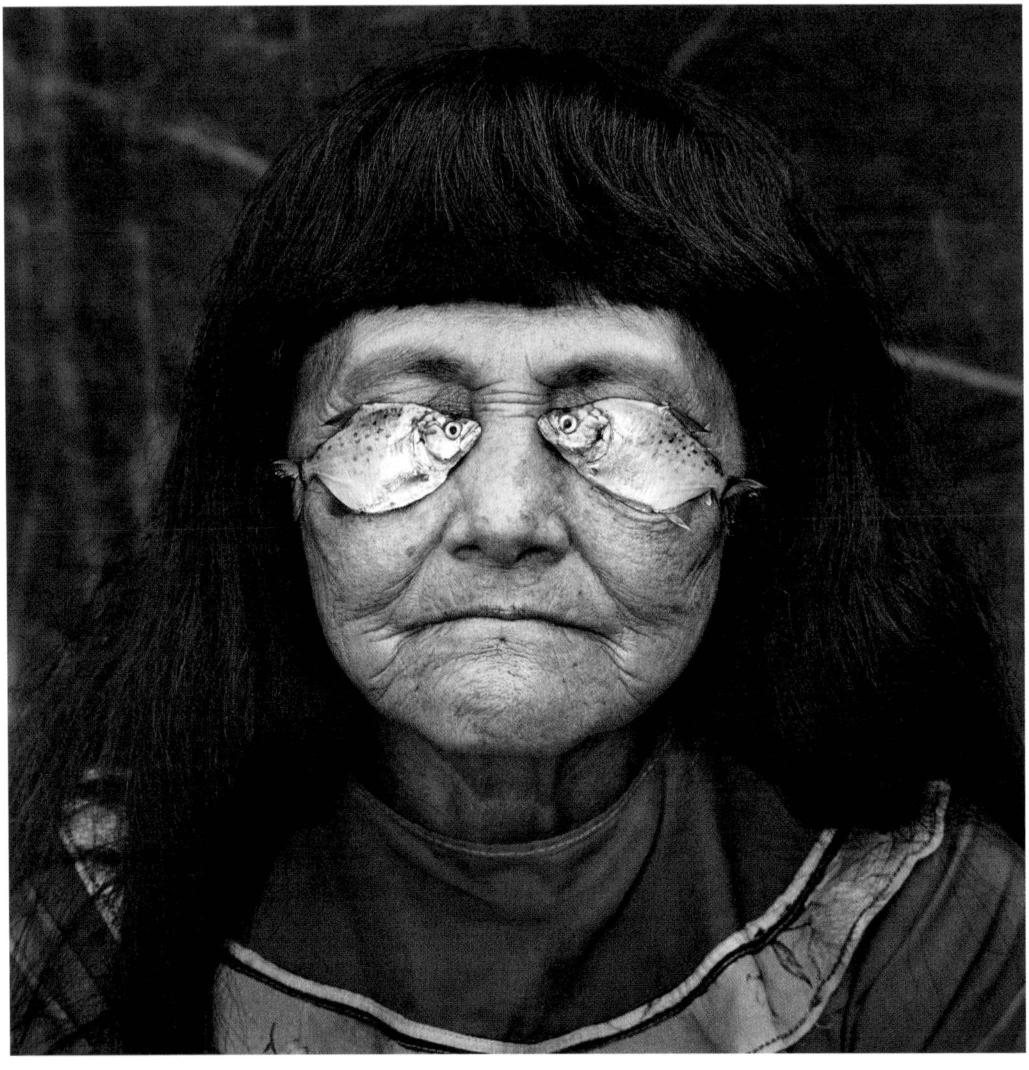

Jan Mulder (Lima, 1949) grew up in a family that gave him a privileged education, divided between Switzerland and Peru, his home country, but his career did not follow any orthodox path. Founder of the Lima Image Center and the El Ojo Ajeno cultural center, he studied photography at Boston University, has had a successful career as a businessman and has a collection, formally started in 2002, of almost 1500 very high-quality pieces that include Irving Penn, Milagros de la Torre, Alfredo Jaar, Graciela Iturbide, Naoya Hatakeyama and the Vargas brothers. Mulder, also instrumental in the original conception of the Lima Biennial of Photography, has found in this medium of expression the ideal vehicle to reflect his view of the world, always contemporary, restless and sensitive. And he did so long before it became fashionable for many international collectors. He says that 'there has been a boom in photography as a language to collect and as a means of expression. When cameras were added to cellphones, it became widespread, and it is wonderful that, of all the millions who use it, a tiny percentage will try to dedicate themselves to photography. There is no more democratic art than it.'

Mulder speaks simply, calmly, and warmly. And, between the Greek origins of his mother and his passion for art, the dialogue flows Zen-like. What made him focus on photography and how did he become a collector? 'I have always had something of the collector, because when I worked at the Roche pharmaceutical company in the seventies, in Basel, I would often go to Strasbourg, visit a gallery, choose something I liked and buy it. Even if they were different media. The attraction was already there. Years later, in a gallery in Hong Kong I saw prints by a Peruvian artist, Cecilia Colichón, which I still have. But the passion for photography goes back further, because my father had a Rolleiflex, and I caught the bug. I've had several cameras, from Brownies to Instamatics. Over time I started studying, I began in Business Administration and after a year I realized that it would not keep me interested, which is why I switched to photojournalism at Boston University, something that I later practiced at *La Prensa* in Lima, until the military government nationalized the media, so I ended up traveling and later working in Switzerland.'

The family's pharmaceutical distribution company was the reason why Mulder, now an associate member of the Board of the Lima Art Museum, returned to his home country in the early-eighties. However, his interest in collecting photography came much later, because he had previously acquired works by painters such as Fernando de Szyszlo and José Tola.

'I first started buying works without thinking about a collection. Art Basel Miami 2002 was the first fair in which I acquired some pieces by foreign artists, until I made the decision to only collect photographs by Peruvian artists such as Luz María Bedoya and Billy Hare. Over time, one builds groups or families of works that revolve around certain themes, such as artistic, urban or nature-focused photography,' he explained.

Some photos are historical documents, while others are pure beauty, proof of the creative greatness of the subject who takes them. 'Photography as a medium is very broad, from the artistic in all its variants with the inspiration it provokes through works that interest me a lot, such as that of Gladys Alvarado, who has technique and visibility, to the documentary and journalistic work of Jaime Rázuri or Daniel Pajuelo.'

As he explained, 'there are photographs that document historical political moments, such as a police strike or the removal of an equestrian statue from a plaza to a warehouse and then to a park: we are talking about an important monument in Lima that changed its location because of the wish of the president's wife. And despite the fact that my history as a journalist was brief, I am sensitive towards this type of work, and the truth is that Peru is a country that has an important history to document.'

Mulder underscores the importance in his opinion of visiting galleries, though not 'to buy photographs in batches,' and also art fairs, although he does not plan in advance which ones he will go to each year. In 2018, he bought two vintage Japanese photos at Art Basel from a Tokyo gallery and some time before he had acquired a piece by a Chinese photographer documenting the cultural revolution from a Toronto gallery, something that has marked him personally, as he had lived between Hong Kong and Vietnam at that time.

What is the ultimate fate of his collection? 'I have not decided yet, but one option would be to set up my own foundation and have my children take over in time. Another option would be to ally myself with an institution in Lima such as the Contemporary Art Museum, which would enable the photography collection to continue growing and would train young people to meet that goal. I don't expect the Peruvian State to come and give me anything, I only expect something in proportion to the taxes that I pay and will continue to pay,' before musing on the state of culture policy in Peru. 'There is no profound concept of what our culture is. We do have an inherited and very important Inca, pre-Inca and colonial culture, but there is no law to promote or support it. And so, it is down to individuals to demonstrate an ability or sensitivity to do something, from a cultural center to a museum. Without the private sector, our international representation would be very poor.'

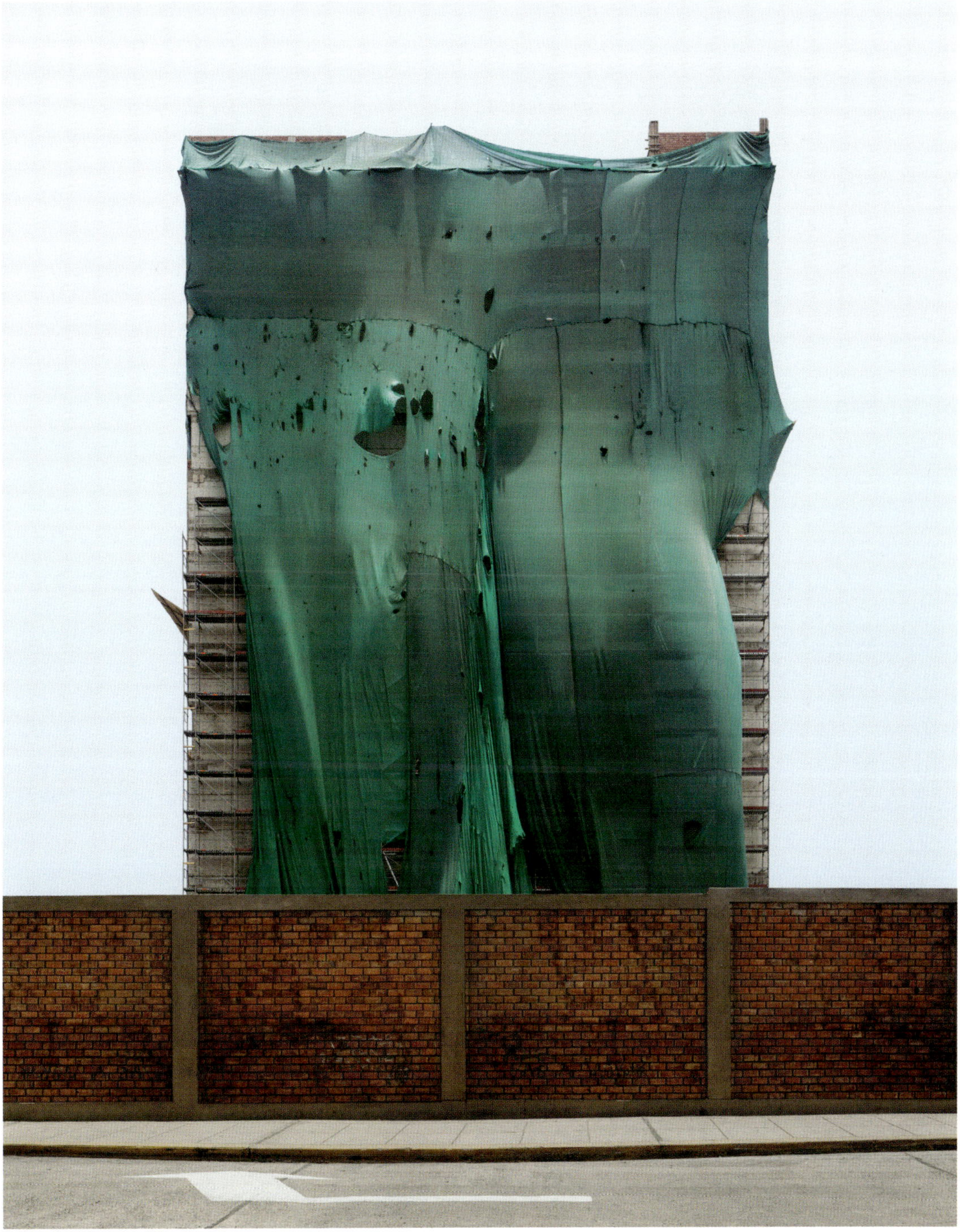

Edi Hirose, *Lima 5928*, 2013

Sheikha Al-Mayassa

'There are some collectors with a lot of money and little knowledge who damage the market'

Richard Serra, *7*, 2011

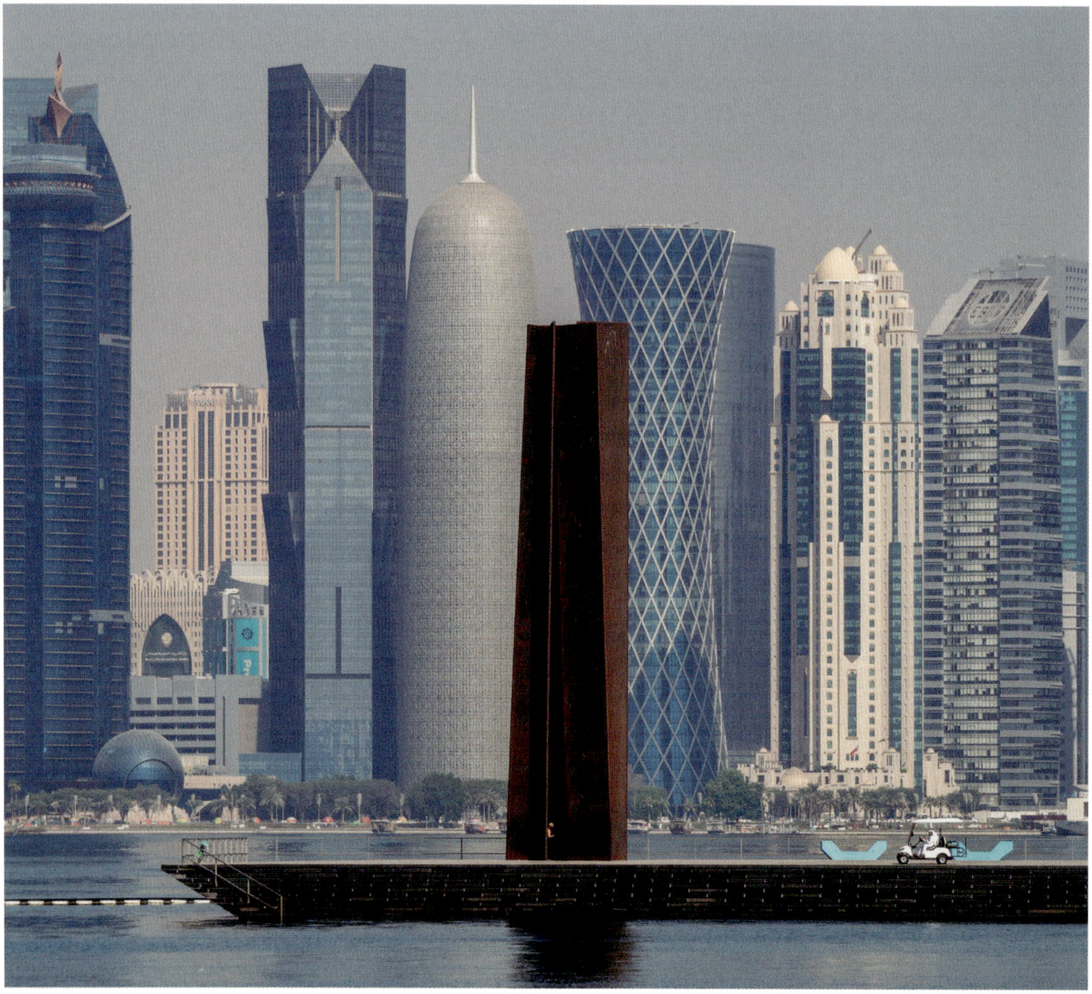

Sheikha Al-Mayassa bint Hamad al Thani (Doha, 1983) is on *Forbes* magazine's list of the world's 100 most powerful women. The sister of the Emir of Qatar and daughter of the legendary Hamad Bin Khalifa al Thani and Moza bint Nasser, she has become the most powerful woman in the art world for her work as head of the Qatar Museums, a position that affords her the ability to acquire works with a practically unlimited annual budget that has shaken up the international market. She has been responsible for bringing to Qatar blue chip contemporary artists such as Takashi Murakami, Damien Hirst and Richard Serra. She is credited with some of the most notorious acquisitions of recent times, hitting authentic records for their economic value, with names ranging from Cézanne to Rothko.

'Actually, I've always been interested in the creative world, but I didn't study Art but Political Science and Literature at Duke,' she explained during a conversation at her palatial home in New York, the day before the inauguration of the Qatar National Museum in Doha, a true 40,000-square-meter wonder of design created by the French architect Jean Nouvel. And she added: 'the main thing for us was to open the museum properly, no matter that it was planned for 2016.'

The force behind the Museum of Islamic Art in Doha, the Arab Museum of Modern Art and the Orientalist Museum, she explains about the genesis of the new museum: 'Jean Nouvel had different plans, one of which was that the museum be underground and that there would be nothing around the palace [former royal palace of Sheikh Abdullah Bin Jassim and home to the Qatar National Museum]. I told him that it was a slightly claustrophobic idea and I asked him to think of something else. Perhaps he was a little offended, but finally he came up with such a beautiful and architecturally complex structure that architects have come from all over the world to admire his daring and talent.'

The eyes of half the world also turned to Qatar for the controversial placement of fourteen giant bronze sculptures by Damien Hirst—thirteen fetuses and a baby that represent the development of an embryo until birth—at the Sidra hospital. 'To be honest, we didn't think it would upset the Qataris too much, but it is also true that we had already had controversies when we opened a major exhibition by Hirst. Part of the public, who were not familiar with his work, thought that his works with embalmed animals had been executed by him, which goes against our religion,' she explains, before clarifying, 'If you let your children have Barbies, what is wrong in us exhibiting sculptures that represent babies? The work is part of the hospital and we are happy with it, although I would like to make to it clear that our goal was never to provoke and that, once the controversy began, we tried to dialogue with the people who were offended, knowing that there is not

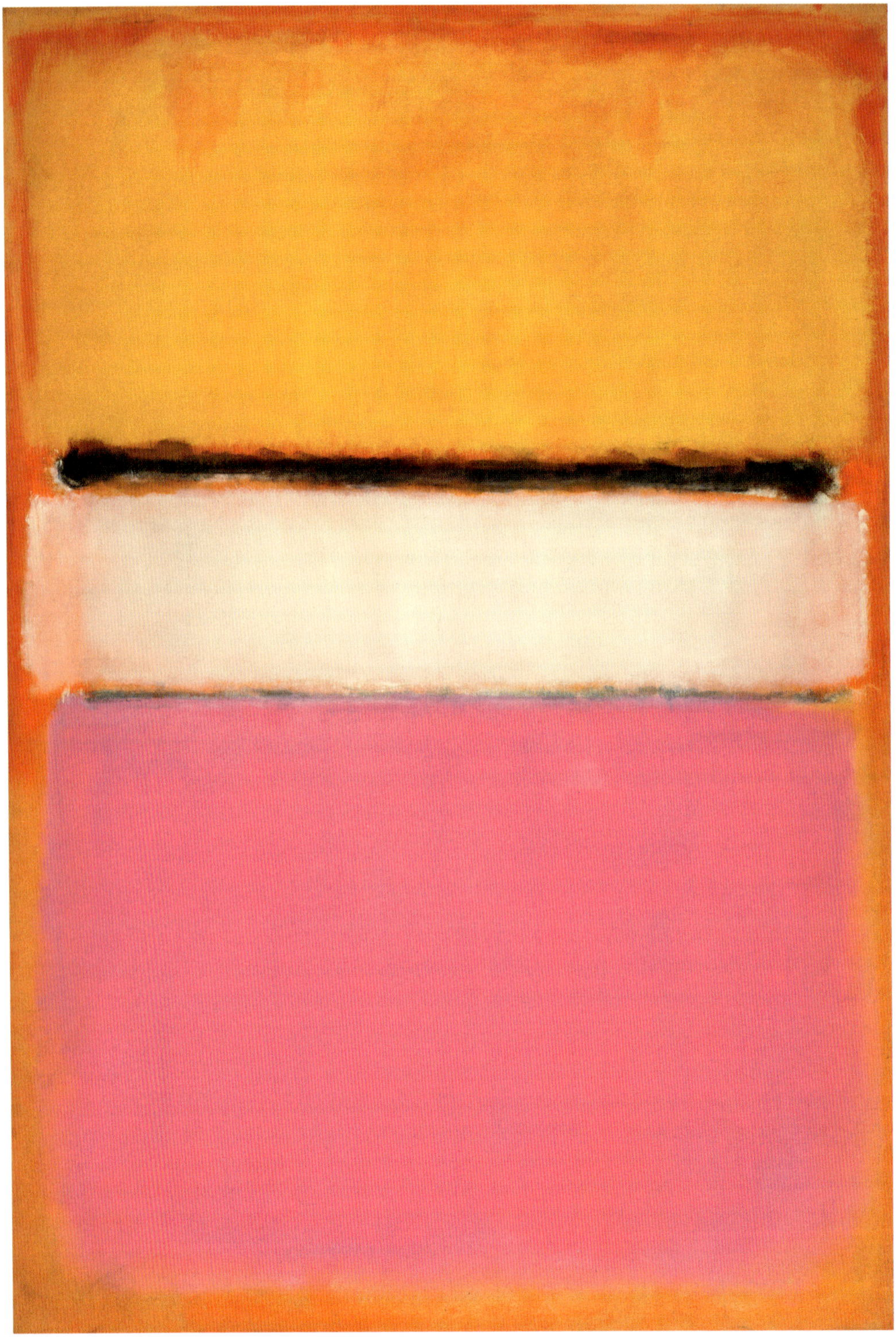

Mark Rothko, *White Center (Yellow, Pink and Lavender on Rose)*, 1950

one single piece that everyone likes. Enjoying art is contagious and some works may be viewed differently in twenty years' time.'

But what does she think of the worrying phenomenon of a few private collectors acquiring works of historical value that iconic museums cannot aspire to because of their asking price? 'This phenomenon is not unique to the art world, which is a market like any other. Having said that, we do not want to inflate it. Some of the things that have been said are absolutely false, like, for instance, that we offered a lot of money for a Da Vinci when in fact we never even bid one dollar,' she says in reference to the *Salvator Mundi* bought by the Louvre in Abu Dhabi. 'There are some collectors with a lot of money and little knowledge who damage the market and can destroy the careers of great artists. All the actors involved want to inflate this artificial and unhealthy bubble which I believe will be punctured at some point by the market itself. In addition, museums are not only the owner of artworks, but also exhibit them, frame them within a context, place them in a catalog that has a certain meaning and help everyone enjoy art.'

Al-Mayassa makes a point of stating that she is not a collector herself, among other reasons, to avoid possible conflicts of interest, and that all her plans are medium-to-long term. 'I like it when people can see what is behind a dress, a chair or a painting, because knowledge can be used so that life, which is so short, can have another meaning. To that end, you have to think about the reasons why things happens, instead of assuming that they just simply happen.'

Luiz Augusto Teixeira de Freitas

'I hope that the art market as we know it will be torn out from its roots'

Carlos Garaicoa, *De cómo mi biblioteca se alimenta de una realidad concreta*, 2006

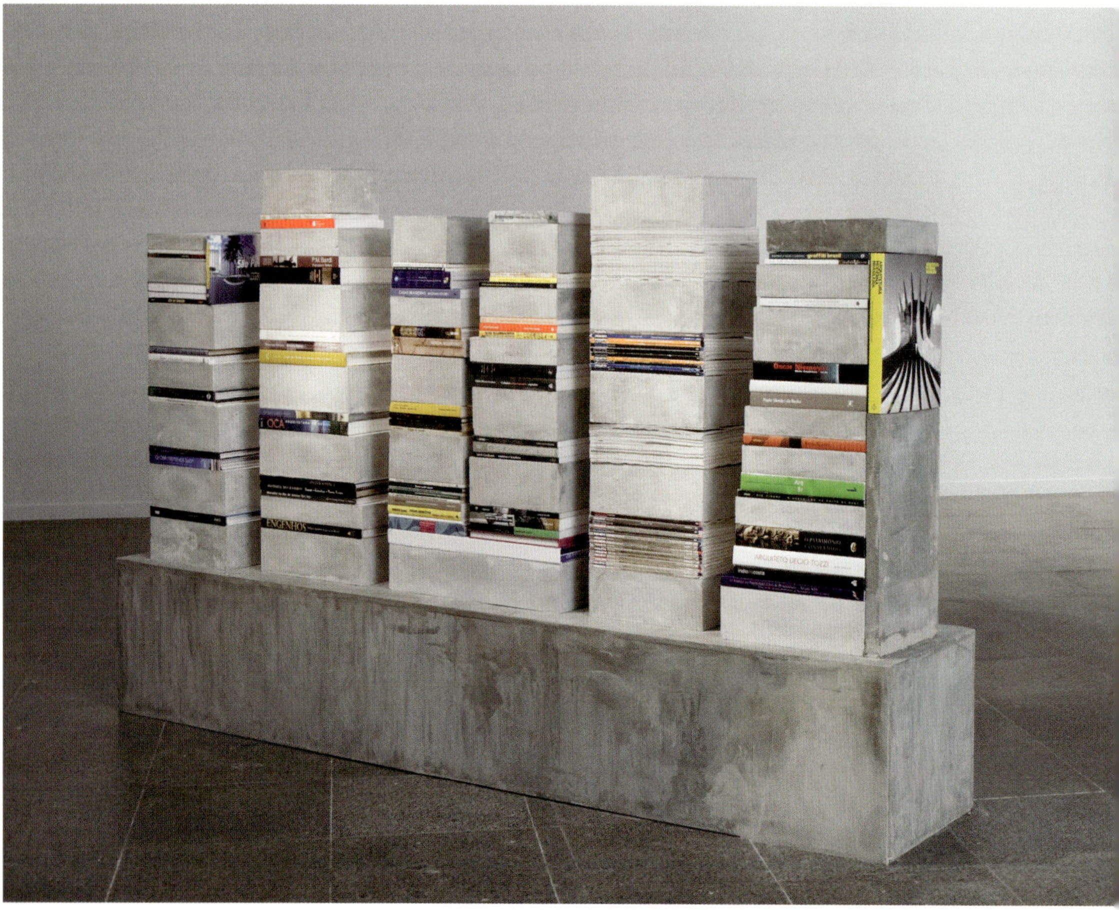

At some point in the late-nineties, Luiz Augusto Teixeira de Freitas bought two major works by Howard Hodgkin and Hans Hartung at auction. This was the beginning of a coherent and fascinating collection, a reflection of the unique taste of its maker. Today the Teixeira de Freitas Collection has works by Cildo Meireles, Jonathan Monk, Jorge Macchi as well as Robert Breer, Armando Andrade Tudela, Alighiero Boetti, Esther Ferrer, Thomas Ruff, Jonathas de Andrade, Juan Araujo, Gabriel Sierra and Abraham Cruzvillegas. In 2019 Fundación Banco Santander's exhibition hall at Ciudad Financiera in Boadilla del Monte hosted *No habrá nunca una puerta. Estás adentro* [There will never be a door. You are already inside], a fantastic show of over 300 works—painting, drawing, photography, video and sculpture—by 190 contemporary artists.

Teixeira de Freitas received us at his home in one of the most beautiful and oldest neighborhoods in Lisbon. The host opens the door, still wet from the shower, laughing at our excess punctuality. The walls are bare, quite unusual for a collector who possesses more than 3000 artworks. 'I am taking advantage of the fact that my favorite works are in an exhibition to paint the walls white and reflect. Besides, I don't want to hang other works here,' he explains. Black loafers, beige pants and a light-blue shirt set off Luiz Augusto's white hair and beard, as he observes the world from the balcony of his house with confidence, ease and satisfaction behind the dark glasses that mask sleepless nights. Never before had the collector agreed to show in one exhibit the result of his compulsion, but he acquiesced when the curator was his own daughter Luiza, who is perfectly acquainted with the heart of this lonely hunter.

'I am an atheist, but I collect artists' bibles. The most important is the Marcel Duchamp bible, a fascinating *catalogue raisonné*,' he explains. Teixeira de Freitas is critical of what he considers a scandalous 'lack of regulation' in the art market. An unorthodox collector, he believes that artists loses purity and autonomy when they live exclusively from their art and that collectors are secondary. He admits that, when his walls are not bare, what we would see are works by artists such as Lynette Yiadom, Tauba Auberbach, Robert Kinmont and Marcel Broodthaers. And he adds, 'the one that is never missing is Damian Ortega. He still does something for me.'

The lawyer, for whom snobbery is anathema and obsession a constant and accepted presence, has donated an important work precisely by Damian Ortega to the Reina Sofia Museum. He doesn't hesitate to define his collection as though it were his own life: 'my ideas, my thoughts, my contradictions, my utopias, my encounters, my frictions and my nightmares.'

His appreciation of the respectful and sensitive spirit with which the exhibition at Boadilla del Monte was organized does not mean that Luiz is going

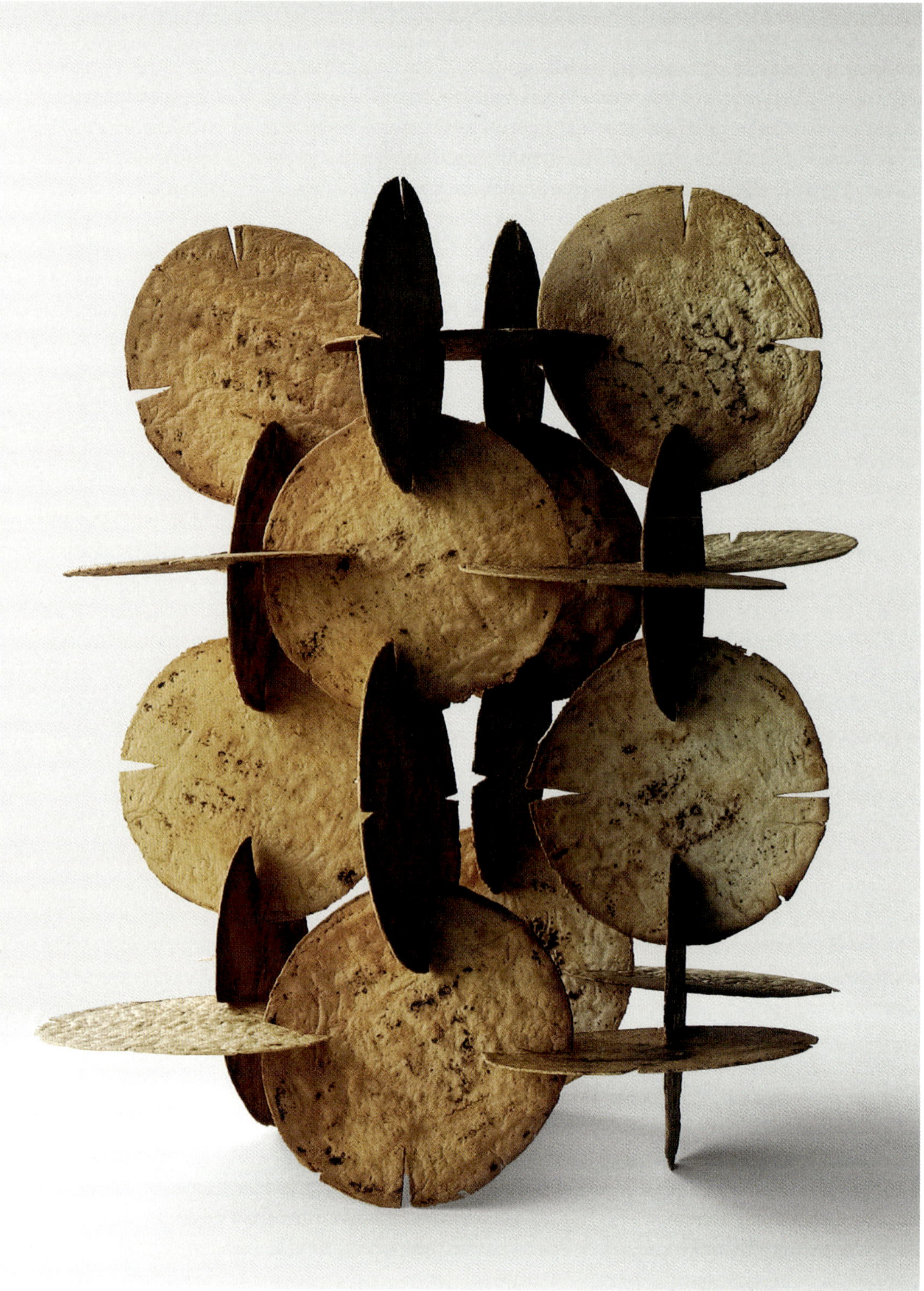

Damián Ortega, *Módulo de construcción con tortillas*, 1998

to abandon his low profile. 'I've had the satisfaction, having a chance to see those works displayed a certain way, dialoguing with each other, and, as Herman Daled says, "to have the immodest vision that the lot of them could be just one work of art" which I would like to create if I had the ability to be an artist. But showing my collection to the public is not something I would like to repeat.'

Making this concession in Spain is no mean feat for someone who has also declared: 'My collection, for which the initial input of Paulo Vieira, a friend who started collecting before me, was very important, as was the curator Adriano Pedrosa, is not an accessible collection, not even for many people interested in art. I know it is not instantly appealing because it can seem too conceptual. I know I am not representative and that my vision of the market isn't either, but this kind of art interests me more and more.'

Luiz Augusto laments that, at the moment, 'artists are the object of speculation for many people who buy them when they are very young and put pressure on them to produce more. Many collectors approach them in a disingenuous manner, only to resell their works a bit later. This shopping mall approach to art is a tragedy and I hope that the market as we know it will be torn out from its roots, so we can start to rebuild it from scratch. This is why, even if it sounds presumptuous or a pipe dream, I buy things because I consider them to be good for humankind and interesting to the eye.'

Jarl Mohn

'If you hear a song and you love it instantly, it may not age very well. The same thing goes for art'

Larry Clark, *Untitled*, 1971

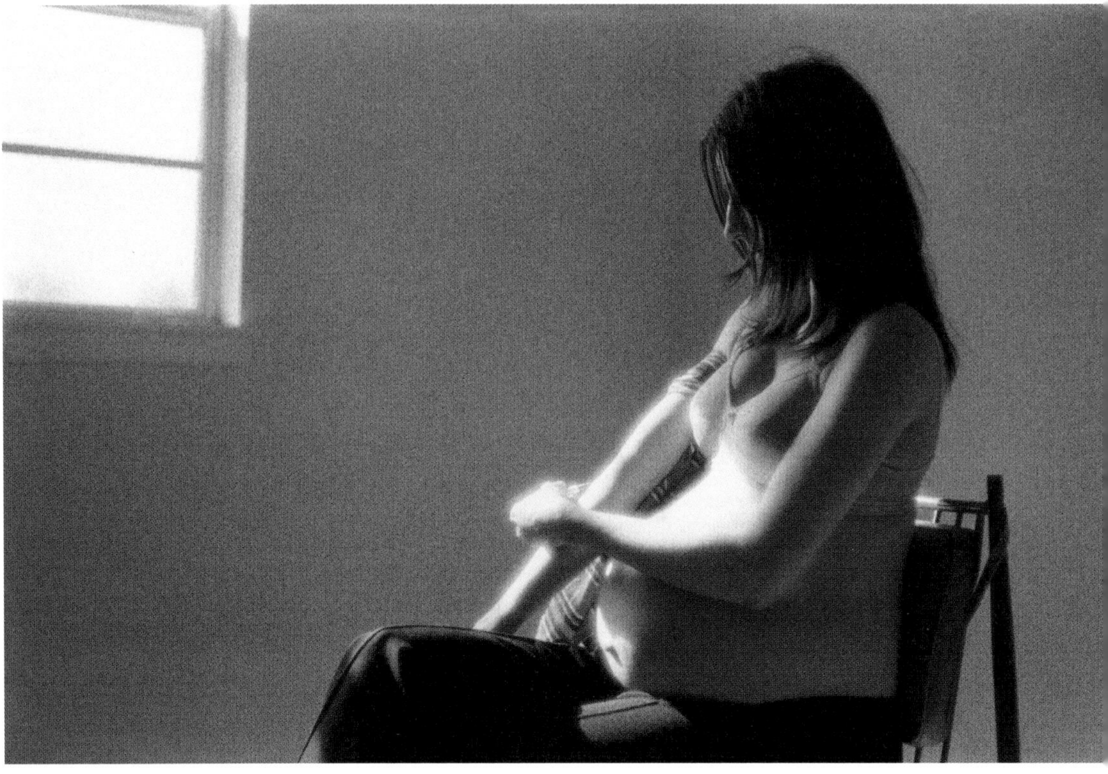

Calmness and passion are not attributes that usually go together, and yet they sit so naturally alongside one another within the privileged sanctuary offered to them by Jarl Mohn. Although born in 1951 in Doylestown, a small town in Pennsylvania near Philadelphia where 8,000 people live, his life story is closely connected with New York and, above all, with Los Angeles. Mohn spends his life between the two cities and, together with his wife Pamela, he opens the doors to his houses in both places so that curious art lovers can enjoy an impressive collection which, though focused on minimalism, does not exclude more classic artists. The collector receives us at his home in Georgetown, District of Columbia, dressed in a light-blue striped shirt, beige chinos and a navy-blue sports jacket.

Jarl Mohn is a man with a profound interest in public affairs, whether in his personal political activism—as a fervent Democratic supporter—or in his professional activity as CEO of the giant National Public Radio (NPR), before which he had spent time DJing for WNBC under the alias Lee Masters, founding E! Entertainment Television—whose transmissions of the red carpets for the Oscars have been seen across the globe—and in top executive positions at the legendary television networks MTV and VH1. Mohn's philanthropic work is carried out from the Mohn Family Foundation. Some of its most noteworthy actions are an award for emerging artists it organizes jointly with the Hammer Museum and specific contributions to institutions such as LACMA or the J. Paul Getty Trust.

'It's a bit embarrassing,' he replies with a laugh when asked why he started collecting. 'I really have to give my wife the credit because, after we moved into a new home in Los Angeles, she said "with all these bare white walls, we should put up something really nice and start thinking about collecting." But my answer was that the art world was made to take advantage of people like us, that they would take a lot of money from us and that we would not choose the right works!' recalls Mohn.

Nothing changed until the early-nineties, when a good friend who was well acquainted with the New York art world took him to a few galleries, where he chose three works by a certain Larry Clark, today a highly acclaimed photographer, from a series he did on drug addicts. His wife's reaction was instant rejection. 'What's the problem with you? One is of a pregnant woman shooting up in a recliner, another has an addict with a gun, and another has a dead baby, a drawer, and a priest! You can't hang these on the wall!' a very level-headed Pamela reproached him. And they didn't hang them for years, although Jarl bought them and today they are in the house of one of his daughters, who coincidentally was born in Tulsa, Oklahoma, where those photographs were taken. 'If you hear a song and you love it instantly, it may not age very well. The same thing goes for art, because it usually takes time for you to appreciate the best things, but when you do, it is with even greater force,' he argues. Nine years after buying those photos, he was smitten by an exhibition of sculptures by John McCracken. And the spell it cast was never to be broken. Ever since, minimalism—both contemporary and classic—took hold of his mind, his soul and his heart. Apart from James Turrell, West coast artists like Robert Irwin and Doug Wheeler dominated a coherent whole marked by this art movement, sprinkled with the odd star from the East coast.

But the architect of the collection puts his stamp on it even when talking about art, a discipline whose theory he has soaked up, perhaps later in life but no less deep for all that, but also in the practice, meeting the artists he collects face to face. 'When prices started to rise and investments became risky, I was forced to learn more in order to know not only who to invest in, but also the condition of the work I wanted, or what series would be the right choice. Besides, throughout my life I have always relied on the advice of experts who have helped me a lot,' Mohr explains before confessing that 'I would love to be able to buy a Donald Judd *Stack*, but I can't afford it.' In Mohn's opinion, 'what's happening with the art scene in Los Angeles right now is comparable to what happened in New York in the 1950s, in Paris in the early-twentieth century and with Florence during the Renaissance.' His interest in supporting local artists with whom he identifies through the acquisitions he makes and his award for emerging artists is palpable in his every word.

On a more personal note, he says 'my wife is irreplaceable for me, but I am the one who makes the decision about which works to collect. Pam didn't like minimalism, and now she loves it.' She once told him, with her great sense of humor, 'It will be your collection, but it's my investment!' And he concludes: 'This path is an exciting adventure, very different from what I had imagined. And although I have evolved, because at first I didn't understand contemporary art, at bottom I am a very curious person. Incredibly, my father, despite loving culture and being a teacher, never took me to a museum. Nevertheless, I always knew there was something there that could be rewarding. That's why I always say that the key is to observe, to observe and to observe. Then, over time, your unique personal gaze emerges. But you don't have to be a collector to appreciate art. Just visiting a museum for two hours is amazing.'

As the French writer Robert Escarpit once said, 'the ability to marvel, which the English call the spirit of wonder, is in the hearts of men from the moment they open their eyes to life.' Jarl Mohn, more than anyone, needs no reminder.

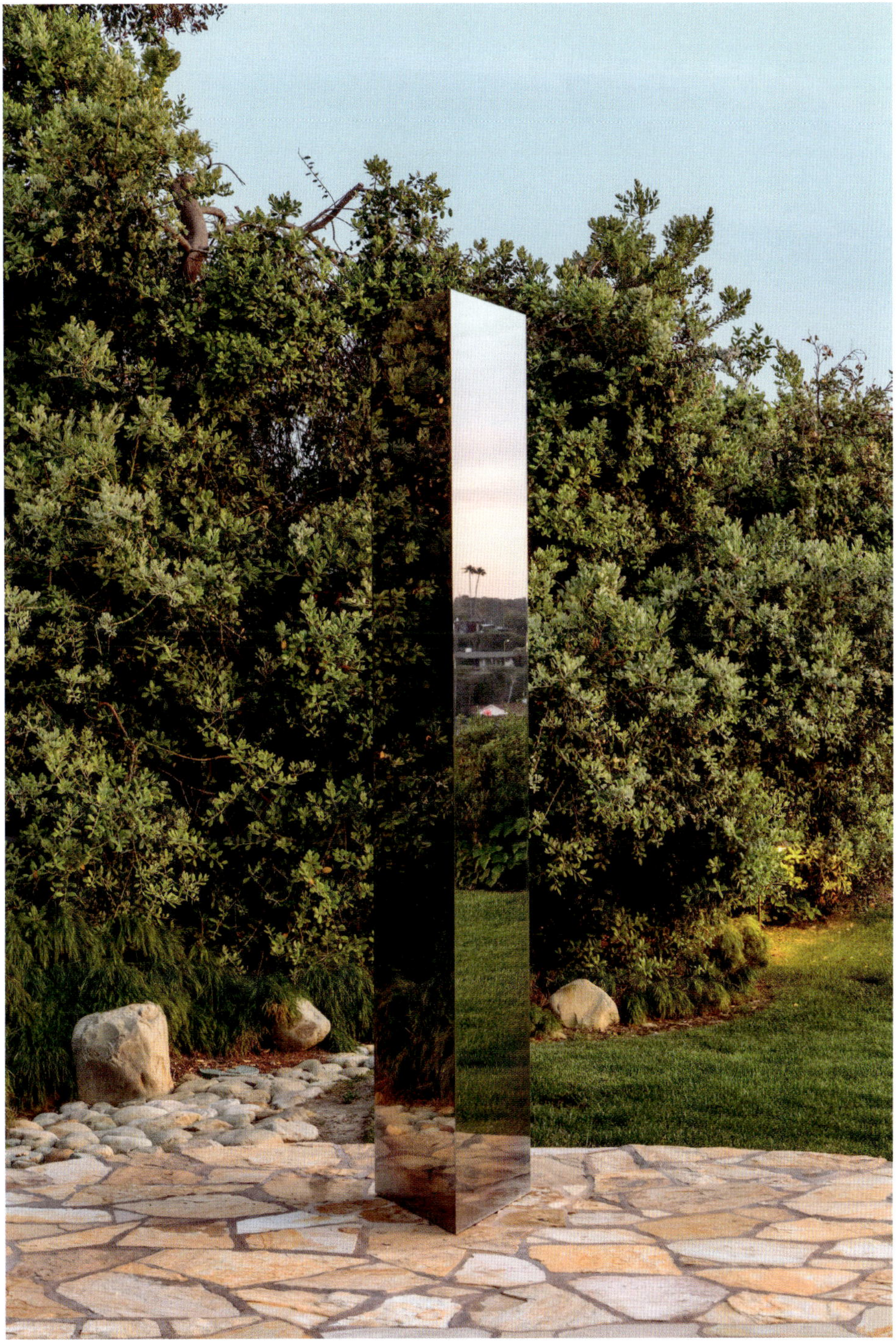

John McCracken, *Magic*, 2008

Mitchell and Emily Wei Rales

‘We have no intention of being the richest people in the cemetery’

Louise Bourgeois, *The Birth*, 2007

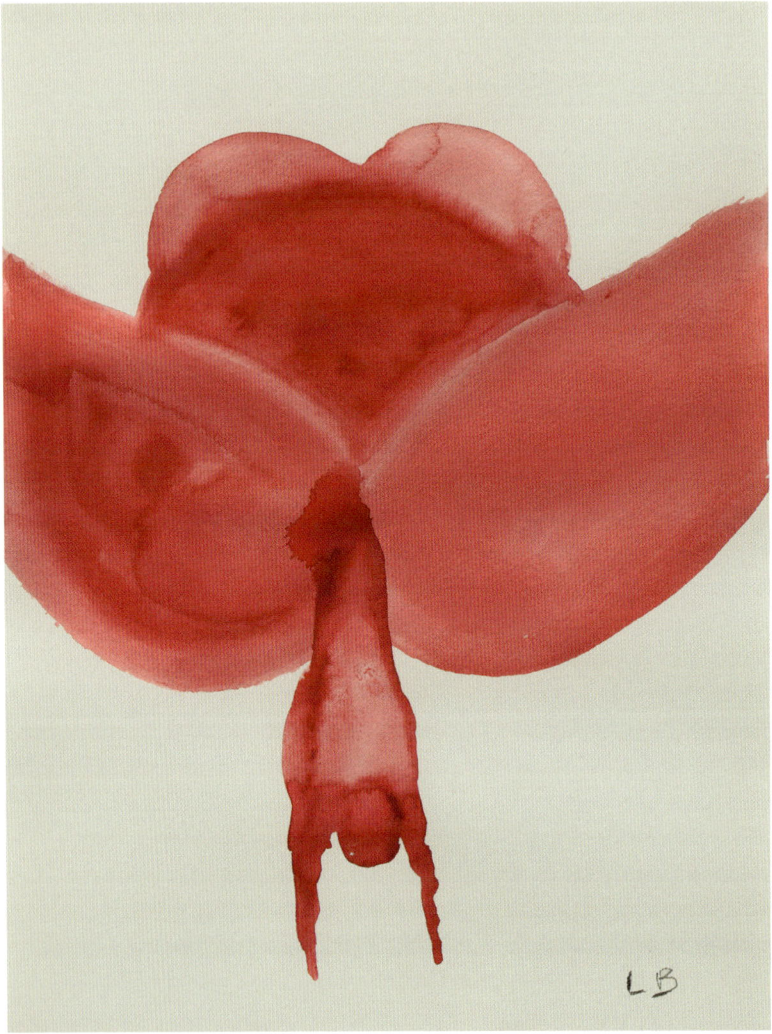

If you were to judge by the dominance of one voice over the other, you might think that this extraordinary couple is quite mismatched. Yet, that would be a big mistake because Mitch and Emily Wei Rales make a perfect albeit unconventional tandem. He is a low-profile billionaire well respected in Washington, D.C. His father, Norman Rales, founded a real estate emporium from nothing, fulfilling all the movie clichés of the American dream. At the age of 23, Mitch and his brother followed in their father's footsteps, and started to buy companies and quickly became front line industrialists. From there, it was just one small step to becoming an elite collector and wanting to leave his mark in philanthropy. And Emily was to have a fundamental role in this transformation.

Mitch is in his element: relaxed and dressed in casual pants and a light-blue shirt. He is accompanied by his wife Emily, an accomplished art historian and the chief curator of Glenstone, a private museum with no admission fee in Potomac, Maryland, where the Rales showcase their magnificent collection. We are in the offices in the basement of the 20,000-square-meter museum designed by the architect Thomas Phifer, whose recent extension, opened in 2018, cost 200 million dollars, not to mention the new 400-square-meter wing added in 2022 to house Richard Serra's sculpture *Four Rounds: Equal Weight, Unequal Measure* from 2017.

The large windows overlook gardens designed by Adam Greenspan and Peter Walker which invite the viewer to slow down, to stroll and contemplate before arriving to the galleries. These minimalist and balanced indoor and outdoor spaces match the concept the Rales have embraced, made up of equal parts of austerity and elegance. More than 1300 modern and contemporary artworks form this collection, situated just half an hour from downtown Washington. Yet it is not the quantity but rather the quality and the character what distinguishes this cultural center, where there is no shortage of gems by artists of the stature of Alexander Calder, Mark Rothko, Louise Bourgeois, Andy Warhol, Jasper Johns and David Hammons.

How did this fascinating story begin? Very simply, Mitch assures us: 'I built a new house in 1990 and found myself with bare walls. I felt the need to put something on them but I had no background to fall back on because I did not grow up with art nor did I go to museums. I was more interested in sports.' This wake-up moment was enough for the entrepreneur to start a relationship of 'love, attraction and intrigue' with collecting, choosing his words carefully.

'A secret I seldom tell is that the first two works I purchased, a Picasso and a Matisse, did not wow me. It wasn't until I discovered abstract expressionism that I really fell in love. It's funny, because in their time, while Cézanne

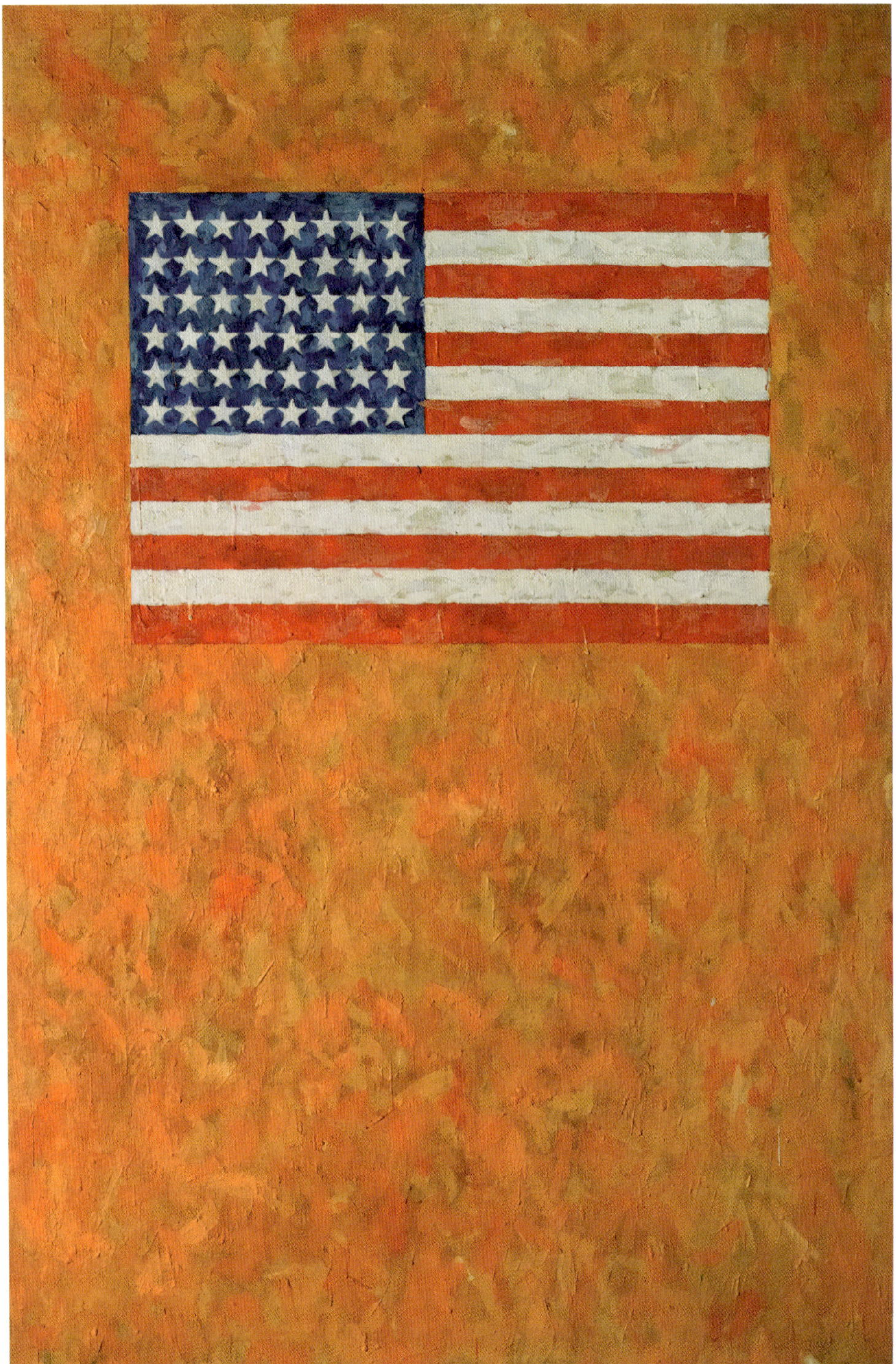

Jasper Johns, *Flag on an Orange Field II*, 1957

was fully renowned, those revolutionary artists were poorly understood and had very little prestige, as though what they did was to conceptually splash lots of colors onto a canvas. I feel very connected to that sentiment because when I was young and started buying and innovating in the business world with my brother Steve, people had no faith in us either. Today, I appreciate Picasso and Matisse, but I'm not interested in collecting them the way I am mesmerized by the abstract expressionists or contemporary works' he added before highlighting that 'like in all unregulated markets, you can be hoodwinked in the art world. So, the fact that a dealer of the category of my friend Bob Mnuchin was my guide made all the difference.'

But art has not captivated Mitch only through its masterpieces. As Emily explains, while laughing, 'I was working at a contemporary gallery in Chelsea, in New York, and Sandy Rower, a common friend and grandson of Alexander Calder, introduced us, deliberately setting us up because he thought we would be a good match. I come from a more intellectual background than Mitch, who entered the art world through the secondary market, which is to say, by acquiring works that had already been in other collections. My professional experience was related with the primary market, with organizing exhibitions and working with those creative and sometimes unpredictable individuals who are the artists.'

Back in the museum, Mitch declares that the experience for visitors to Glenstone is unique, because of the surroundings and the works, 'especially the large installations that can only be seen in museums and which we believe are extremely interesting. To get to this point, it was necessary to find our passion and realize what it is that is truly essential in our lives. We wanted to create something lasting, a unique experience and to contribute to the good of society. We have no intention of being the richest people in the cemetery. Thanks to Glenstone we can share our collection with visitors in perpetuity, thus leaving a lasting mark for generations to come.'

Lekha Poddar

‘The interest in Indian art today has a real side but also something of an artificial boom’

Bharti Kher, *Angel* (from *Hybrid* series), 2004

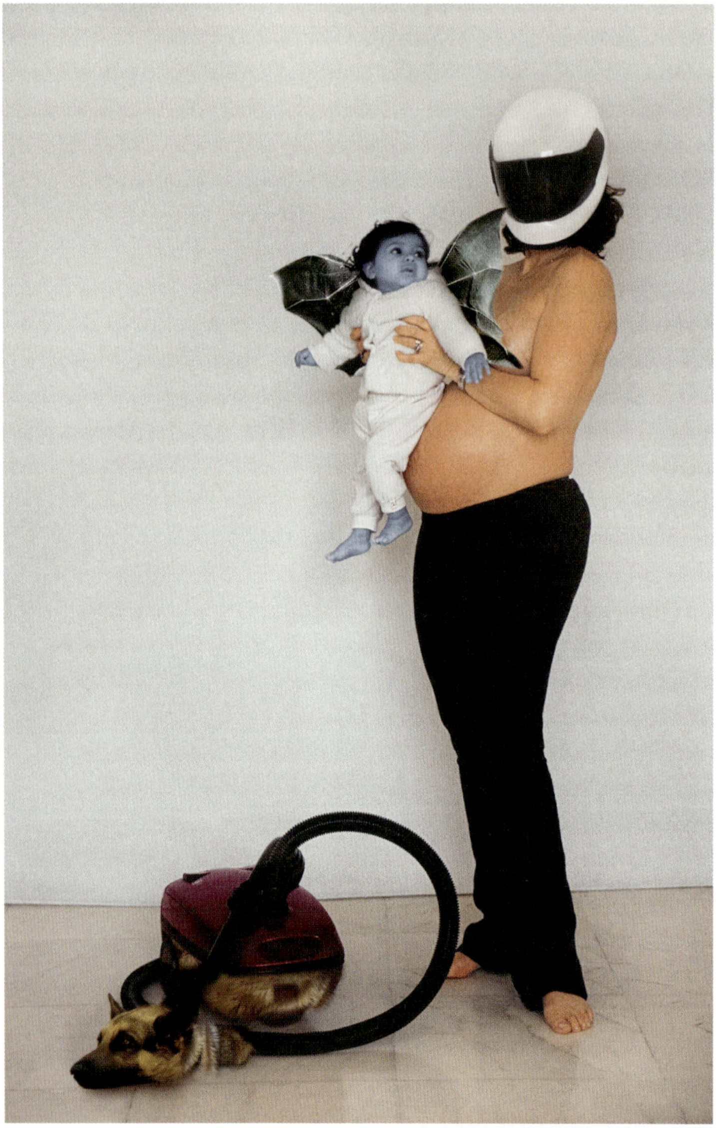

Lekha Poddar has placed Indian contemporary art in the international spotlight. Before her, no one had tackled this feat, one she took on with the assertiveness of a collector who is not afraid of challenges. That assertiveness is evident during our conversation at her home in London. A home with understated elegance, in contrast with her house in New Delhi, a postmodernist building designed by Inni Chatterjee in which tribal objects are combined with uninhibited ease and good taste.

As the promotor of the Devi Art Foundation, her interests have become more and more defined: 'Basically, my interests are centered in India, Pakistan, Sri Lanka, Bangladesh and Iran, and this has become even more so since my son graduated from university and started collecting on his own. Later, we joined efforts and agreed on criteria.' Lekha has allowed herself to be led by the instinct of her son Anupam Poddar, who at the age of 23 began to take note of many unknown Indian artists, admired today thanks to the efforts of these two collectors. For Lekha it took a bit of adjusting as she was not familiar with videos and installations.

The collector contends that until recently there were only two important galleries in Delhi, and that they bought directly from artists that no one seemed to be interested in. 'The interest in Indian art today has a real side but also something of an artificial boom,' she explained, arguing that collectors interested in the artists that big galleries and museums are fighting over would be better served looking in their own backyards. 'The opening of the economy helped to widen this circle.' And she admits that Indian art has become more interesting, complex and sought-after thanks to their contribution. A contribution that for Poddar has an uncertain future. In spite of the educational programs she promotes that allow 16-year-old orphaned youngsters to engage with art, learn from it and express themselves through any of its forms, this patron laments the fact that the institutions in her country have neither the infrastructure nor the professionalism to absorb all her works. She is very frank responding to my question about why she doesn't open a museum in her country: 'Even though my collection has weight and some of the artists have nothing to envy the best known in the world, if I open, lots of people would turn up for the vernissage but the next day, who would come to see it, and how would I deal with that?'

Lekha Poddar has sold some of her works: 'One evolves and your eye becomes more discerning. Besides, I need to make room. Although I'm not so sure because I sell one and buy five. There are works I don't see regularly, they are in storage and require adequate conservation. Around 99% of what I have is in storage.' Finesse is the trademark of her collection: 'I may have works that are violent, loud, bloody, but in the same way as I prefer upbeat movies to gore, I try to find art that connects with my soul and my sensibility, that is minimalist and peaceful.'

Susana Lloret

'You have to make a connection between the human facets of the artist and of the public'

André Kertész, *Distortion #40*, 1933

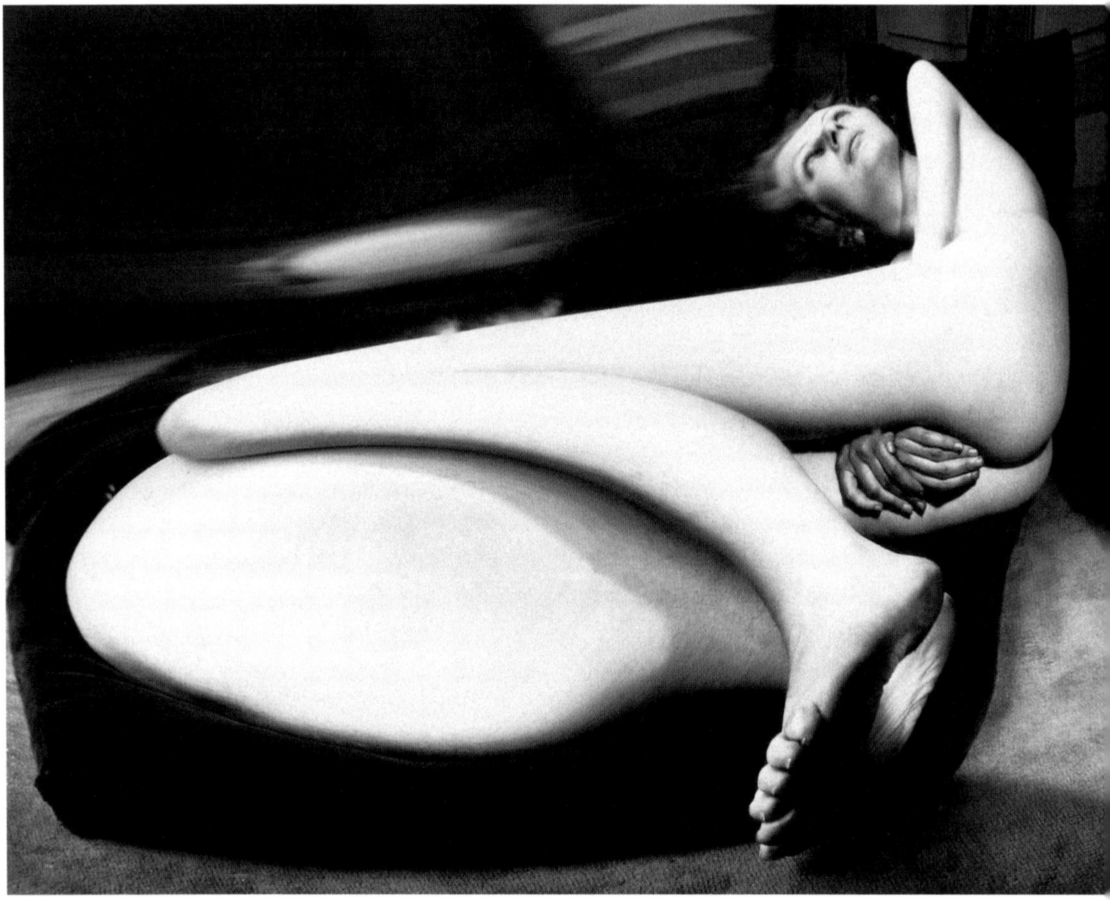

The great Truman Capote said that 'style is the mirror of an artist's sensibility, more so than the content of his work.' And Susana Lloret can be defined by her style. Style in speaking, in dressing, in welcoming visitors. But, above all, in conceiving art from a modern, relaxed perspective, accessible to people and, as she herself has declared, anti-elitist. Lloret is a formidable patron who is genuinely excited about showing her collection to non-specialized audiences, 'simply for the love of art and others.' With inimitable expressiveness, she welcomes us to Bombas Gens, an abandoned hydraulic pump factory in Valencia now transformed into a thriving and hypnotic museum where world-class exhibitions coexist with classrooms to provide education to local children in risk of exclusion.

A high-flying executive, general director of the Fundación Per Amor a l'Art and collector of 2,250 works from about 220 artists—a collection that has earned her the A Prize from the ARCO Foundation, but which she assures us that there is no profit motive behind it—this woman knows what she is talking about. Which becomes abundantly clear when she is asked how she got started. 'The driving force behind the collection is my husband, who has always been passionate about painting and, above all, photography. But we teamed up very early on. My background is in humanities. I'm a psychologist and I have dedicated a lot of time to research. I worked at the university, and my interests were always to do with the possibility of knowing more about people and the human mind. And this has a lot to do with contemporary art because, the more abstract what you see is, the more the spectator needs to make sense of it. But even though my husband was the one who started it, we were soon going to visit galleries and art fairs together, and it's really hard to pinpoint exactly when we started. There comes a time when you realize that what you are trying to build can have a greater significance and reach, as well as a purpose other than your own personal satisfaction. In any case, it's true that Vicente Todolí's expert advice was a turning point in this story. After falling in love with a certain piece, we have always gone to Vicente for his opinion and it has always been spot on. Now I could say that our collection is in fact a product of the three of us, and is intended to be open to the public for free.'

On the impact of patronage on society, she explains 'our interest in art encouraged us to want to share it, but we also had other concerns of a more social nature. We supported research into rare diseases, providing shelter for the homeless and for children at risk of exclusion. Art fits in with that desire to give something back to society. So we looked for a way to make all those activities work, which was the foundation, and a place, Bombas Gens, which is where the foundation fulfills its mission related to art. Here is where we show our collection. But we also share it with other centers, we carry out free activities and try to raise awareness among as many people as possible, also trying to help people to understand, which is why we have mediators. After all, art is not only for connoisseurs. Everything starts with curiosity, and that is why our idea is for the public to be able to appreciate the human dimension of each artist, to relate to their work and ensure they don't walk away indifferent.'

Humanist and cultured, Lloret sums up her idiosyncrasy as follows: 'You have to make a connection between the human facet of the artist, the difficulties they face and the risks they take, which are often invisible, with the human facet of the public. If you create that bond, the work will be seen with different eyes, because the artistic context alone is not enough. There is no need for this kind of support for people who are already interested in art, but the person who is not informed can be won over by putting art in the human context in which it has arisen.'

Surrounded by the fabulous atmosphere offered by the exhibitions of the great Indian artist Sheela Gowda and the Japanese photographers Tamiko Nishimura, Toyoko Tokiwa and Isiuchi Miyako, Lloret repeats that nothing she has achieved would have been possible without the joint work carried out with her husband, José Luis Soler, who penned the following revealing lines in a recently published catalog: 'What is here is part of my present, the discovery of a secret that many people are lucky enough to practice, and that is to share.'

Always insightful, Lloret also underscores the virtues of her team: 'Something that sets us apart and is one of the great merits of the director of Bombas Gens, Nuria Enguita—and of her replacement, the Portuguese curator Sandra Guimarães, following Enguita's appointment as the new director of IVAM in 2020—is the focus on research. As collectors, many galleries and fairs offer us certain works, and that leads to a work of research that helps us grow. A result of it, for instance, is the incorporation of more women artists into the collection. There is a disproportion between the number of men and women artists in museums and we are interested, without falling back on positive discrimination, in finding women artists who are producing excellent quality work but who, due to their gender, have not had the same impact. The building is finished and has given us a lot of satisfaction. But we must decide how to guarantee its sustainability. We are in an ongoing process every day which means that, together with the hard work of our team, we have to put all our efforts into trying to make society better, so that children don't believe that art is for connoisseurs, but a means of communicating something they like, they dislike, that surprises or shocks them. And, of course, we are proud. Those of us who are lucky enough to have, also have the responsibility to share.'

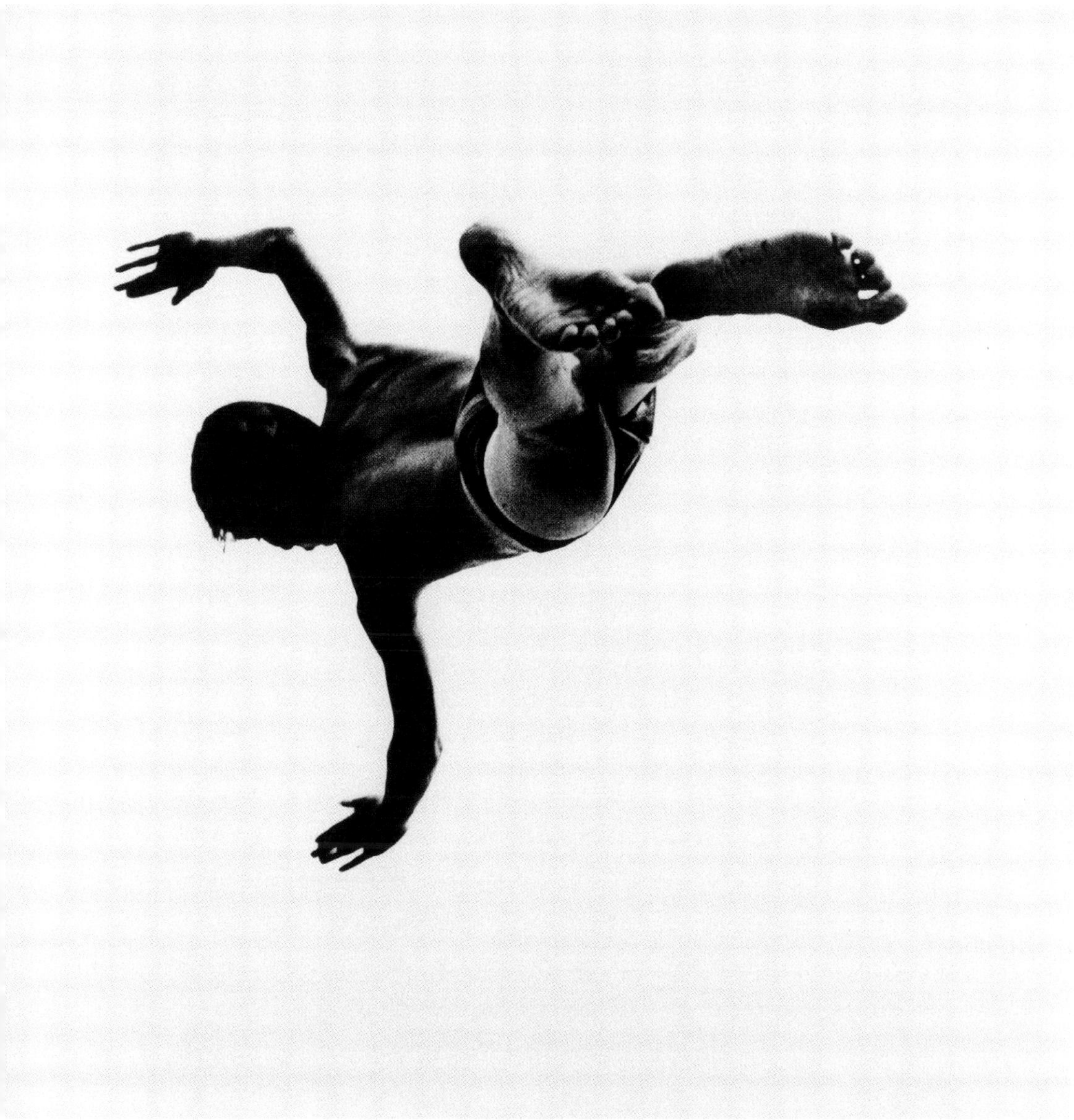

Aaron Siskind, *Pleasures and Terrors of Levitation 37*, 1953

Don and Mera Rubell

'We want art to be as meaningful to the public as it has been for us.'

Julian Schnabel, *Sad Vase*, 1983

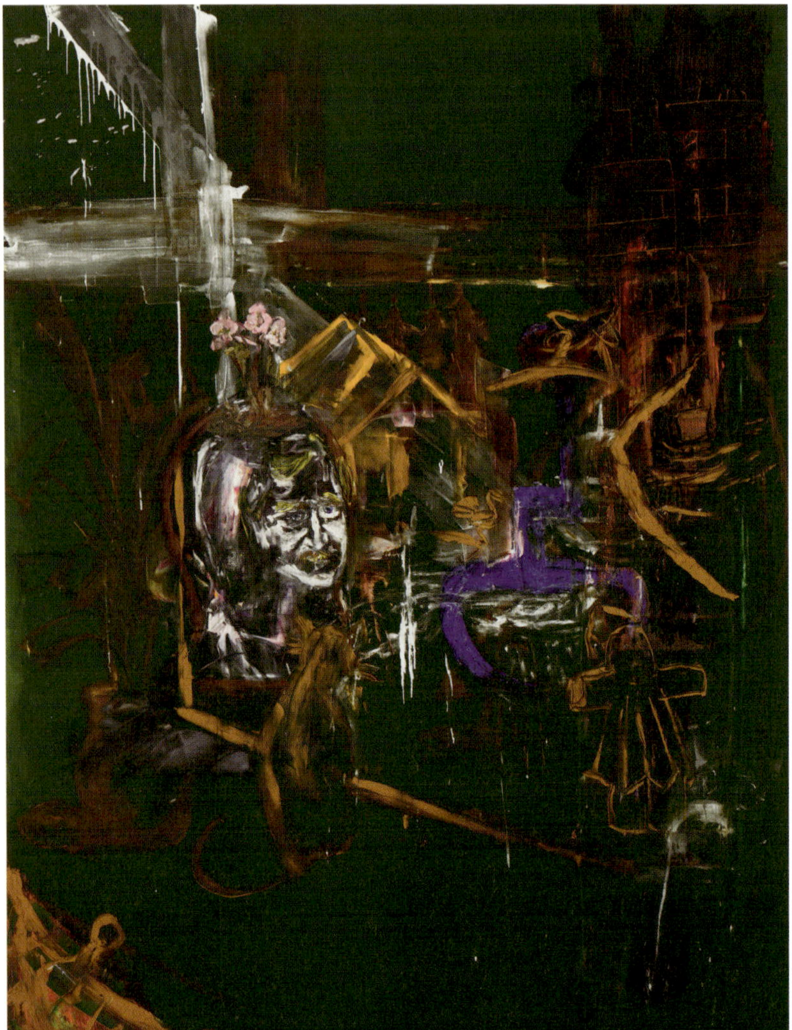

In a city as artistically thriving as Miami, Don and Mera Rubell are the couple that no one can afford to overlook. The two head the Rubell Museum, a lavish, warehouse-like building that holds works by artists like Damien Hirst, Maurizio Cattelan, Anselm Kiefer, Lyn Foulkes, Kara Walker, and James Marshall. Located in the Allapattah neighborhood, not too far from downtown, the museum—which occupies six former industrial buildings and was reconverted in two years by the Selldorf architecture studio—boasts no fewer than 7,200 works by 1,000 artists and is a reason in itself to explain why Miami is becoming more and more attractive.

The couple are totally at home in this context, aware that much of their prestige resides in a risk-taking, keen and sensitive eye, characterized by a unique sense of opportunity, which has allowed them to sniff out talent very early on, like Richard Prince and Jeff Koons, now superstars of the contemporary art world.

Dressed in black and with an innate sense of sophistication, Mera effortlessly guides the conversation. We take her lead, follow her around the museum, exploring and learning about the different rooms. And also its incredible library, a go-to reference for many Miami students and art scholars. Our eyes are constantly taken by surprise by pieces waiting around the corners of an endless labyrinth, creating all kinds of illusions. The art they collect reflects the couple's worldview and conveys it instantly to the beholder in a relentless torrent.

Which should come as no surprise, seeing that Don and Mera were behind the mythical *30 Americans* exhibition which traveled around the globe, showcasing the work of African-American artists at a time when it was necessary to take that step. But their facet as pioneering collectors is fleshed out by their abiding concern with the work of contemporary visual artists, and all the better if they are young.

Don and Mera have been married for well over fifty years. They began collecting together when they lived in New York, and later garnered fame in Wynwood, Miami's artistic neighborhood where they brought their collection in 1993. Perhaps the only thing that essentially tells them apart is the way they talk, Mera effusively while Don—passionate about the history of collecting, from the Middle Ages to the present day—takes his time, as if he weighs up each word before uttering it. Yet this contrast between them does nothing but add to the nuances of a couple that has never lost its freshness. Don puts things in perspective: 'In a way, the rooms in this museum don't just show art, they tell our story as collectors. Naturally the paths we've taken have changed, but we have never sold a work, and we have had strong influences that we always wanted to make evident. If people try to second

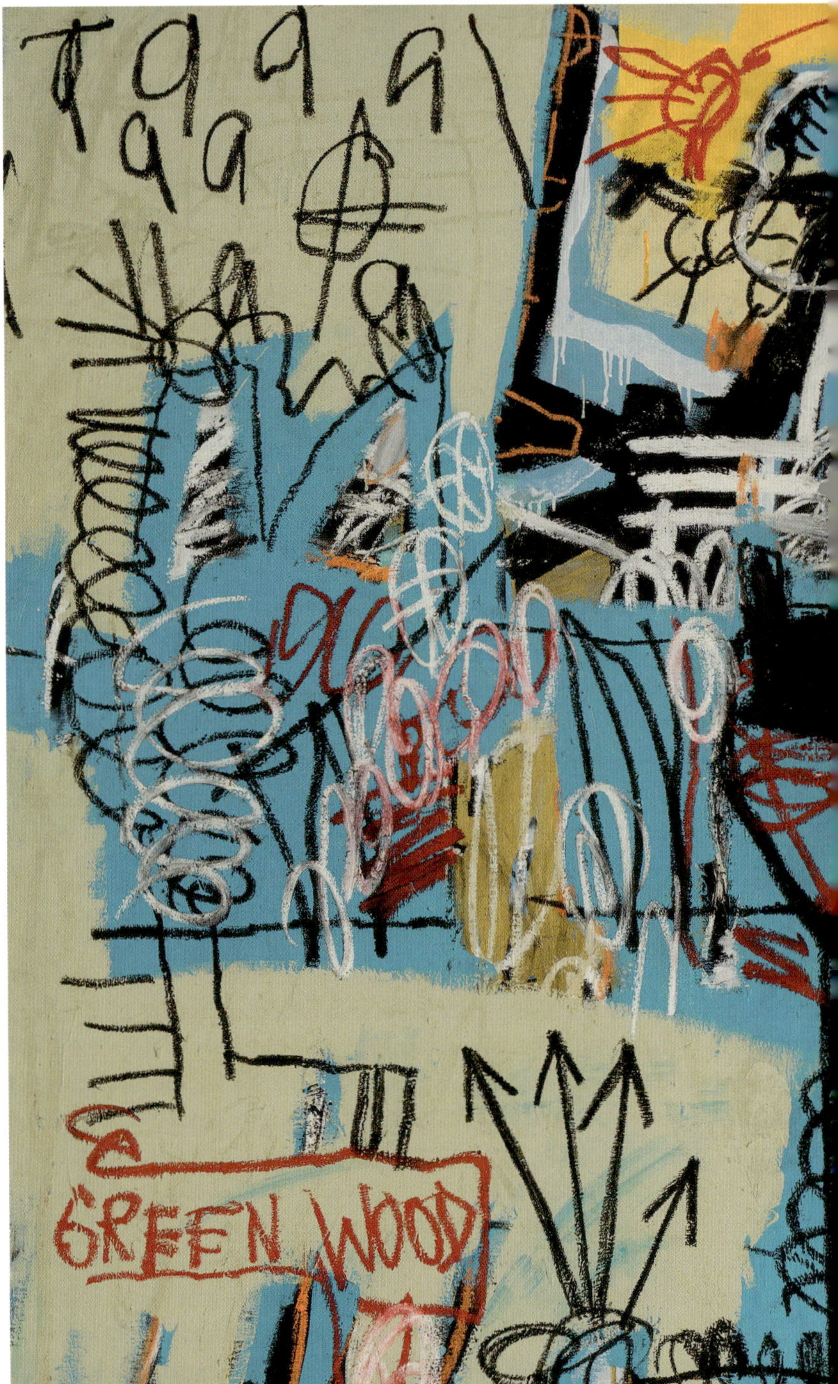
GREEN WOOD

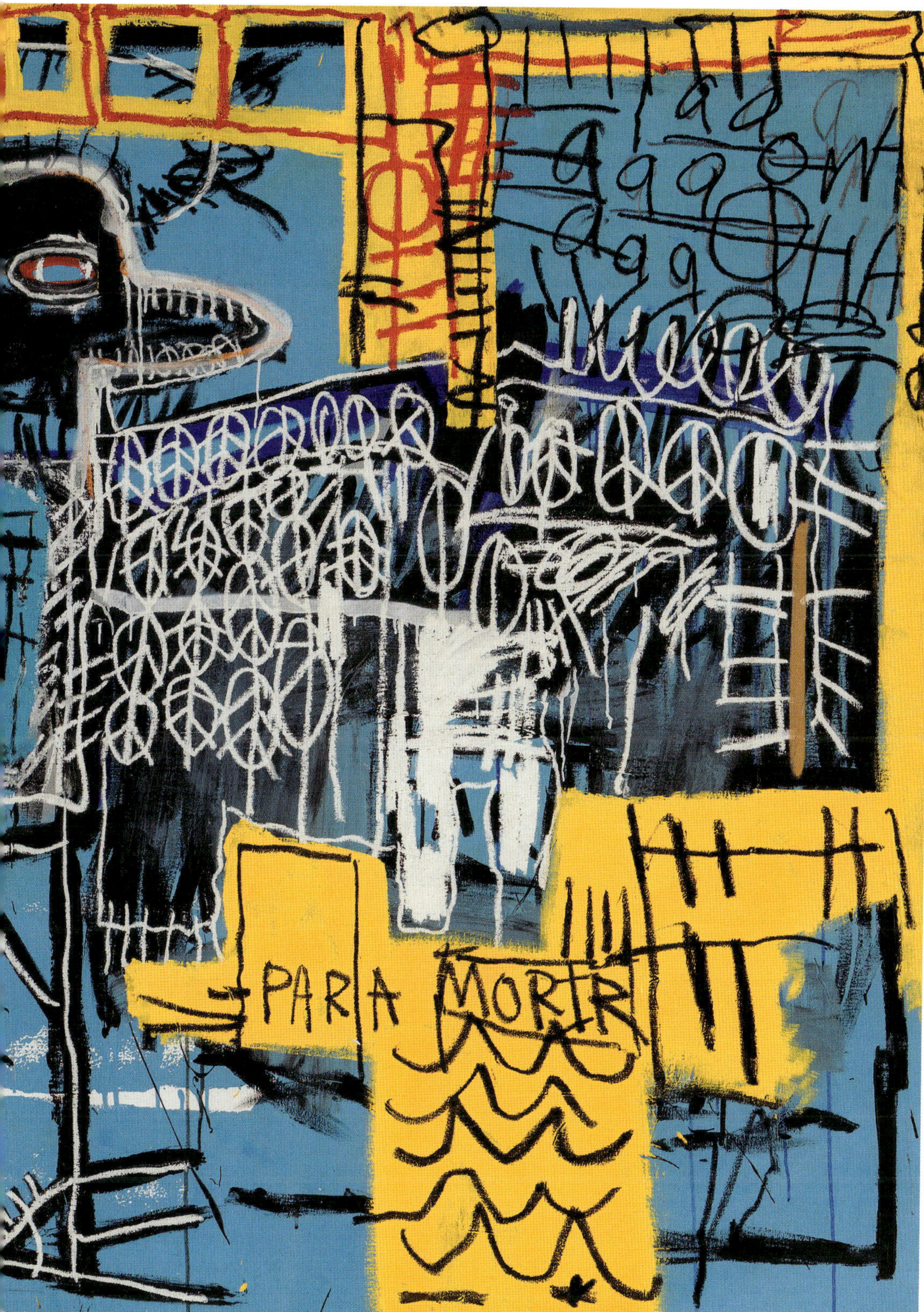

Jean-Michel Basquiat, *Bird On Money*, 1981

guess our taste, they generally get it wrong, because as much as possible we have tried to remain open to the changing world that contemporary artists try to reflect. What we want to do is to collect works that capture our time faithfully, rather than adapting what we buy to our taste, like people who collect paintings of objects that please them, such as flowers. Our goal is to engage the viewer with the artists, because we want art to be as meaningful to the public as it has been for us.' To this end, the museum—whose policy of subsidized admissions is conceived so that anyone who really wants to can visit it—has a plethora of different ways of collaborating with public schools that Mera can describe with surgical precision.

This is what the whole tour of the museum with Mera is like: animated with images thrown up by her mind and others when, for example, the visitor comes across one of Jeff Koons's earliest seminal works. 'I truly believe that every private collection is a unique fingerprint that reflects the talent, ambitions and history of those who have created it. If you add to the equation the influence of our son Jason and, of course, of a daughter like Jennifer, who works professionally in art, in addition to the concerns of a couple who have been together for fifty-five years, then, whether you like it or not, that unique character is accentuated.' Her husband wryly adds: 'Every bad marriage is the same, and every good marriage is different. It is the same with collections: they are perfect reflections of the collectors as individuals. It is much more interesting to collect than to earn money in the activity in which you originally dedicated yourself.'

'We collect young artists who have recently started to show their work, and we like to meet them personally and establish a relationship that lasts over time. For this reason, the way in which we began to collect is related to our life, with the economic limitations that we had at the beginning and with a path that was made little by little, because we did not have a large house whose walls we had to fill.' Maybe that's why, for the Rubells, it's hard to think of art as decorative. 'There was no premeditation or philanthropic pursuit here, but a genuine interest in original works of art, which for us has always been and still is magical.'

What works will stand the test of time? 'There is a fantastic three-volume book that traces art from the fourteenth to the eighteen century, and one of the conclusions that can be drawn is that no work maintains its value or interest over time, and that includes old masters like Raphael. For me, the interest in these works is more important than the fact that they stand the test of time. For example, why do people now respond enthusiastically to Modigliani in a way that they didn't when he was alive? We don't know,' Don explains before Mera elucidates further, 'I like to put historical and contemporary artists together. Egon Schiele is a consecrated artist who I

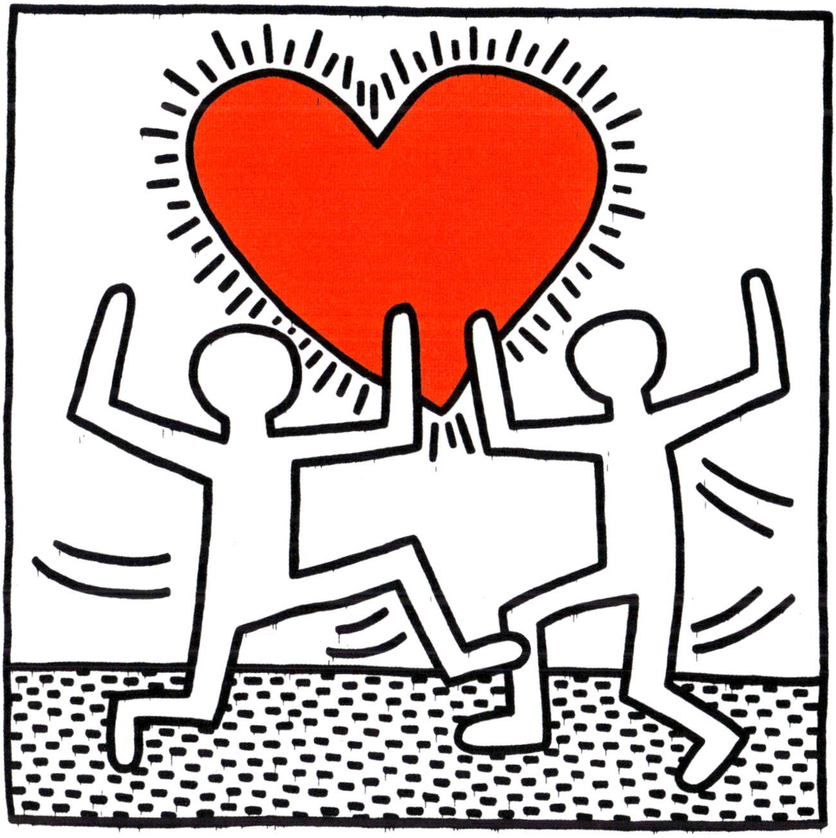

Keith Haring, *Untitled*, 1982

have reconsidered because a young artist I am interested in has recovered him. The history of art has continuity, and it is impossible to believe that what an artist does today is not influenced by what a master did hundreds of years ago. Picasso said that good artists copy but great ones steal. Having said that, not everyone is able to steal and, at the same time, manage to make his art unique.'

'Artists are very smart. And it is only natural that they are the ones who recover their own predecessors, then passing on their interest in artists like Marcel Duchamp to us,' concludes Don, who together with his wife has accumulated more miles than an astronaut and who has never given up an old vice: a daily game of tennis.

Elena Rueda, Marcos and Rafael Martín

‘The collector must always think big’

Eric Fischl, *Untitled*, 1986

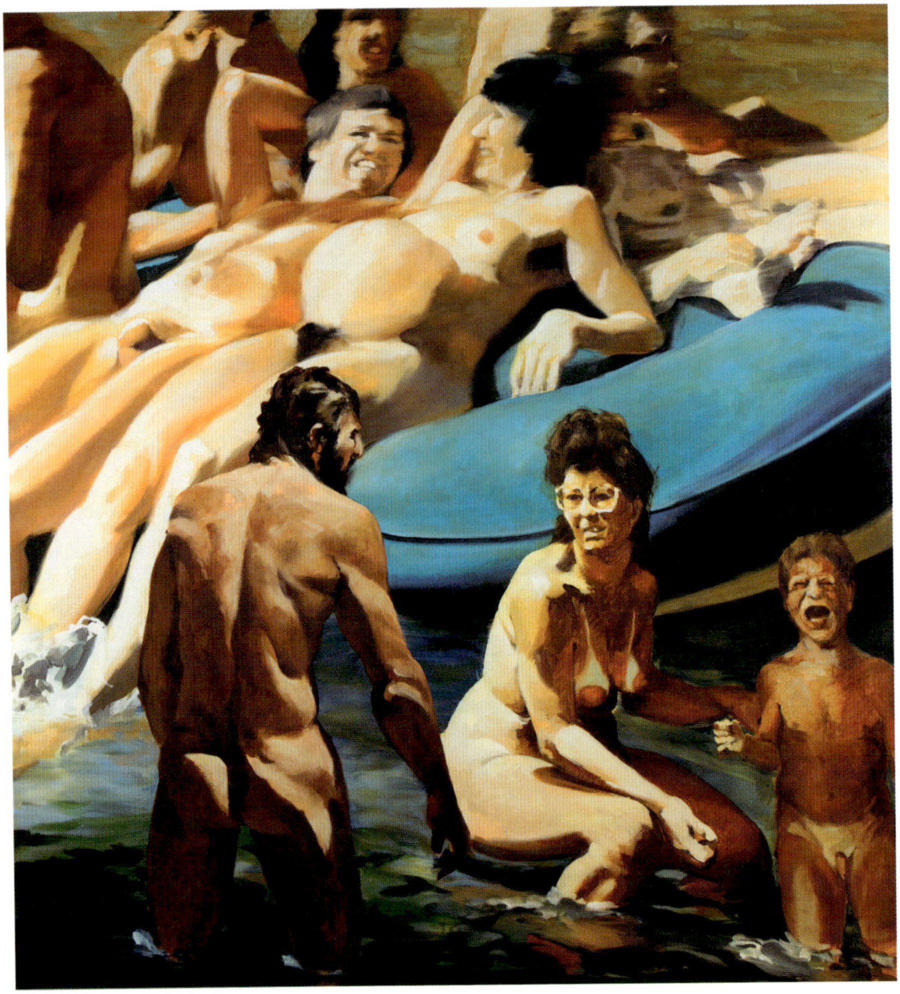

The story of the family formed by Elena Rueda Rodríguez and Marcos Martín Blanco is the story of the celebrated MER Collection, but essentially it is that of a wonderful self-made couple who came from humble backgrounds. Today, following the death of Marcos in June 2022, and with Elena fighting stoically yet lightheartedly against the health problems that afflict her, there is no better translator for their always youthful ideas than their son Rafael, a natural successor to their legacy, and not only because of the filial bond. Which also explains the acronym MER, standing for Marcos, Elena and Rafael.

The house in which the interview takes place is from the seventies, an important decade for Segovia, where it is located, as it was for the rest of the world. Inside it is a labyrinth of contemporary works of the highest quality, selected by the couple with courage, a counterculture spirit and an admirable sense of diversity. More than 700 works are housed in basement. After all, there is no collector who is not burdened by the lack of sufficient space, and so some of them are still in the original boxes in which they were delivered.

But neither Elena nor Marcos became rich with art, but rather the fruit of what they earned from their business selling suckling pigs and cold meats. After a long, hardworking and improbable career as agricultural entrepreneurs and, in the case of Marcos, as an economic consultant and former head of the Ministry of Public Works' Economic Advisory, they invested in this area with such keen insight that, despite their scant prior experience, today they are surrounded by a set of works of incalculable value, many of which they acquired when nobody was paying attention to the artists.

In this marriage, Elena has been the driving force and Marcos, the vision. And it is in this contrast that one can find the core of the synergy they have established, now brought together in a splendid catalog, and in which the sum of the parts forms a coherent and, above all, personal and hypnotic whole, dotted here and there with gems by artists as dissimilar and exceptional as Julian Schnabel, Jenny Saville, Eric Fischl, Juan Usle or Andrés Serrano. Winner of the ARCO Award for Collecting in 2004, MER, focused more on subject matters to do with the human body than on a specific chronology or aesthetic school, is a truly impressive collection. But it is no less interesting to talk to Rafael, one of the apexes of this triangle whose other two members, his parents, were classified by Dan Cameron as 'ecstasy collectors.'

'My father comes from a very small town in Segovia where no one went to college, but even as a child he always wanted to study, so thanks to great effort he graduated from high school and went on to study Economic Sciences. From the moment his economic position changed, he began to do a lot of international consulting related to infrastructure, roads, hydraulic planning, etc., for which many of the people he hired ended up occupying key roles, for example, in the government of Felipe Gonzalez. He had great vision both as a consultant and in his investments. After they got married, my parents visited my grandmother here all the time, and while they were looking for houses they came across this one. Their initial intention was to build three houses: one for my uncle, one for my grandmother and one for themselves. But the original plan changed, and just when they did not have a penny left, Gerardo Rueda appeared in my parents' lives. In 1979 he accepted the commission to decorate their house. And among the things he brought were works by contemporary artists, which at first they didn't understand because their gaze wasn't educated. Gerardo did not impose anything but rather acted somehow like Pygmalion, opening up the world to them and a way of looking at art, which took shape over a number of years.'

Marcos and Elena have confessed that contemporary art transformed them as people: 'Gerardo Rueda gave us the bug, and then we decided to visit galleries and museums at least one afternoon a week. After three years we began to understand something, like babies starting to talk. And then the pleasure arose.' And also a very personal gaze and taste. As Rafael explains, 'the effort they made to visit galleries, the way they came across Soledad Lorenzo and María del Corral, and the way they entered the world of art, it's amazing. My father set out on this new path with my mother in the same way as he applied industrial technology to cattle breeding. That led them to meet contemporary artists who were overlooked at the time but whose work is worth a lot today.'

But what is collecting for Rafael, beyond the passion he shared with his parents? 'Well, when there is no room to hang the paintings, and you have to stack them, it means there is a passion. In the case of my parents, the initial attraction to painting hooked them completely. And they began to realize that some works had grown in value, and their quality endorsed, but that the opposite also happens, so that they purged between 100 and 150 works in auctions. That opened up a market for them, both selling and then buying. They showed that with limited resources the evolution of their collection could be exponential, because many of the important works in the collection have been bought at the expense of selling others.'

The dream of a first-class museum is one of the few that the family has not been able to materialize. This is bad news, more so for Spanish society than for them personally. 'It makes no sense to have works stored away. You may own them, but what right do you have to keep them stacked away as if it were in a mausoleum? The logical thing is to make them visible.'

Regardless of the medium, whether it be drawing, photography or painting, why has Marcos focused so much on the human body, without eschewing explicit approaches on occasion? 'My father always had a strong *cabaretesque* streak, so it is no surprise that the majority of depictions of the human body are of women. I think he leaned towards the ironic side of figuration. In any case, when it came to collecting, apart from his eye, he always applied an analytical mind and the guidelines he learned in business, believing that the collector must always think big and make a big personal and economic investment.'

A few years ago, Marcos said: 'We have often thought of throwing in the towel, because most of what we were seeing looked like a joke. But after you keep looking and looking, you gradually adopt. Whether it is because you like it, because it inspires you, because it gives you pleasure, because it fills you.'

Marilyn Minter, *The Last Pam*, 2010

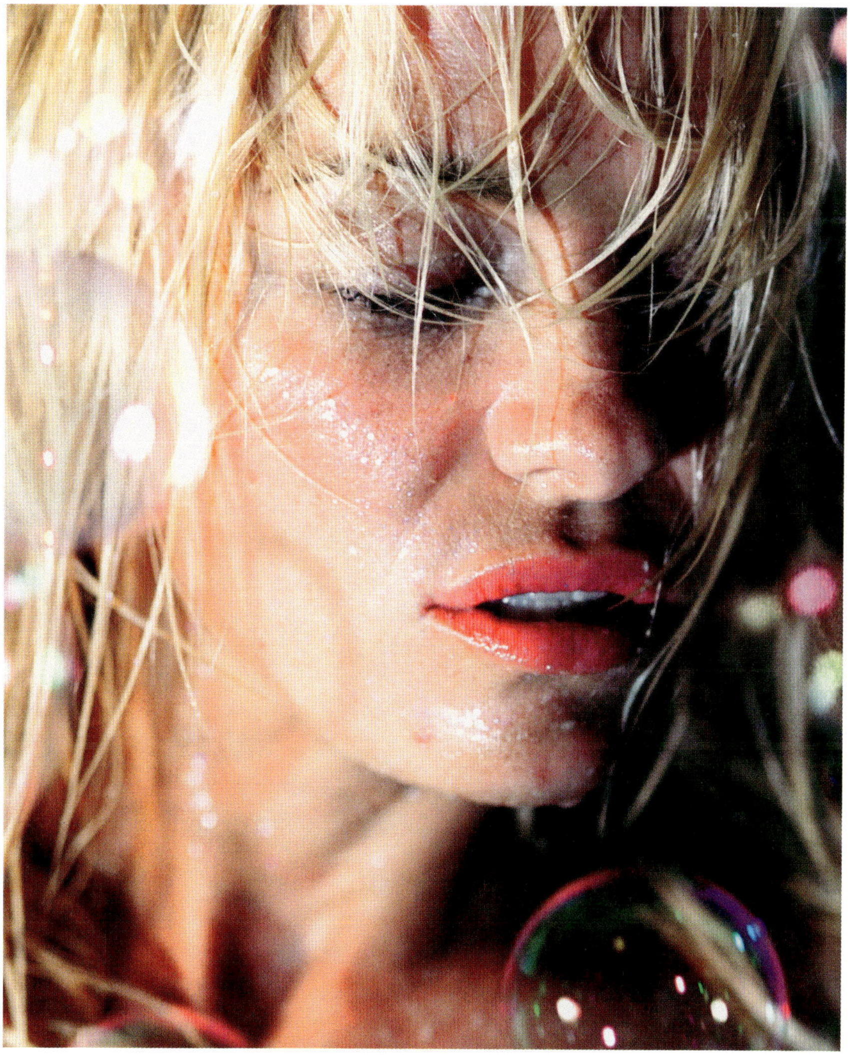

Eugenio López Alonso

'I am interested in the art world more for passion than for investment.'

Gabriel Orozco, *Atomists: Making Strides*, 1996

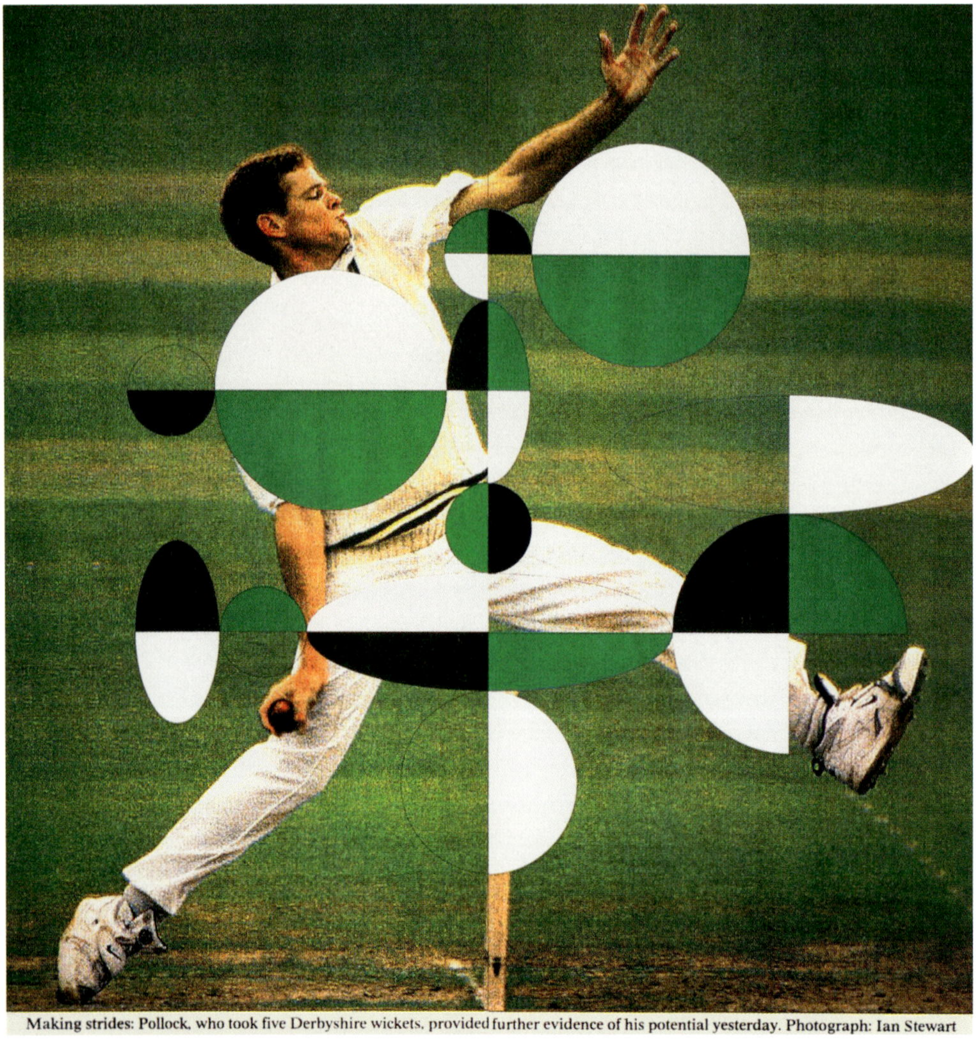

What does a great collector do and why are there no two alike? No one knows for sure, but there is a consensus that certain attributes are mandatory: aesthetic passion, a keen discerning and pioneering eye, a conception of the collection as a whole that, when taken together, reflects its time and asks the spectator unavoidable questions, and of course, a factor of risk. But, how much risk? That depends on each case, although if we are talking about Eugenio López, the more the better. The mettle of this patron, philanthropist and collector has paid off, and the value of his works has multiplied manyfold, something he is proud of. Yet, what is much more important to him is that his undertaking has given people access to the work of contemporary artists of the highest quality who would otherwise not have had it, and ultimately that it is able to move them profoundly.

López Alonso is not an orthodox collector. He was never destined to be one. Because he says whatever he feels like, because he gives very few interviews and because his profile is more rock star than high-brow. In addition, he speaks intelligently, entertainingly and seductively. And in this case, he talks for over an hour at his fabulous home in Lomas de Chapultepec, Mexico City, built in 1976 and renovated in 2015 by Luis Bustamante. Everything here could not be more contemporary and, yet, because of the excellence that surrounds us, one comes away with the impression that each detail was conceived solely and for the greater glory of some unexpected and tireless reincarnation of Lorenzo de Medici.

At the beginning of the interview this Mexican collector, dressed completely in black, gives off the impression of apparent vanity. However, as we start to chat, the shell soon drops away. Behind the façade López reveals a very personable character, proud that things have gone well in his life and, above all, a socially, personally and artistically sensitive man.

The inheritor and multiplier of one of Mexico's great fortunes, López acquired works of incalculable value during the downturn, including some by consecrated artists such as Cy Twombly and Roy Lichtenstein. Moreover, he never speculates with the works he purchased. Rather he followed the instinct that guides all great collectors, and democratized access to art through his Jumex Foundation for Contemporary Art and later with the Jumex Museum, a wonderful legacy for his country designed by David Chipperfield and opened in 2013. The Jumex Museum has exhibited James Turrell, Marcel Duchamp, Jeff Koons and Andy Warhol—the splendid Warhol of the 1960s—among many others that form part of the 3,000-plus collection belonging to López, a member of the board of such major institutions as the Tamayo Museum and MOCA Los Angeles and the recipient of multiple awards and tributes for the excellence of his collection and his philanthropy. Maybe that is why each answer he gives is direct and sincere. 'I bought my first work,

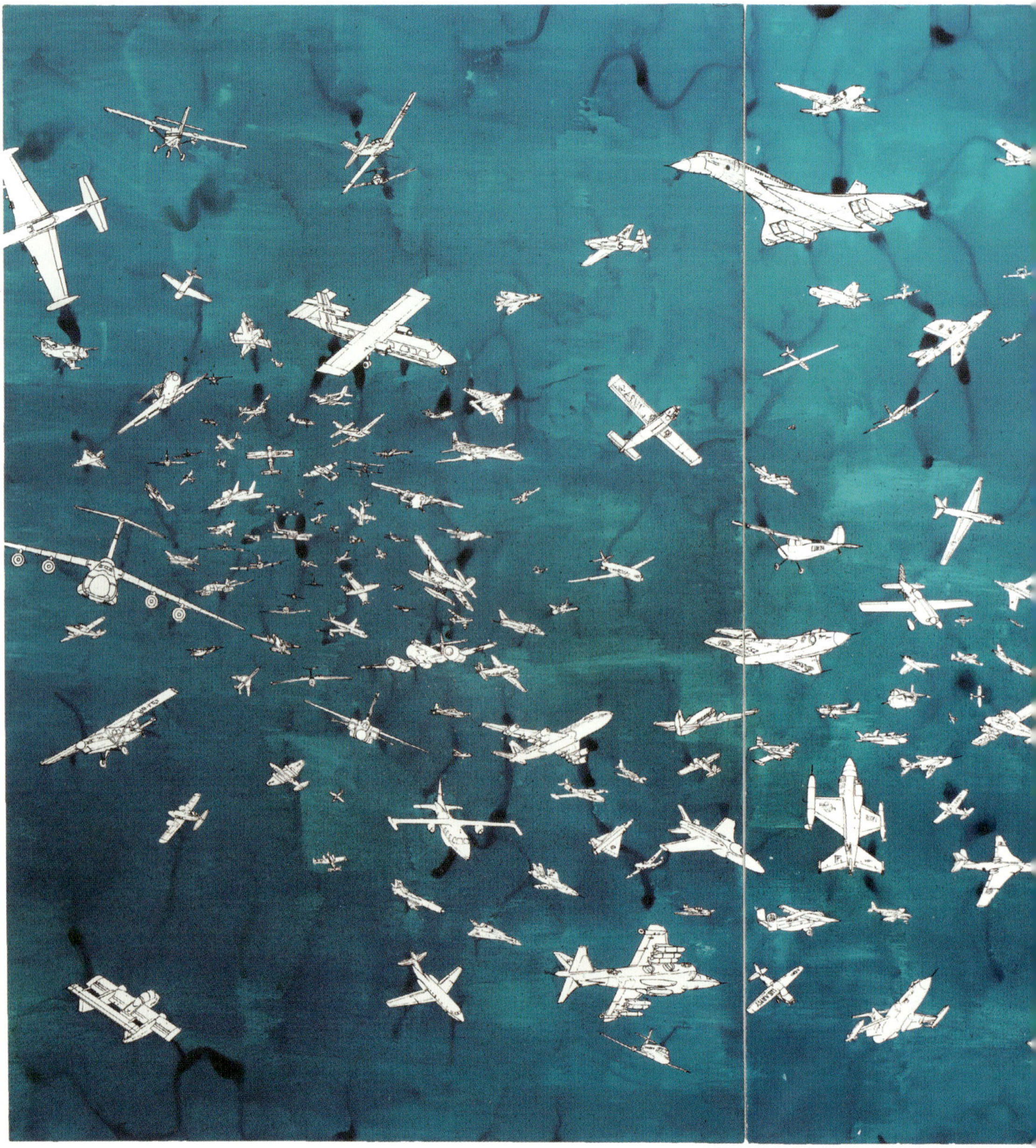

Alighiero Boetti, *Aerei*, 1988

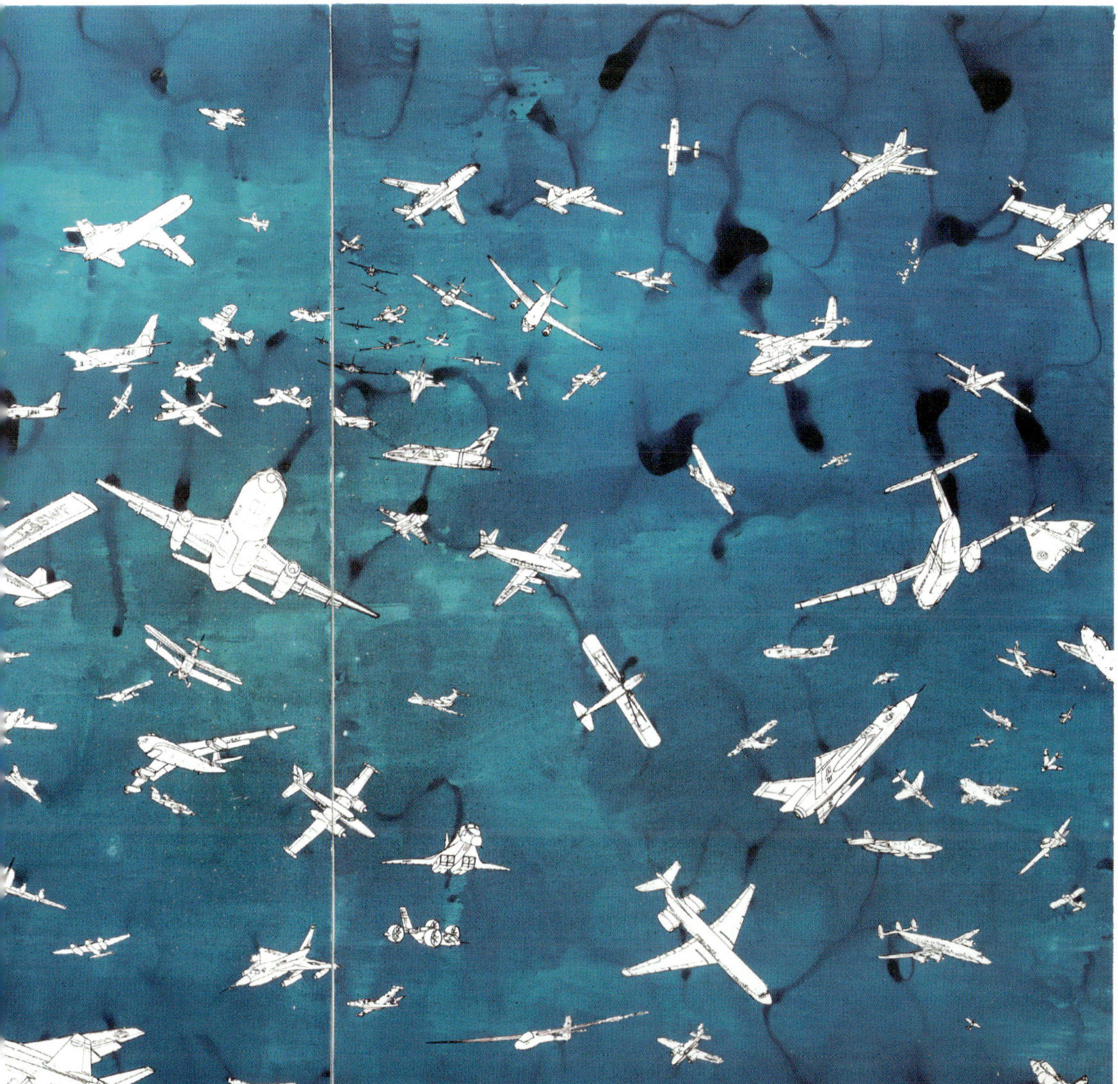

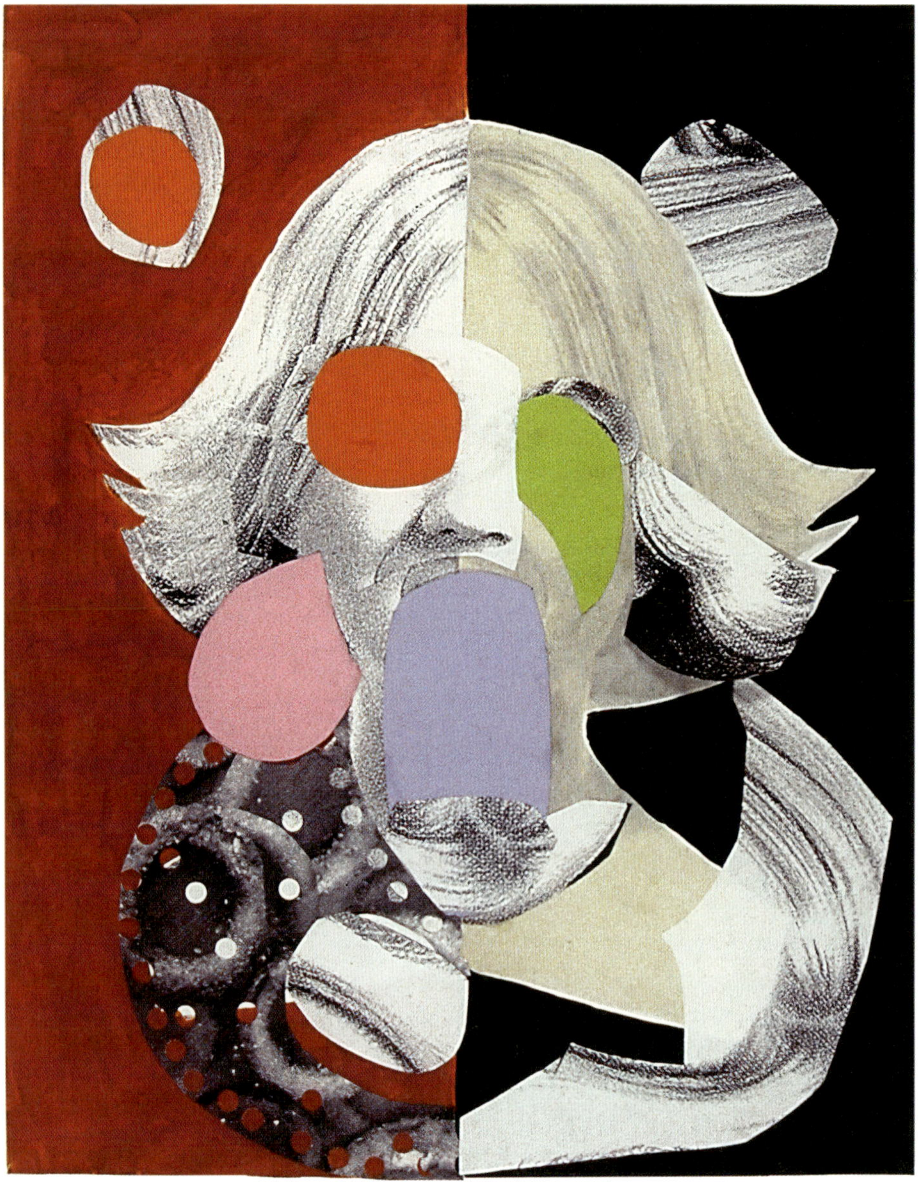

Meg Cranston, *The Myth of Symmetry*, 2006

a painting by Roberto Cortázar, in 1990. I had been drawn to his work and from the time I first saw it I began to feel the need not only to collect, but to have something attractive and beautiful, something that would be mine. At that time I was just twenty-two years old. However, I did not start collecting seriously until 1994 when I came to the United States. Seeing artists I knew nothing about was a fantastic stimulus and made me very happy,' he claims. He went on to add: 'At the beginning, Esthella Provas and Patricia Marshall helped me, but I didn't fully understand what it was all about until

I went to an auction house. There I understood that there was something more to it and that I had to get to know it better. The most amazing thing that has ever happened to me is to have had the parents I had, who, once again, showed me who they really were. On that occasion, my father, who knew the old masters like Goya and Velázquez but had no idea about contemporary art despite his intelligence and infallible instincts, supported me.' 'In the early-nineties, there was a big dip in the art market. I saw some wonderful works and I traveled to meet gallerists, to visit museums and biennials, and started to read incessantly about the history of art. So, even though the economic factor was important to me, and it is true that there are works that twenty-five years later have increased their worth enormously, I am interested in the art world more for passion than for investment.'

He says that he is normally more attracted toward abstraction than figuration, and he collects pieces from renowned as well as emerging artists. 'In the marketplace there is a vast offer, there are fairs, auctions and galleries. It's impossible to buy everything from everyone, right?' he adds with a smile. With high praise for some of his personal favorites like Jasper Johns, Willem de Kooning, Antoni Tàpies and Cy Twombly—'the first time I saw him I was hooked; the truth is that there is no one who held such fascination for me'—he pinpoints the starting point for his collection in abstract expressionism. Toward the late-nineties, because there was no more room in his apartment and because of the importance his collection had acquired, it became part of the gallery of the Jumex factory in Ecatepec, and later became the Jumex Foundation, an accomplishment much applauded by the international press before it was recognized at home. All this eventually led to the opening of the museum, which had such a deep emotional impact on López Alonso that, laughing, he compares it to a postpartum experience.

What happens after a birth, even if it is years later? One answer is that each individual philanthropist decides what will be the ultimate destiny of his collection. 'The idea is for the collection to stay in Mexico and for it to continue growing. How to fund this is something I have yet to decide,' he underlines.

The collector's more social facet can be seen in the scholarships on offer for young people to study abroad or in the system he uses to subsidize free admission to his museum. With conceptual coherence, Eugenio López adds, 'if things go well in the country, in business and in my personal life—because one does not depend solely on oneself—the future will be brilliant. Over and above the vanity of what one does, there are moments that surprise you to the core, like when a very emotional woman thanked me for giving her the opportunity to see a Jeff Koons in person in Mexico. I remember the way she said it and it gave me goosebumps. That's when you realize that it is all well worth the effort.'

José Darío Gutiérrez

'My concern is far from being aesthetic'

Antonio Caro, *Cristo efervescente*, 1980

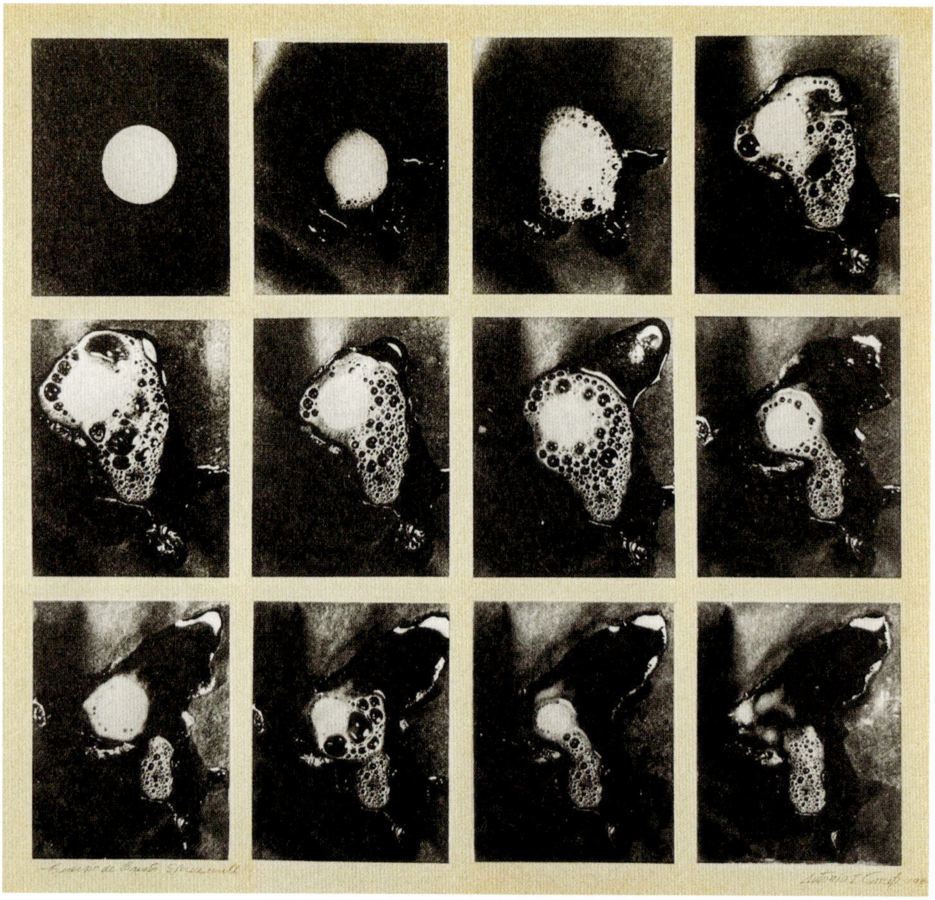

The world of a collector speaks as much about the works he surrounds himself with as it does about the mind and heart of the person who has brought together this unrepeatable set of works. In José Darío Gutiérrez, the fruit of that passion is unique, but what are the pulleys that move it? This humanist Colombian began collecting Matchbox cars and postage stamps, before coming belatedly to the visual arts. In addition to studying Law, he became passionate about literature. This was a logical result both of his own inclinations and of the magnetic environment in which he grew up, between the drawings and clay moldings of his father and the lessons of his mother, a high school music and art history teacher, which Gutiérrez would never forget.

'Art was always something normal in my house,' he explained and 'although my parents were not collectors as such, our home was full of art and the works were chosen for artistic and not decorative criteria. Even still, I find it hard to get to the bottom of my drive to collect. It is like a mental or psychiatric condition: a desire for control, or the pleasure of being surrounded by things that invite one to think. In principle, it is not a very generous attitude, and more like hoarding. But what history has shown us is that the collector is a temporary custodian who puts together a collection that is sometimes so valuable that it cannot be sold, and ends up becoming part of the national heritage.'

Gutiérrez is the driving force behind the ambitious Bogotá-based research initiative into Latin-American art called the Bachué Project. In his apartment, it is easy to delineate the beginning and end of each of the periods he collects. But if we lose ourselves in the labyrinth of pieces Gutiérrez has accumulated, the spell begins to take effect and one no longer knows what is what, engrossed in so much beauty, so much excellence, so much insightfulness and, as if that were not enough, with such refined criteria.

During the long conversation on Zoom owing to the pandemic, the effect is equally hypnotic, as we skip from Alfonso Suárez and Camilo Lleras to Fernando Botero, Leopoldo Richter, Alipio Jaramillo, Leonel Castañeda and José Alejandro Restrepo. From the cycle of Colombian modernism to the arrival in the collection of an emblematic, eclectic work by Rómulo Rozo Peña from 1925, misunderstood at the time, passing through the development of the aforementioned Bachué Project and a subsequent more profound examination of concepts which helped to enrich the context and essence that give meaning to each work.

Contrary to what one might suppose, the spell cast by the collection ends up being natural in a country where another magician, Gabriel García Márquez, showed us how his most fantastic stories were in fact realist.

'The concept of collecting has a gathering and hoarding spirit. But the point on which I later reflect, and one that led to the moment in which my project is formalized, has its origin in a concern about the national identity of a country like Colombia and, fundamentally, about its entry or not into modernity, because I believe that this is still a pre-modern nation. This concern with what is proper to us has always intrigued me, probably because of my family DNA, perhaps going back to my grandfather Benigno Abelardo Gutiérrez, a self-educated enlightened man from the beginning of the last century in Sonsón, a town in Antioquia where, in addition to manager of a mining company, he was a photographer, a liberal in a conservative place, and founder of one of its newspapers and also of the Public Improvement Society. He made the first study of the town, placing it within the overall context of Colombia, and started to compile local folklore from Antioquia, a task he continued at the helm of a nationwide publishing house based in Medellín,' Gutiérrez explained, and listening to him is almost like reading Juan Rulfo.

'I didn't have a close relationship with my father, also an engineer, who always wanted to do something related to the legacy of my grandfather, but art and literature were always a natural part of my background, just as music was on the other side of the family, passed down from my great-great-grandfather to my grandfather, my father and my mother,' he confesses before adding that he began studying piano at the age of seven along with his cousins.

However, and affording us an inkling of his personality as an elite collector, he declares: 'I don't define myself as a connoisseur of art. Generally speaking, my concern is far from being aesthetic, and at times leans toward the opposite, because I am more attracted to something that offends or shocks me. So why did I get mixed up in all this, so early and so forcefully, wanting to be surrounded by things that I felt comfortable with, but which were also unsettling and created unease? I think that because, just as my grandfather was a compiler, I am an editor who identifies social phenomena, which in this case are manifested in the visual arts. So, I want to know about the environment in which they were produced, what was behind the work and, above all, why certain works which I believe have great anthropological value are not appreciated by the art world, and that has allowed me to collect wonderful works that that world does not view as being extremely valuable.'

As a kind of involuntary custodian of a sacred though still misunderstood art, he declares: 'My project is not personal, but rather a challenge to the institutional model imposed on us from above. That is why it is also civic, since it seeks to raise people's awareness and criteria, so that they act as citizens, in the Greek sense of the word.'

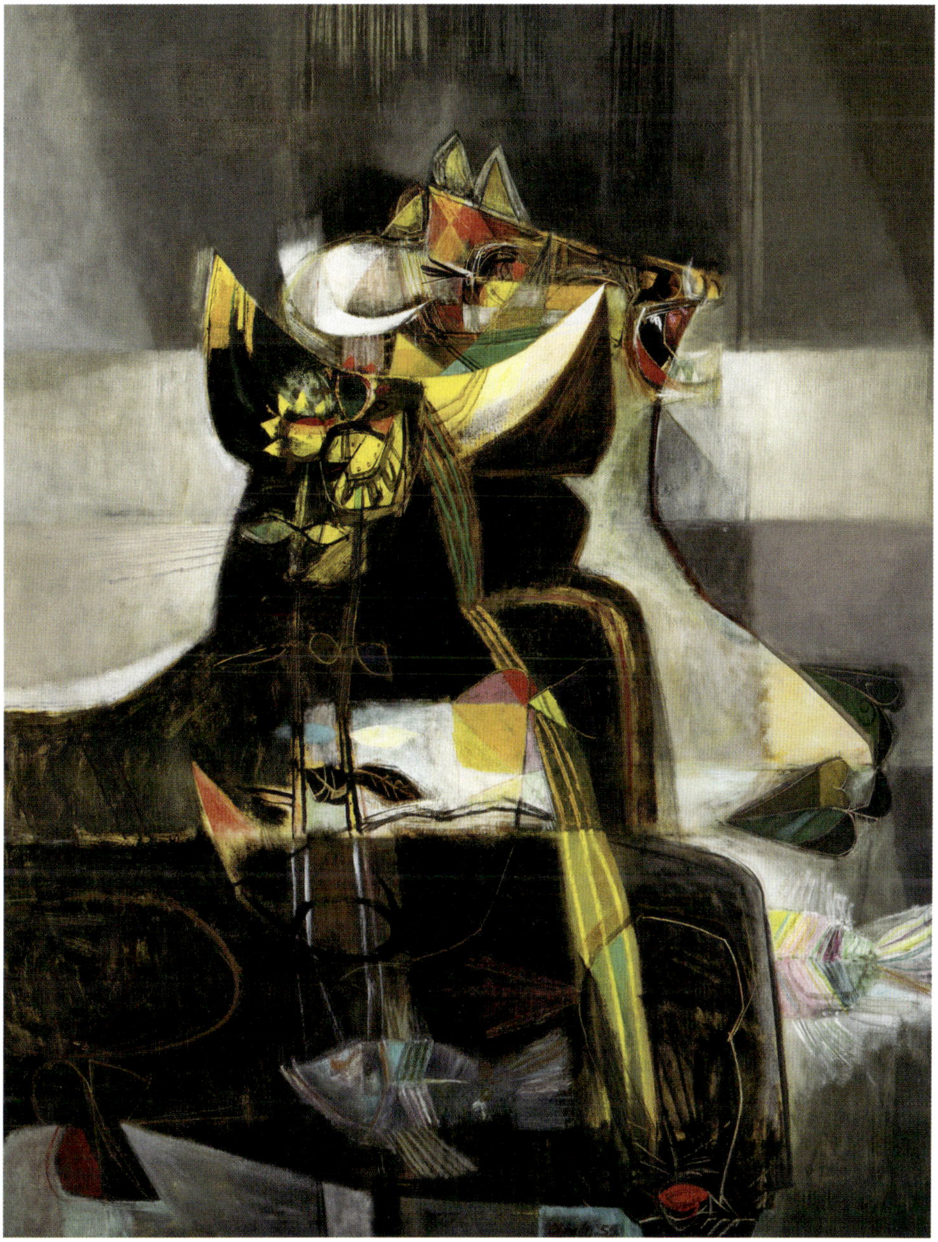

Alejandro Obregón, *Ganado ahogándose en el Magdalena*, 1955

But what does he expect the viewer to find in his collection? In the first place, a series of elements that complement the more widely shared concerns of the establishment. 'I get a sense of morbid satisfaction in attracting a person, whatever their level, who acknowledges that there are things that he does not know, things he has never paid attention to or that he had not recognized, and who suddenly says to himself: "wow, I had no idea about this period" or "why is this next piece alongside the work of a consecrated artist," or other such questions,' he tells us.

All notions of snobbery are completely alien to Gutiérrez. Perhaps that is why he has no bones in openly stating: 'Colombian art has absolutely no, and I repeat, no, international projection. There is one institution that has done something for Latin American contemporary art, but normally it is very hard to see anything other than Botero or Doris Salcedo.' Perhaps that is why he believes it is so vital to provide context to chaos, not only in Colombian art but in Latin-American art and, then, more specifically to the field of contemporary art, which he accumulated with criteria and special zeal between 2000 and 2019.

'I found it difficult to make the shift from modern to contemporary art, but I was helped by several artists working today who are asking questions about who we are and what kind of country we want to be, which is not a political crisis but a case of nation-building. So artists working in this line, like Nadin Ospina, Carlos Castro, Fernando Pareja and Leidy Chávez, or

Fernando Pareja and Leidy Chavez, *Untitled*, 2009

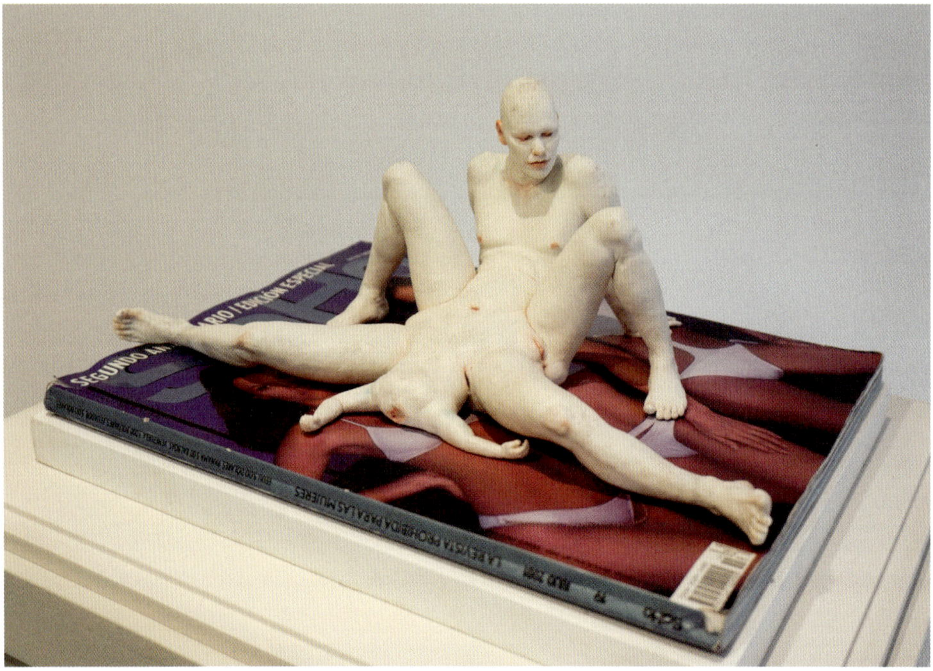

José Alejandro Restrepo, fitted in with my criteria. The kind of contemporary art that interests me not only looks at what is happening today, but is also interested in the origins of humanity and its concerns. For me, geometry or abstraction do not exist as such, but are the expressive decisions of artists. So, going back to people like Restrepo, I was introduced to a new discipline and felt that I could take decisions following my own criteria and not second-hand or because of other people's recommendations. That's how I started to build my own collection of contemporary art, which runs parallel to the general taste without pandering to it; so much so that one university editorial said that it was in bad taste,' as Gutiérrez, a true thinker in these times of intellectual laziness, gracefully confesses.

Despite this, he goes on to clarify: 'In the contemporary world I have to select and be very critical, because there might be 500 artists and I have to choose which ones systematically reflect on the issues that interest me, regardless of the way in which they resolve it visually. Those contemporary artists help me to tell a story, whereas modernity was not so anthropological and played out as it happened. But there are artworks today which, because of their theme or materials, I cannot live with, but which are nevertheless necessary reflections that I must collect. Perhaps because I am not interested in universal art that does not contribute to an idea of a nation.'

A surprise confession interrupts what seemed like a strong ending. 'I have works in storage that I would like to have on view at home, but I am not able to take down one piece without needing the other. It is a challenge.' And he adds with a mischievous dig: 'Unlike some institutions that have the sense to program their exhibitions, the great museums of Bogotá believe that giving space to a collector is to increase the value of their collection, but then what? Will they buy it from me? That is pure selfishness and insecurity.'

The driving force behind in-depth research into modern art and national identity with anthropological and sociological aspects, a businessman, patron, publisher, entrepreneur, collector and intellectual: José Darío is all of these things. And perhaps he would not have gotten to where he is today without a certain determination and a critical sense, though not devoid of kindness.

So it can only be gratifying to hear the way he ends a conversation that could have gone on forever: 'Antioquia feels like a different country from Colombia. It is in search of independence and can boast the great achievements of those who make great efforts. But it also has the problem that it is inward looking, always gazing at its own navel. I criticize these circumstances, even though, as I've said, I consider myself to be from Antioquia. I am a product of that identity in my character, in my ambitions and in my aspirations.'

Ernesto Poma

‘I have never bought art as an investment’

Belkis Ayón, *My Vernicle o Si yo no te olvido,* 1998

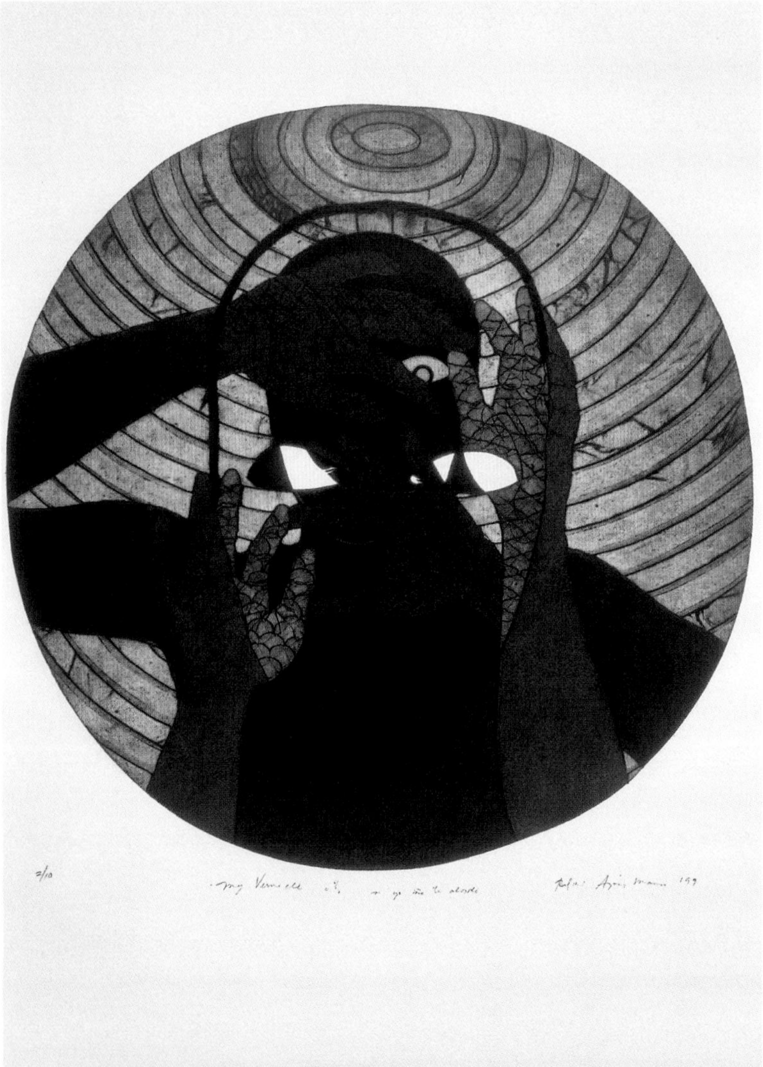

Ernesto Poma is experiencing the pandemic, a strange and dystopian time whose scope we have not yet fully understood, at his home in Aspen, Colorado, a true haven of good taste. Two pleasures can be discerned from our conversation. The first consists in unraveling the soul of an elite Latin-American collector who, because of the magnitude of his collection, could be from anywhere. And the second lies in the pleasure of talking with a leading figure from the world of business and patronage whose conversation is hypnotic, more typical of an era when bars were places for social gatherings during which time was held on pause. And this one acquires greater value if we bear in mind that Poma has chosen to surgically curate his public appearances and declarations.

An entrepreneur in his own right, as well as a member of the family which owns the Salvadoran business holding Grupo Poma, whose interests range from the automobile industry to hotels and real estate, as well as telecommunications, Ernesto Poma and his wife, Cecilia, are members of MoMA's Latin American and Caribbean Fund, as well as Art Basel's Global Patrons Council. His collection defines both a sense of aesthetics and a worldview as well as a love for the continent in which he was born that are quite unique.

'We moved to Miami when the civil war broke out in El Salvador. We went through some very difficult times because, among many other things, one of my brothers was kidnapped. So, we came here in the late-seventies, when I was 17, and I studied in New England, in Boston, and ended up back in Miami, where my family had opened an investment office. In 1987 I married my wife, who is also from El Salvador. Even though a large part of my family returned to El Salvador, where I visit often, I wanted to stay in Miami,' explains Poma. And getting down to the business at hand, he adds: 'Art must be dignified, even in the way works are hung and dialogue with each other, because of the invisible connection between them that makes them so interesting, and because it tells a sort of story. It is something that I learned over time, because even if my parents did not begin as collectors, they taught us to appreciate the beauty in everything that surrounds us, in a sunset or in a flower. Particularly my mother who had a special eye and began to acquire very beautiful pieces of Central-American art.'

'When I was 23 years old,' he continues 'I made the decision to make changes in my life. I went from being a college student who partied a lot to taking a completely different path with other goals. And then I opened my eyes and began to discover beauty around me. It was like a kind of positive catharsis, where I would look around and say, "wow, I can't believe this blue sky." This was the context in which my interest in the art world grew. The first piece I bought was an incredibly well technically executed still life with a pitaya, a fruit with an exquisite color. It cost me $200 and that's where it all started: first I bought work by Salvadoran artists, then I moved on to the idea of the whole Central-American region, and finally I discovered the more global Latin America.'

Thus it was that Poma went from collecting young talents to a deeper—aesthetic, social, psychological, and plastic—insight into great masters like Matta, Lam, Diego Rivera or Rufino Tamayo. And the hypnotic fascination with the maze of endless paths is summed up in a futurist drawing made by Emilio Pettoruti in 1914. 'What I was discovering was telling me a story about Latin America, about art, about its artists, about their context and their influences. And the same continues to happen at fairs, galleries, or artists' studios, from modernism to the contemporary universe. Because I love universal art, but I thought of collecting with a particular approach that spoke to me personally and would stimulate me intellectually and emotionally. I wanted to surround my family with pleasant things that nurture you deeply, but at the same time are appealing,' he underscores. 'My goal was for the collection to be of Latin-American art, and yet I believe that the artists in it are universal artists who have historical relevance due to the weight of their work. There is always something in me of that Latin-American influence, no matter where I am, that is palpable and that attracts me spontaneously.'

As we take a verbal tour of his house in Florida, Poma emphasizes the 'solid Salvadoran contemporary art movement that despite the undoubted influence of instruments that are not proper to it, such as performance, has its own remarkably executed manifestations.' With a highly original although rigorously curated perspective, his collection embraces true superstars such as Roberto Matta, Wifredo Lam, Joaquín Torres García, Diego Rivera, David Siqueiros, and Claudio Bravo, just in the main room, and then moving to the geometric disruption of Jesús Soto, Carlos Cruz-Diez, Iberê Camargo or the Madíes, and finally the contemporaneity of Ernesto Neto, Guillermo Kuitca, Arturo Herrera, Ana Mendieta and Doris Salcedo.

Among these artists, Poma has a special weakness for the Uruguayan master Joaquín Torres García, a champion of constructivism and founder of a school that has given the small South-American country a systematicity and tradition of excellence disproportionate to its size. 'He is a fascinating artist not only because of what he has done in his own right, but also because of the influence he has had on so many artists from generations that followed, including some current ones. It also happens that geometry is something that attracts me a lot.'

Although he likes to personally meet the artists he collects, as happened with Gabriel Orozco, who helped him 'discover new things and find beauty in unexpected places,' for Poma this does not make him love a particular piece any more or less. 'Salcedo's work defines my true interest, because it speaks of incredibly harsh subjects, which I identify with, coming from El Salvador, and it dignifies excluded peoples in a powerful and poetic way. I believe it is absolutely exceptional.'

There is still time for some thoughts on the art market, a thorny issue not just for specialists like himself, but for anyone interested in a constantly changing world, especially at a time when it is seeing unprecedented prices. 'I think, for example, Art Basel has been great not only for collectors in Miami, but for the city itself, making it more international, cultured and sophisticated. The fair gives me a chance to chat with gallerists who are truly trusted friends, and to see new things in a way that can also be fun. Now, due to the pandemic, it is curious to see how major artworks are being sold virtually. I think the market is shifting more toward that. And that trend will allow the market not only to educate itself in prices, but also to become smarter,' says Poma before concluding: 'In any case, the market often acts like a big machine that produces mega-galleries that can put their stamp on something, regardless of its quality, artificially inflating the prices of some artists. But that's not it either: if you spend your money on a work and it goes up in price, then that's great! I have never bought art as an investment, but rather because I love living with it and because it stimulates me. And, more than intellectually, I have done it from a gut feeling. I believe that art is a good place to put your money if you do it with criteria, and the greatest pleasure is the privilege of living with such works. If I want to invest I have other ways.'

Jonathan Ruffer

'The Spanish artists from the Golden Age painted the soul'

Mateo Cerezo, *Penitent Magdalene*, ca. 1665-66

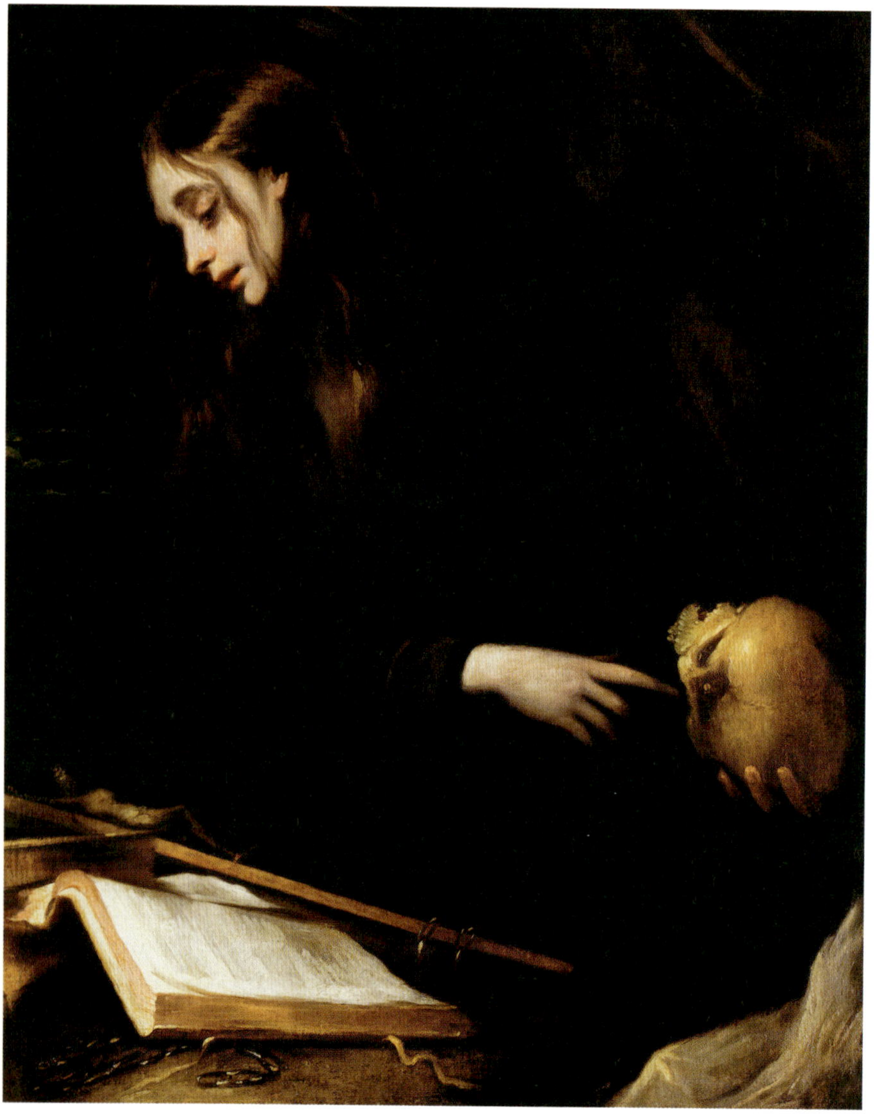

'We are all more like vast subterranean caverns, uncharted even by ourselves, than we are like holes dug straight into the ground,' states the US historian Timothy Snyder in his foreword to *Thinking the Twentieth Century*, the wonderful book by his British colleague Tony Judt, which he co-authored in a very unorthodox way. It is difficult not to return to the soul of this quote when one has been in front of Jonathan Ruffer (London, 1951), another outstanding Englishman, although in different fields: finance, philanthropy and the visual arts.

Talking to him is as, or even more, stimulating than going back over a life path brimming with talent, entrepreneurial capacity and a human sensitivity quite rare in these times. Maybe that's why listening to Ruffer today, when the pandemic ravages the world, is so comforting. After all, how many successful businessmen realistically and modestly preach that no one needs more than £20 million to live, and puts into practice every day an incarnation of Judeo-Christian principles based on selflessness, generosity and care for the common good?

Rare values, indeed, but Jonathan, who was born in London, raised in North Yorkshire, attended public school and began his career as a stockbroker before later becoming a leading barrister, banker and specialist in corporate finance and strategic investing, surely learned those values from one of his greatest references in the world of philanthropy: the prominent William Rathbone VI.

'I have a kind of a collector's gene, and I think the desire to collect things is typically male, because when we meet a girl we want to own her, just as when we come across a work that we like we want to have it, which of course is nothing noble. But since I suffer from this illness, I act as if it were a quality,' Ruffer says with that intelligent and noble humor so typical of Great Britain's most prodigious minds, while he holds forth on another of his passions, opera, and especially Spanish voices, from the timbre of the voice to the mystery that surrounds them and which, as such, cannot be explained.

'In painting we can see the French have been concerned with elegance and the Italians have been interested in beauty, while the Spanish were especially attracted by truth. And that is why Spain had its Golden Age. So it is natural that you like the Italian Baroque if you love aesthetics and that you think that the French are special if elegance resonates with you. But if you care about truth and the soul of things, that era in Spain is extraordinary. Even I, who live life as a joke, have the theory that, if someone wants to know if a genre is authentic, they must see whether it has humor,' he adds, with his trademark wit and grace.

But Ruffer, who spent 18 million euros to prevent the dispersal of *The Sons of Jacob*, a seminal series of portraits painted by Zurbarán around 1640, as well as in refurbishing the fantastic castle in Bishop Auckland, in the north of England, where they are housed, is not interested in collecting as a mechanical and snobbish act. For him it is as natural as breathing, reading, or smiling. And so, he unpretentiously explains what fascinates him about great Spanish painting: 'I am driven by the desire for knowledge, which I systematically accumulate, and the truth is that I believe it is a compulsion. But this would not be the case if it were not for dealer Anthony Mould, a man with an extraordinary eye who has been a fundamental influence and guide for more than fifteen years so that my collection, which now has between 250 and 300 pieces, is what it is today,' says this Cambridge graduate who, despite his modesty, admits an unquestionable facility to provide an historical context to the fine art he admires and collects, from European Baroque to English landscapes.

'When I buy a Spanish painting for Auckland Castle in the town of Bishop Auckland, basically my job is preservation. But when I buy a French Baroque painting, I do it for pure pleasure and for myself,' he comments with all the plainness of someone who throughout his career has assigned resources not only to preserve art, encourage painting and to stimulate the work of curators, but also to help others in ways that, precisely because of the authenticity of his philanthropic spirit, he refuses to go into in any detail.

Fanatical about artists who were unjustly overlooked in their time, but also of acknowledged masters such as Thomas Gainsborough and George Barret, Ruffer, a liberal who detests pontificating, considers that often 'paintings are ideas' and that it is vital 'to look at life through the eyes of others' in order to be able to 'see the difficulties of the other.'

Married to Dr. Jane Sequeira, a descendant of the notable physician Isaac Henrique Sequeira whose portrait, now in the Prado Museum, was painted by Gainsborough, one of his patients, Jonathan concedes that many of his London contacts would surely classify some of his adventures as 'harebrained', he assures us in a personable tone as a way to undercut any solemnity or, perhaps, importance. But then again, a person who generously spends his fortune on the area where he grew up could not be called conventional, and one of his other projects is to invest £80 million on a historical theme park near the castle.

The shadow of Zurbarán and the possible South American destination of his lost paintings hovers over the end of our conversation. Before finishing, this declared enemy of inequality has time to express the pride that comes from having bought and returned *The Sons of Jacob*, a key series of key portraits

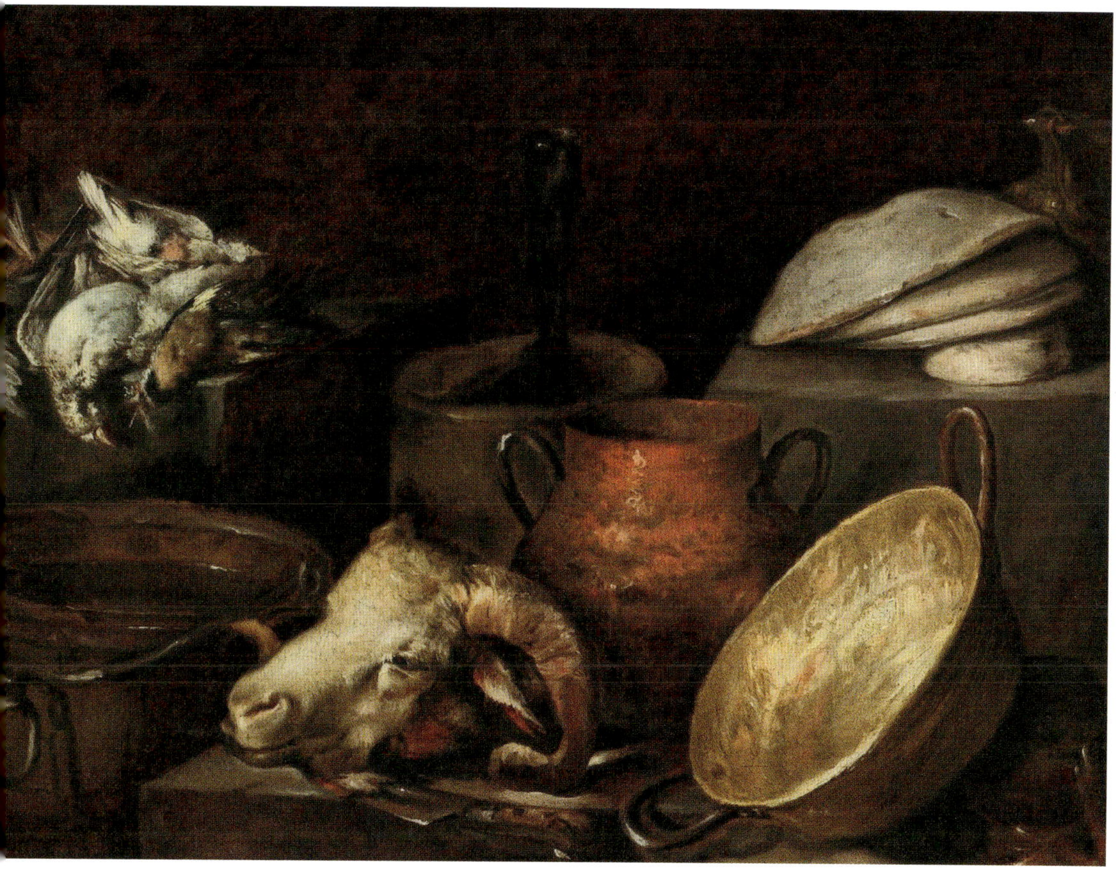

Francisco Barranco, *Still Life with Chocolate and Dead Birds*, 1647

which are an irreplaceable legacy for Spain, and also for Judaism, to the castle that always housed them, and whose ties with the Anglican Episcopate of Durham are so close.

With that warm smile that characterizes him, dressed in a typically English green sweater, a plaid shirt underneath and an insightful series of reflections on semiotics and philosophical expressionism when analyzing some of the works that have made him happy, Jonathan finishes off, not without first praising Navarrete el Mudo, on a characteristically hopeful note: 'Human beings are fascinating. On the one hand we are worms, but on the other we are higher than angels. This dichotomy is very interesting, and if there is one thing that art teaches us, it's that it is greater than all of us. That greatness is what we as a species need so much. Because if people believe themselves to be all-knowing, they become slow, uninteresting, insensitive. But when they know that there are ungraspable things that have a power over them, then they find themselves. And I think that's what I've done.'

Dakis Joannou

‘A museum full of masterpieces is really boring’

Jakub Julian Ziolkowski, *Story of the Eye*, 2010

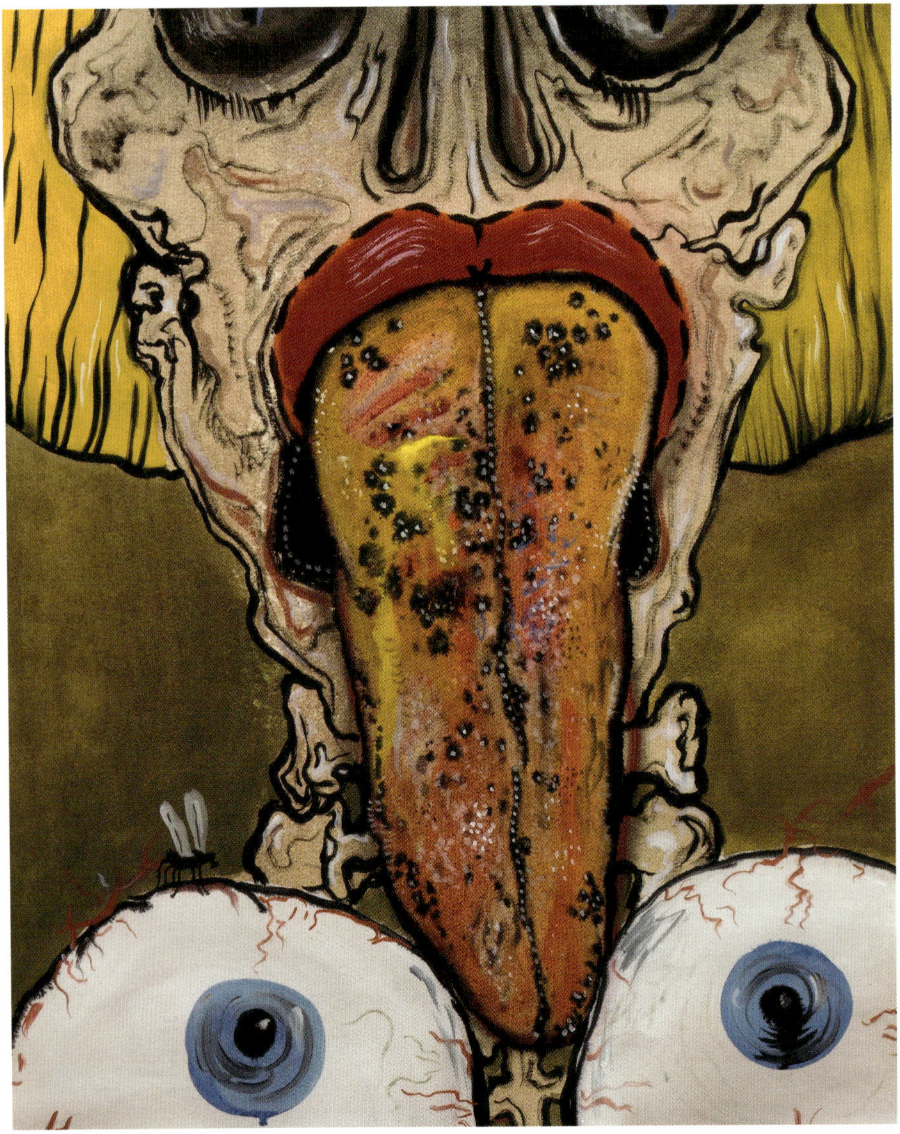

It might seem eccentric. And it is. It might seem extravagant. And it is that too. But there is nothing superficial about *Guilty*, Dakis Joannou's mega yacht. Instead it is bold, countercultural and extraordinary. Throughout its length of 35 meters, it's hard to find a detail that is not unique, and rightly so: its owner, and unorthodox collector, has stamped his character on every corner. Maybe it would not be imperative in another elite collector, but it is in the case of this entrepreneur who seems to be even more elegant with the passing of time.

Like the magnificent yacht created by two geniuses like Jeff Koons and Ivana Porfiri, everything here in his fabulous eclectic summer home is highly personal and welcoming. The furniture and contemporary art he bought when the designers and artists were neither famous nor costly, and which give it such energy, complete the virtuoso triangle whose final vertex is the architecture that some superior being seems to have flung over the landscape of the island of Corfu. Completely at ease, Joannou, a prosperous Greek-Cypriot collector and businessman, responds to each question with a relaxed didacticism.

'Collecting art and sharing it with people, which is materialized through the Deste Foundation in Geneva, is what really matters to me. And, you know what? For me, collecting was not always something I was interested in or wanted to do. It was my dear friend Pierre Restany who, during a lunch by the sea in 1982, gave me the idea of setting up a foundation, and since then I became more and more interested. Back in the sixties, I liked art but in a more personal and less focused fashion. Afterwards, other friends got involved and that allowed the seed to grow. Until one day in an East Village gallery in New York in 1985, I was fascinated by a work which was on sale for 3000 dollars. And, of course, I asked for a discount, which they agreed to and so I reserved the installation, though I didn't want to buy it until first meeting the artist, who I got on very well with and we spent a long time chatting in his studio. It was by Jeff Koons, who is now a good friend of mine.'

The public's reaction to early exhibitions by Jeffrey, as he calls Koons, was initially very skeptical. Today, Koons is one of the cornerstones of a collection that boasts hundreds of works, most of them by other greats of contemporary art like Robert Gober, Maurizio Cattelan, Anish Kapoor, Sarah Morris and Pawel Althamer. 'I only realized I had a collection several years after that beginning,' added Joannou. 'Collecting is a way of communicating and a reminder of who I am and what I am doing. But, above all else, it is part of a much wider interest in art, in connecting with and dialoguing with artists who, if I didn't know them, I would never have collected.'

With regards the way in which, over the last twenty years, some collectors, in conjunction with auction houses and a handful of big galleries, have made the art market practically inaccessible, he argued: 'This is a negative change, because it confuses the price of an artwork with its artistic value, when they are two very different things. Now it seems as if what is most important is that everything is expensive or, on the contrary, to enter into a spiral of speculation consisting of getting your hands on works by new artists which are still cheap but with potential to rocket. I would say it is a social problem, as the middle classes, if you like, of the contemporary art world are shut out. And that is to everybody's detriment because we lose the wealth that comes from a range of voices that runs from young promises to established masters. After all, a museum full of masterpieces is very boring.'

Is there a solution for this loss? 'It's hard to see any. Nobody accepts responsibility for it. In the USA, the state is much less involved in running museums than in Europe. And, on the other hand, too many museums are more worried about footfall that the quality of exhibits. So it is not a simple issue. In addition, galleries have lost the close contact they used to have with artists and the commitment to promote them, so they are increasingly becoming more like simple dealers. However, it has to be said, art fairs have improved enormously. Then again, as if the above were not enough, some artists are overwhelmed because they are forced to keep producing all the time, and that is not natural because creativity requires downtime.'

Have he thought about what will happen to his collection when he is no longer here? 'There is no sense in donating it to a museum, because it would lose its spirit and each artist would end up being classified in the alphabetical order of their surname. I have given some isolated major works to museums, but the truth is that I haven't ultimately decided what to do. My children and grandchildren really like art but they don't share my passion or commitment with collecting.' He reaffirms this commitment 'first of all, by acquiring more works by some of my usual artists, like Maurizio Cattelan. And then with some developing talents in whom I really believe, like Jakub Julian Ziólkowski and Kaari Upson who died an early death in 2021.

Before finishing our conversation, he defined his curious passion for fashion and for furniture, with a special mention for Ettore Sottsass, as a natural prolongation of that first passion.

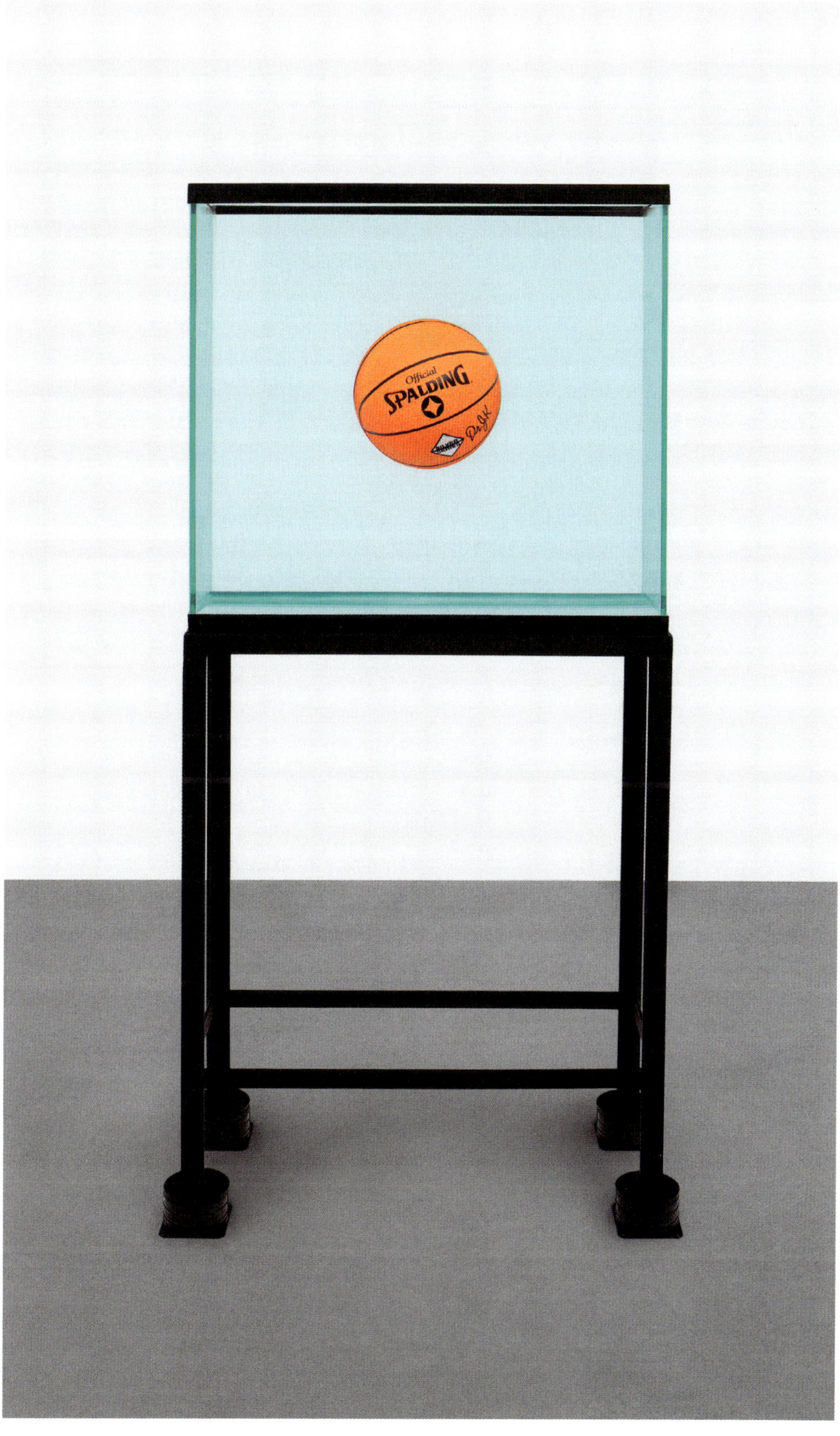

Jeff Koons, *One Ball Total Equilibrium Tank*, 1985

Lia Rumma

'I want to be part of what is going on right now and to encourage young artists and collectors'

Michelangelo Pistoletto, *Mappamondo*, 1966-68

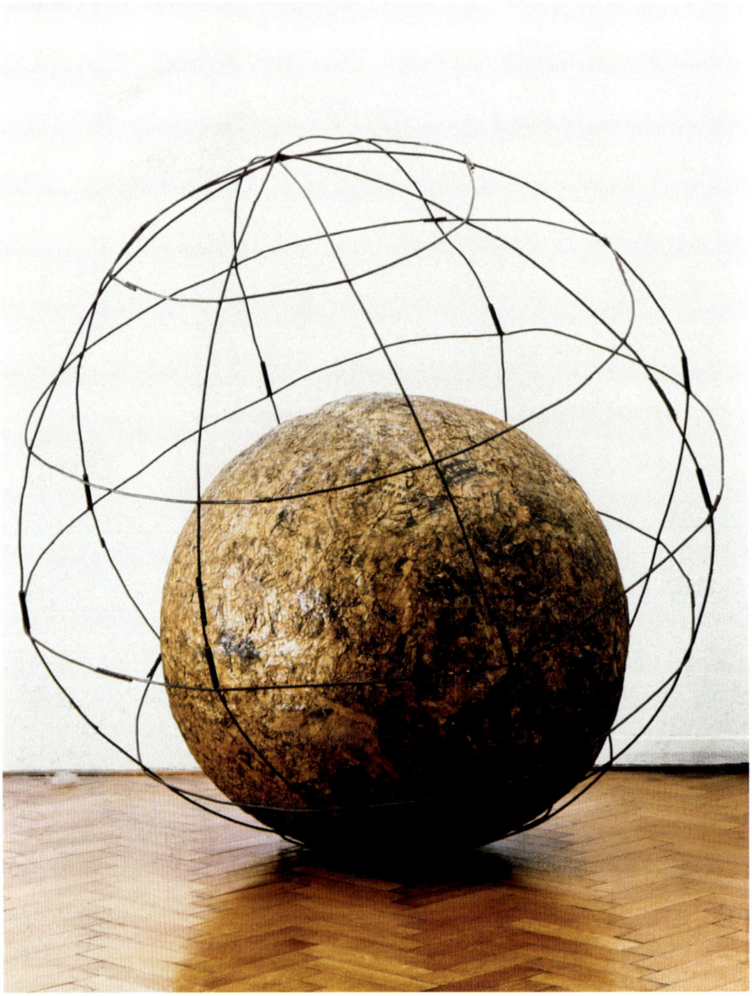

Just as Carmen Balcells played an instrumental role in promoting the Latin-American boom on both sides of the Atlantic, Marcello Rumma, the influential collector and patron who died in 1970 at the age of 27, was a catalyst for *arte povera*, the hypnotic movement that would turn Italian art on its head in the seventies. It took its name from the exhibition curated by Germano Celant, who perceived a revolutionary use of humble, everyday materials. Half a century later, its flame is kept alive by his wife, Lia Rumma, famous for collecting with character, taste and criteria, and for her aplomb in overcoming adversities.

An entrepreneur in her own right, Lia Rumma lives in an apartment in Donn'Anna, the magnificent palace built in the eighteenth century by Anna Carafa, Duchess of Stigliano, who was married to the celebrated Spanish nobleman Ramiro Núñez de Guzmán, viceroy of Naples.

Now in 2018, the original project *Arte Povera + Azioni Povere*, a three-day event held in Amalfi in that tumultuous year of 1968, is half a century old. And since then, as an eye-witness to the passing of time, Rumma has accrued enviable experience, giving a very special boost to contemporary artists of the stature of William Kentridge, Giovanni Anselmo, Vanessa Beecroft and Anselm Kiefer before they went on to become superstars of the global art market.

With her natural elegance and dressed all in black, she welcomes us with Vesuvius looming in the background. Lia is not afraid of the passing of time, as demonstrated in our conversation, held in Italian, and she grows in confidence as she relates the story of the movie into which her life has become. As she said, 'although my vision is international, I have always worked with Italian artists, both famous and still unknown. And now I am following a group of young promises such as Domenico Antonio Mancini, Marzia Migliora and Luca Monterastelli.'

Daughter of a Latinist father who was a fanatical scholar of Dante, she grew up travelling the globe. And so, between fantastic gardens, famous artists, renowned intellectuals and the not inconsiderable number of nine siblings, she cultivated a streak that led her to lose herself in nature and to give free rein to her imagination, yet at once always eminently practical: 'I am a gallerist because I am a collector and, even though I find it difficult to let go of my works, if I want to buy I have to sell.'

A benchmark in elite collecting for her bold, modern, lucid and risk-taking yet not reckless insightfulness, Rumma endorses and puts into practice an old saying by Picasso: 'You don't make art, you find it.' She gets emotional when remembering her father's obsession with culture as the ultimate

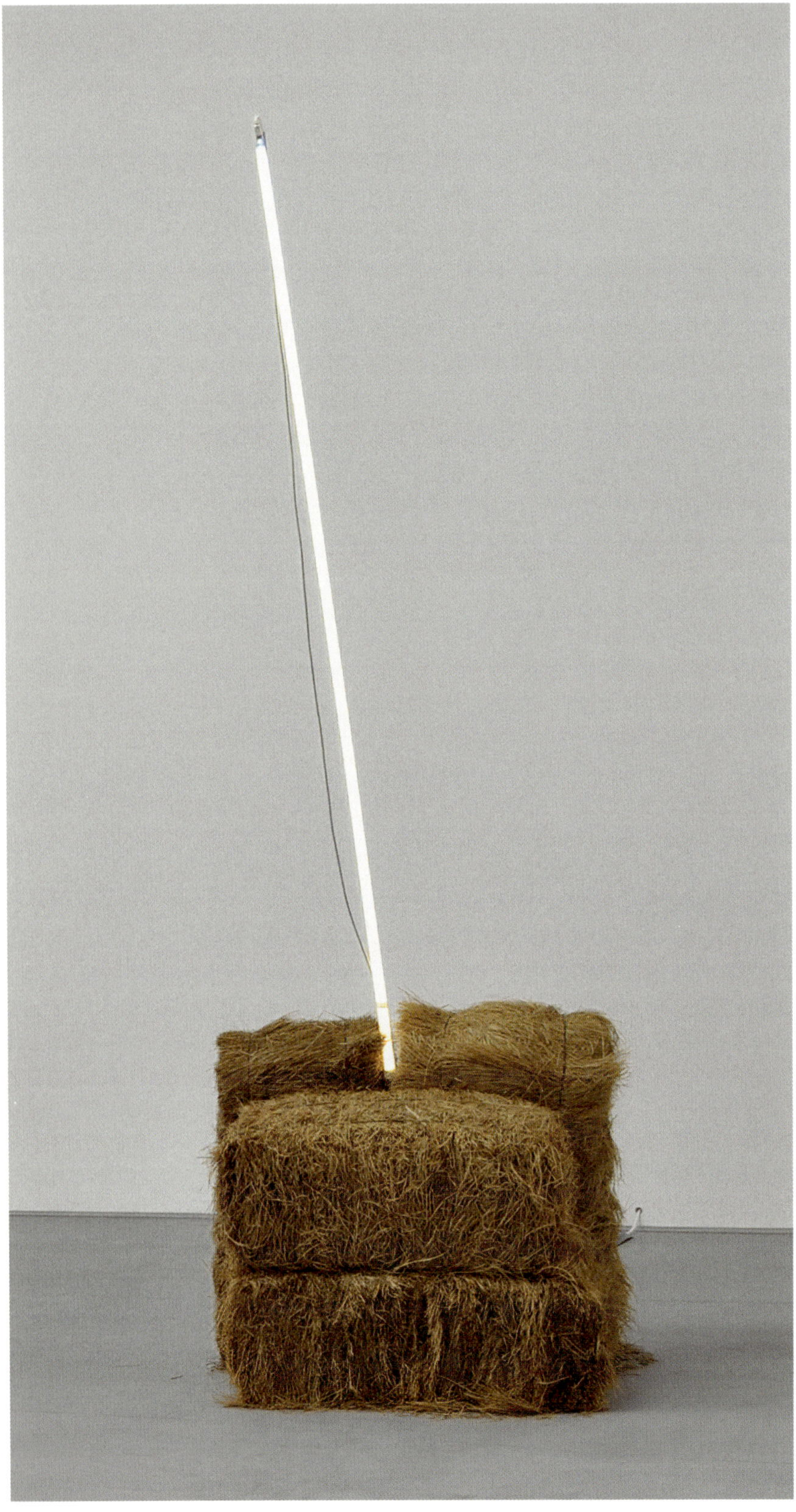

Mario Merz, *Untitled*, 1969

source of personal freedom. And when she recalls how she met Marcello, 'a brilliant, good-looking and visionary young man' after her family moved from Salerno to Como. 'The two of us came from intellectual backgrounds, though at the time he was more interested than I was in contemporary art as compared to classical. With the little bit of money we were able to put together we started to buy works by our friends in installments,' she explained.

Full of dreams and fraught with economic hardship, those beginnings gave rise to various exhibitions that were to lead to the birth of *arte povera* and the subsequent consecration of its legends (Mario Merz, Jannis Kounellis, Luciano Fabro...) and then, later, to a publishing house that would bring out canonical texts on art, aesthetics and philosophy by Eugen Fink, Marcel Duchamp and Michelangelo Pistoletto among others.

In October 2018, Salerno, Amalfi and Museo d'Arte Contemporanea Donnaregina (MADRE) in Naples paid tribute to Marcello with a number of activities and exhibitions recalling his storied legacy. Lia feels proud and thankful, though she cannot avoid remembering how, after her husband's tragic death, the Rumma family turned up at the apartment she shared with Marcello and took all the works that they had collected together with great sacrifice over a span of five years.

The fact that so much has happened between that depression and this light that now shines from her with natural sparkle is little short of a miracle. 'I have a gallery in Milan and in Naples, and of course I sell, but what matters most to me is to promote my artists,' she declared before adding 'my main ambition is not to exhibit the collection outside Italy. What I really want to do is to set up a studies center for Italian contemporary art. I am pouring all my efforts into this endeavor and I hope to have the health and energy to be part of what is going on right now and to discover and encourage young artists and collectors. Luckily, there is no end to dreams.'

This comes as no surprise to those who have discovered Thomas Ruff thanks to her, who have seen the William Kentridge mosaic installations that Lia made possible, or have enjoyed Anselm Kiefer's stunning *The Seven Heavenly Palaces* at Pirelli HangarBicocca in Milan, based on a project by Rumma.

Juan Carlos Maldonado

'My idea is to educate through art'

Tomás Maldonado, *Composición*, 1950

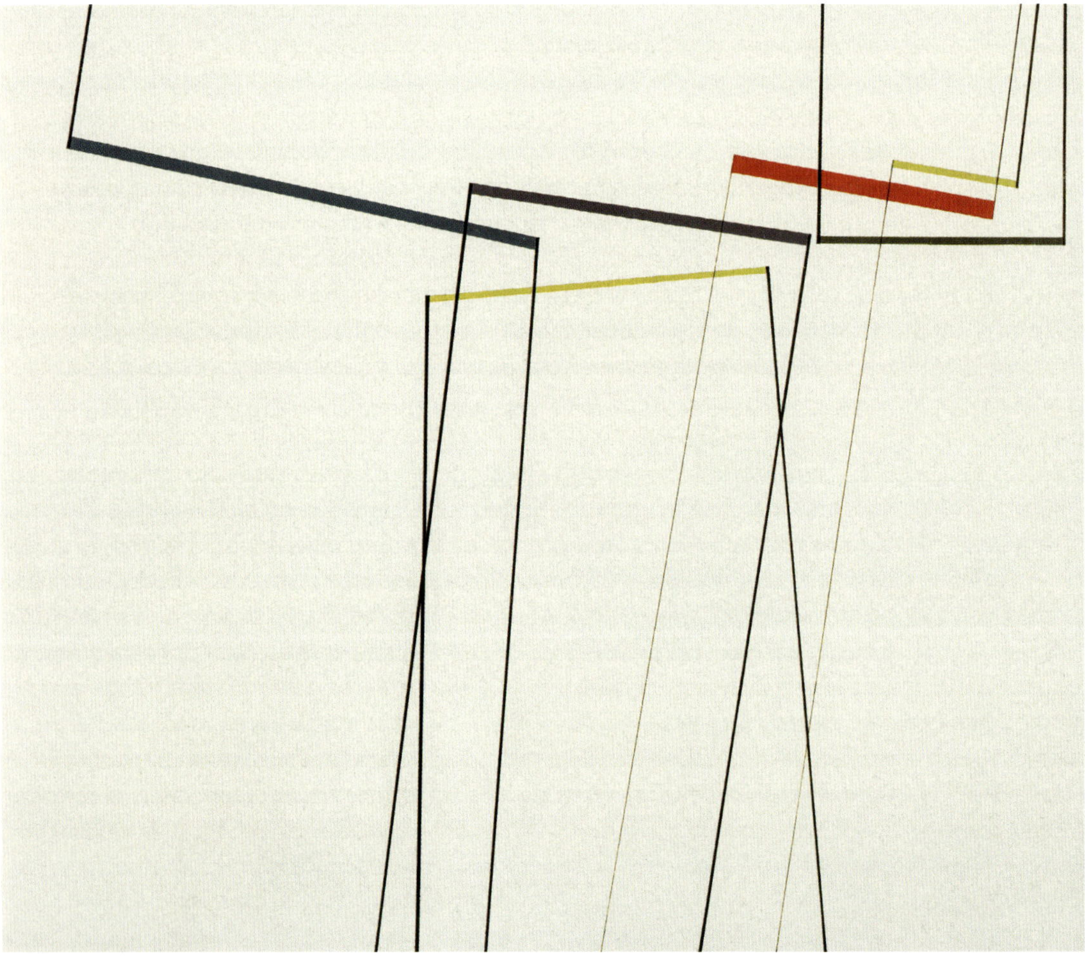

'The humility of the greats' is an expression trotted out too often in much of Latin America. However, it is difficult to find a better one to describe Juan Carlos Maldonado Bermúdez, whose success as a collector, patron, businessman, and even as an involuntary leader is striking. Maldonado leaves to one side his evident modesty when he welcomes us in Miami, surrounded by *Iridescent Geometries*, a superb exhibition by Cuban artist Ernesto Briel at the Juan Carlos Maldonado Art Collection (JCMAC). We had already been given access to his private collection of gleaming Latin-American geometric art, in a beautiful apartment in the Madrid neighborhood of Salamanca, decorated by the interior designer Belén Domecq.

Abstract geometry of modern Latin-American masters, especially those who shone brightly between the 1930s and 70s, is the star attraction of a collection that brings together some of the greatest artists of Colombia, Argentina, Brazil, Mexico and Cuba, in addition of key pieces by European and American icons such as Victor Vasarely and Alexander Calder.

A major player in the insurance market in South America, the businessman lays bare his roots. 'I was born in Puerto Ordaz, in the state of Bolívar in Venezuela, where Jesús Rafael Soto comes from, but at the age of four I moved to Caracas, where I have lived all my life, including most of my school years, except for university. I went to Wofford College in South Carolina, and later MIT, where I did my MBA. I worked at Citibank for many years in Venezuela as well as in New York, where I dedicated myself mostly to asset trading and management. In 1995 I returned to Venezuela to join the family business, a large insurance company, and worked there for 15 years until I became CEO. But in 2009, ten years after Chávez came to power and having seen everything that was happening, including the expropriation of an important family estate for the conservation of animals, we finally took the decision to sell the company. I then focused on my own projects, particularly in the insurance, health and banking sectors. So the dynamics of buying and selling companies is not new to me. I enjoy taking over businesses that are in difficulties, changing them, improving them and, after ten years, evaluating the results. I have had the ability to build things quickly and to be able to identify a business's strong points. I am motivated not only by the business aspect but even more so by the social and cultural responsibilities,' Maldonado claims.

It was not until 2005 that he began to collect, 'although my aunt Milagros Maldonado is a great collector of Latin-American art, so I have always been exposed to the work of artists like Wilfredo Lam and Roberto Matta. She was always my point of reference in the family. She lives between Paris and Miami and has a very interesting space in Wynwood that works with many young artists. We are still in touch and I value our conversations very much,' Juan Carlos adds.

On the unique direction of his own collection, he explains: 'I began with the serious intention of collecting Venezuelan artists first, with a preference for geometric abstraction rather than figuration and, within it, for kinetic art. That movement, its forms and ways of handling space caught my attention. But it was not until 2009, with the sale of the company, that I decided to invest heavily in the movement, not only focusing on Venezuelan artists, but also on other Latin Americans, ranging from Torres García's constructivism to Brazilian concrete art or the Madí movement, because, ultimately, geometric abstraction is universal. And I was keen to see the exchange of artistic concepts between Europe and Latin America, conditioned by crucial historical processes, such as the Second World War.'

A journey, it should be noted, in which Maldonado established a whole network that began with hiring the services of María Carlota Pérez, a New-York based curator who helped him understand what was happening with geometric abstract art in Latin America, so that he could select the most significant works from such a vast and fruitful movement. 'That process, which is so interesting from a cultural point of view, was also an incredible learning curve for her too. Oddly enough, she was not an art expert at the time, because she came from the financial sector. I sent her all over the world to meet collectors and gallery owners, as well as to learn about artists' estates and to go directly to the sources. For example, we bought *Bicho* by Lygia Clark directly from her family. And in the case of a work by Tomás Maldonado, we made our way to the last owner, who was closely associated with the family. It has been a long journey of study and research to get here,' he says.

Maldonado is planning to open another major art space in Miami, for which he has brought on board the Spanish architect Juan Herreros. 'My idea is to educate through art. For me, the most important luxury that a human being can have is education. I am not interested in my collection being just for one man, but rather for everyone and for it to be seen. This is why we made the effort to create this space here. I want people to come to look for themselves, to question and to be a part of the cultural community that Miami has to offer. This could not be achieved without the scholarship program that we are preparing. We want to be an all-round institution for those who are interested in the arts, especially in universal geometric abstraction. And I'm particularly interested in working with artists who have something to say, and in understanding where they are coming from. When you understand the life of the artist and then see the final product, everything is much simpler.'

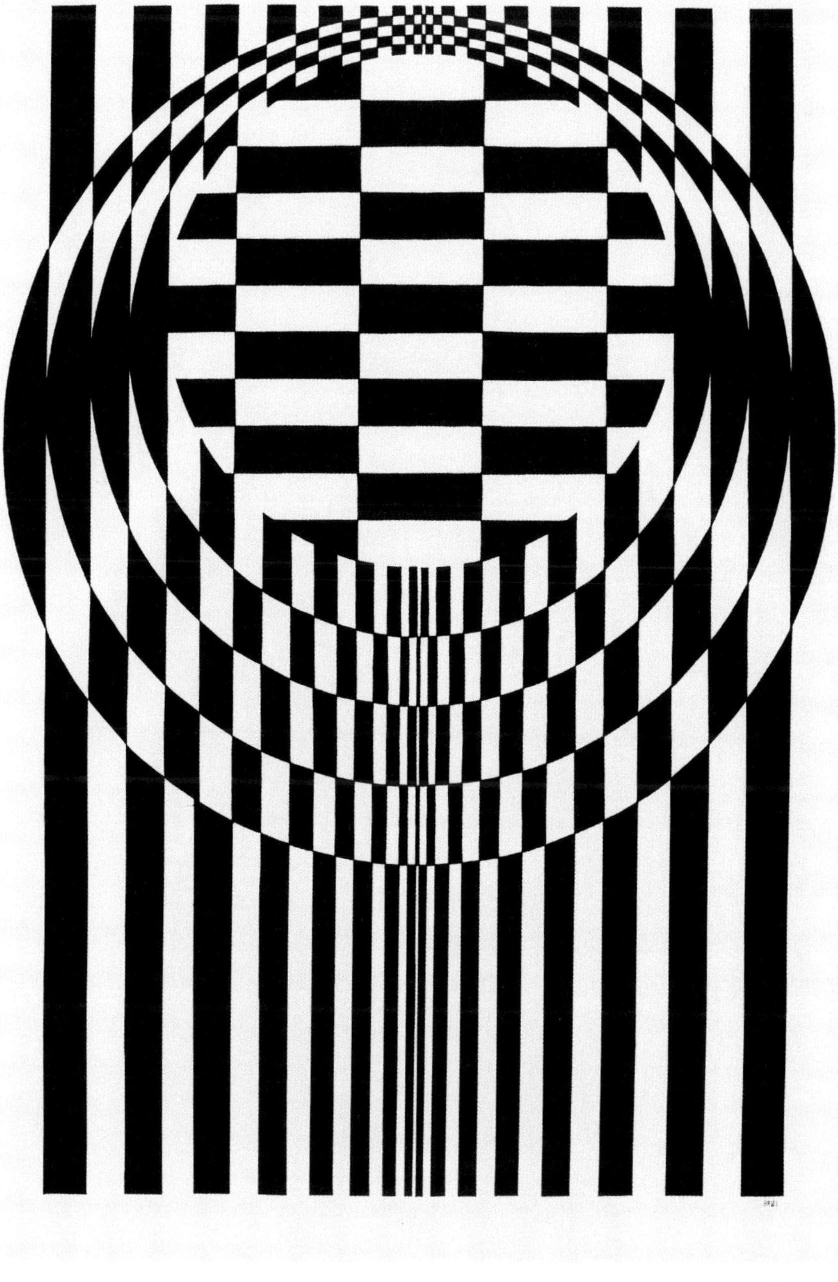

Ernesto Briel, *Untitled,* 1970

Anita Zabludowicz

'What interests us is to see the effect art has on society'

Gillian Wearing, *Dancing in Peckham*, 1994

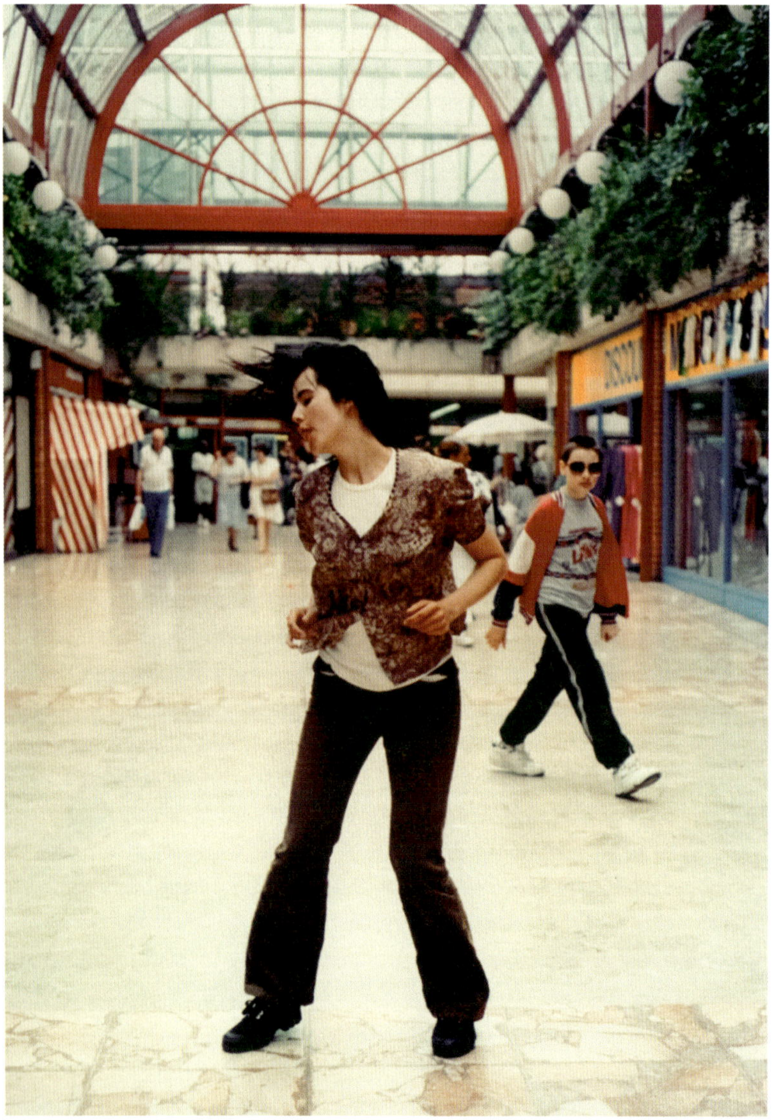

Few people in the arts are as driven as Anita Zabludowicz, an elite collector. Born in 1960 in Newcastle as Anita Steinman, this British daughter of a wholesaler and an art historian has spent her time building an enviable career. Recognized as one of the 100 most powerful women in the art world by Artnet and a worthy recipient of the Most Excellent Order of the British Empire, Zabludowicz has promoted numerous fairs and exhibitions. Together with her husband, the Finnish-born English businessman Chaim 'Poju' Zabludowicz, she has undertaken projects such as the creation of the Zabludowicz Center for Autoimmune Diseases at the Sheba Medical Center in Israel, the donation of funds for the ultimately rejected planned Guggenheim Museum in Helsinki or the construction of a collection of more than 5,000 works by 500 different artists.

The Zabludowicz Collection in London (with branches in New York and Sarvisalo, Finland) offers an invaluable insight into the universe created by the couple, which Anita talks to us about with passion, proving herself to be direct and approachable. She does so during a videoconference in which she narrates how her love affair with contemporary art, especially emerging art, came about in the not so distant 1990s. 'I was educated in an artistic and creative environment, because my mother was really passionate about art and she was always keen to make things interesting and to stimulate that same passion in me. At one time I thought I would like to paint, but I found it quite boring. The same thing happened to me when studying Art History. I dedicated myself to interior design for ten years, which I really enjoyed. This is how I met a series of fascinating people who guided me along what would be my definitive path: to become an art collector. My time at Christie's, where I studied Modern Art and Auctions, was very exciting, among other reasons because it gave me a chance to get a profound knowledge of the contemporary art world,' she says.

Laughing, she adds, 'first, I thought we should concentrate on works by the modern British artists like Lucien Freud, Francis Bacon or Barbara Hepworth. But very soon my husband derailed me when he purchased a work by the contemporary artist Matthew Barney! So we explored the field of photography in the mid-nineties with great enthusiasm. We met Thomas Dane, at the time a gallerist and now a consultant, who has been an invaluable guide who gently nudged us away from the predictable, which is to say the Young British Artists such as Damien Hirst, but rather toward photographers like Wolfgang Tillmans.'

Video art quickly captured the attention of this discreet yet restless woman, who studied Fine Arts at the College of Arts & Technology in Newcastle and who went from fervently accumulating works by Jim Lambie, Gillian Wearing or Thomas Struth, to considering that her collection was too experimental and that, therefore, 'something could be missing.'

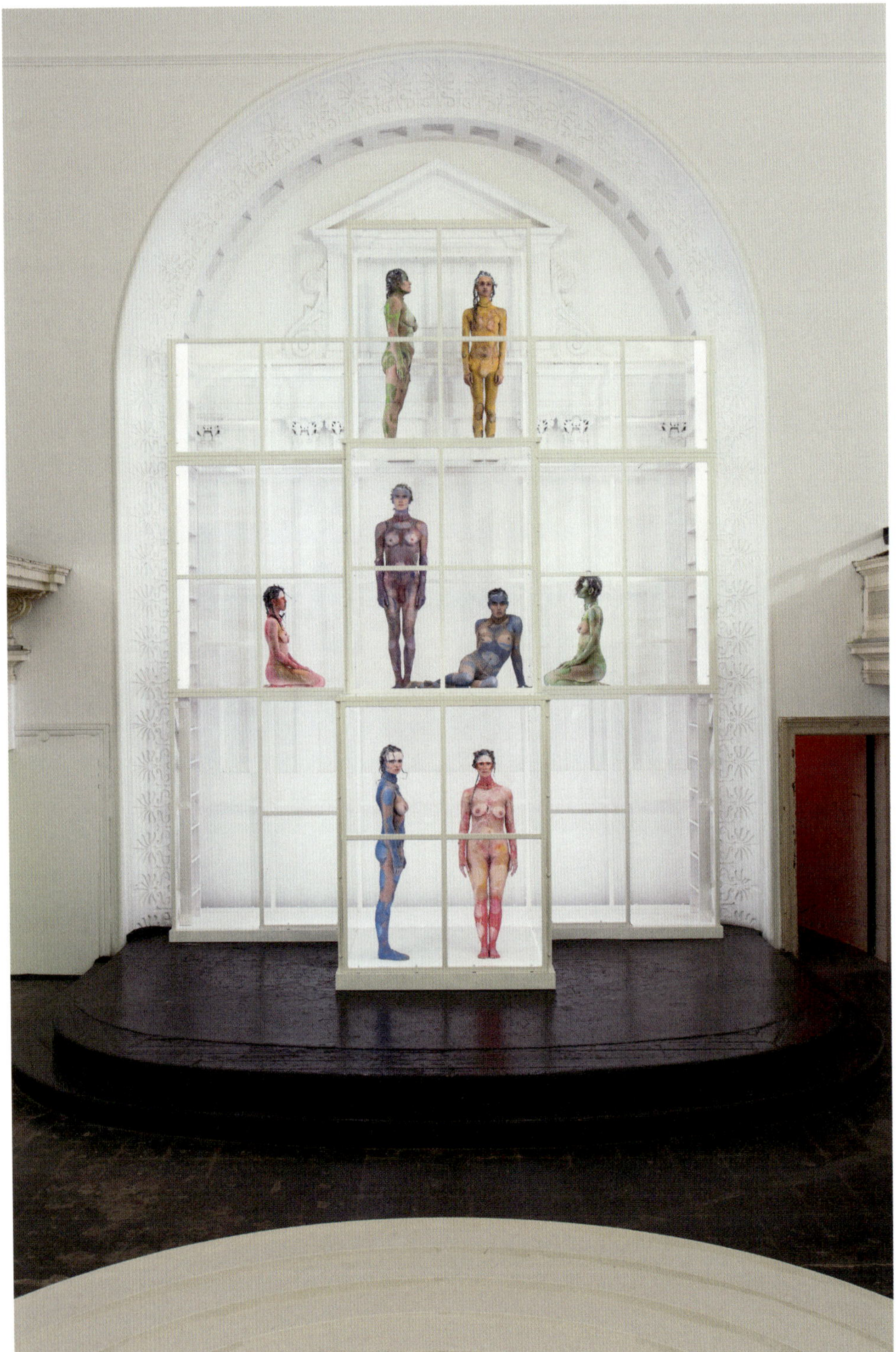

Donna Huanca, *MELANOCYTES/ETHERIC TEMPLATE*, 2016

'We really liked imaginative, technological, inventive, and conceptual artists, but it didn't seem appropriate to have that kind of work stored away in a warehouse. So we decided to open our own space, for which the expert and humble help of curator Jenni Lomax was key. In this way we could show what we possessed and share it with the community and the public in a more institutional rather than personal place. I knew what I was doing, but I couldn't explain it exactly.' The collector chose London as the headquarters and Elizabeth Neilson as director, despite the fact that, at the time, she was only twenty-six years old. 'Fourteen years later, I think it has been a success, accruing a significant audience and notable influence; we have helped nurture the artistic ecosystem. In short, we have done more good than bad. And above all, I can safely affirm that for us art is not a commodity, a product or an investment, but rather that what interests us is to see the effect it has on society, as well as to observe the way in which each artist advances in their professional life. All this has been a true journey,' she says proudly.

As Anita speaks enthusiastically about her daughter Tiffany, who has left her own mark as a curator on the Times Square Space in New York, she tells us about some of the educational programs she has run with children and young people. She also talks about landmark shows, such as the Donna Huanca exhibition in 2016 at the Zabludowicz Collection, the ongoing collaboration with top-level universities and the residences that, from the United States to Finland, have allowed her to establish a deep and intimate dialogue with the artists, in addition to understanding their processes and motivations.

With exhibitions at the collection's three venues, she has managed to define an authentically contemporary collection: 'My husband and our daughter are very involved in the fine arts aspect. But I prefer the more experimental and technological side, and I also see this task as a way of supporting creativity beyond borders, since the very nature of digital work, for example augmented reality, allows it.' A big fan of immersive experiences, Zabludowicz says that 'working with these technologies and ideas gives us a chance to understand a lot about the future, but also the past, in a new way.'

Eddie and Sylvia Brown

'The boom in African-American art will continue to grow'

Martin Puryear, *Arabesque*, 2006

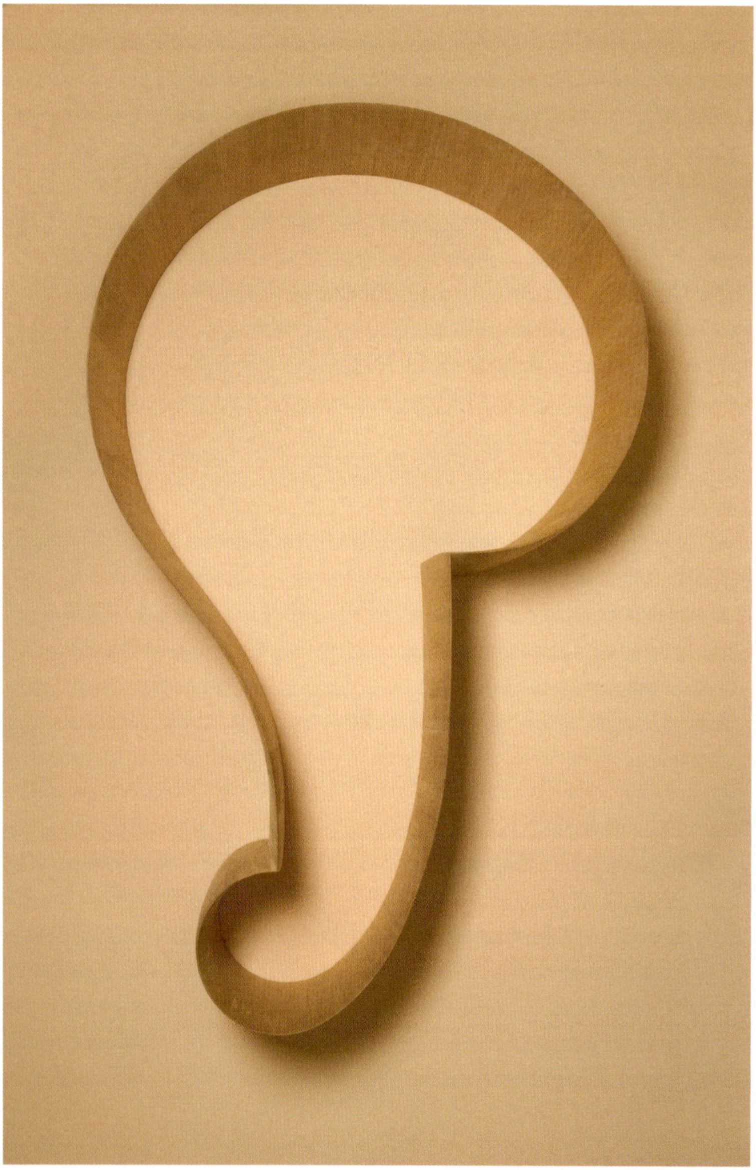

When we talk about 'philanthropy' we generally think of large donations, selfless actions, and in the best of cases, the will to do good without others knowing it, but this beautiful yet often abused word is actually defined in the dictionary as, no more nor less, 'love of humanity.' This is precisely the spirit that drives Eddie and Sylvia Brown, prestigious US patrons of the arts, collectors and philanthropists. The couple met many years ago at Howard University—he was studying Engineering, she Physical Education—and since then they have gone on to build the Brown Center at the Maryland Institute College of Art (MICA), to collaborate in funding the Bloomberg School of Public Health and, as if all this were not enough, to put together a collection of African-American art grounded in a passion for excellence, with close bonds to Baltimore, the city where they set down roots, and home to one of the couple's most beautiful projects, The Ivy luxury hotel nestled in the heart of the city.

Simplicity is a virtue that makes the great even greater. The truth of this statement is borne out by the Browns, as clearly evinced in a recent conversation in which they explain what they are all about, the essence that allowed Eddie to set up Brown Capital Management and for the two of them to harvest what they sowed in this collection, the first seed of which was planted in Philadelphia, when they acquired a work from a small gallery specializing in African-American art without 'knowing anything' at the time.

They may not have known it then, but they already saw something that others did not see and felt what they themselves describe as an intense 'emotional connection' with that work and others that came later.

'We separated years ago, and very well, just like Church and State,' says a smiling Eddie. And he adds: 'Jennifer, our daughter, manages our family and personal affairs under the name The Brownstone Project, and during the day I take care of my company, specialized in investments. We have been collecting for decades. And that has a lot to do with the fact that Tonya, our eldest daughter, became interested in art and then graduated from the Leroy E. Hoffberger School of Painting at MICA and devoted herself to painting. The truth is that, along the way, we met many professionals. But a core of three people in particular helped us better understand the world of collecting: Steven Jones, Jackie Copeland and David Driskell. Around 90% of our collection is made up of African-American art, although there are some exceptions for Caucasian artists, like Grace Hartigan, who has a very special significance because she was Tonya's professor at university. The emphasis and focus of the collection is on the African-American universe, from consecrated names to emerging talents, including mid-career artists who cannot yet be considered masters. Let's say we have about 300 works that could be considered museum quality.'

Sylvia infuses the conversation with a deep and mysterious style, and Eddie with pragmatism and intelligence. In combination, they delight anyone interested not just in patronage, but in the art of storytelling. Perhaps that is why they so naturally reel off some of the big names whose works they treasure, long before collecting African-American art became fashionable.

They continue, and judging by the shared chemistry it is irrelevant to distinguish who says what, 'we have a private collection and it's also true we receive a considerable amount of visitors. We have begun to catalog our collection, something that is not easy because it calls for research by experts into each artist, which can convey to people who don't know what we do, an interesting sense of unity.'

Donors to many initiatives they believe will enrich the community, not just in Maryland, but throughout the United States, the Browns reply with caustic humor, eschewing the perennial vice of solemnity, to the question of what the mission of their foundation is. 'To give away all the money we have,' they say with contagious laughter before adding, more seriously: 'We have three clear goals: to help educate children from underprivileged socioeconomic backgrounds and, if necessary, to give them scholarships; to expand the visual and performing arts to all those places where possible; and to alleviate disparities in access to health. Looking specifically at the artistic part, we donate money to the Baltimore Community Foundation, and they do the background work to ensure the professionalism and the aims of the organizations that ask us for money. We want to broaden the horizons of children brought up in critical contexts beyond the poor neighborhoods in which they grow up. The children who study in The Crossroads School, an excellent public institution in Baltimore, are sponsored through Turning the Corner, a model achievement program that for the last fifteen years has been helping to solve their families' social problems, so that the cohesion of each family has a positive impact. The children attend symphonic concerts and first-class museums, in search of stimulus for opportunities and to give them access to a world they do not know. This involves social workers, teachers, mentors, and artists. And we are proud to have sponsored the best program at the Johns Hopkins Bloomberg School of Public Health, and to have recruited the best and brightest professionals to help improve the life and health of those who live in the most underserved communities in the city.'

Getting to know this side of the Browns is as exciting as talking to them about art. And even when speaking about slavery, the Holocaust, the economic inequality and racial injustice that still plague the United States, or the way the public identifies with what they see in contemporary art shows, they do not lose their sense of humor or friendliness. 'Collecting is

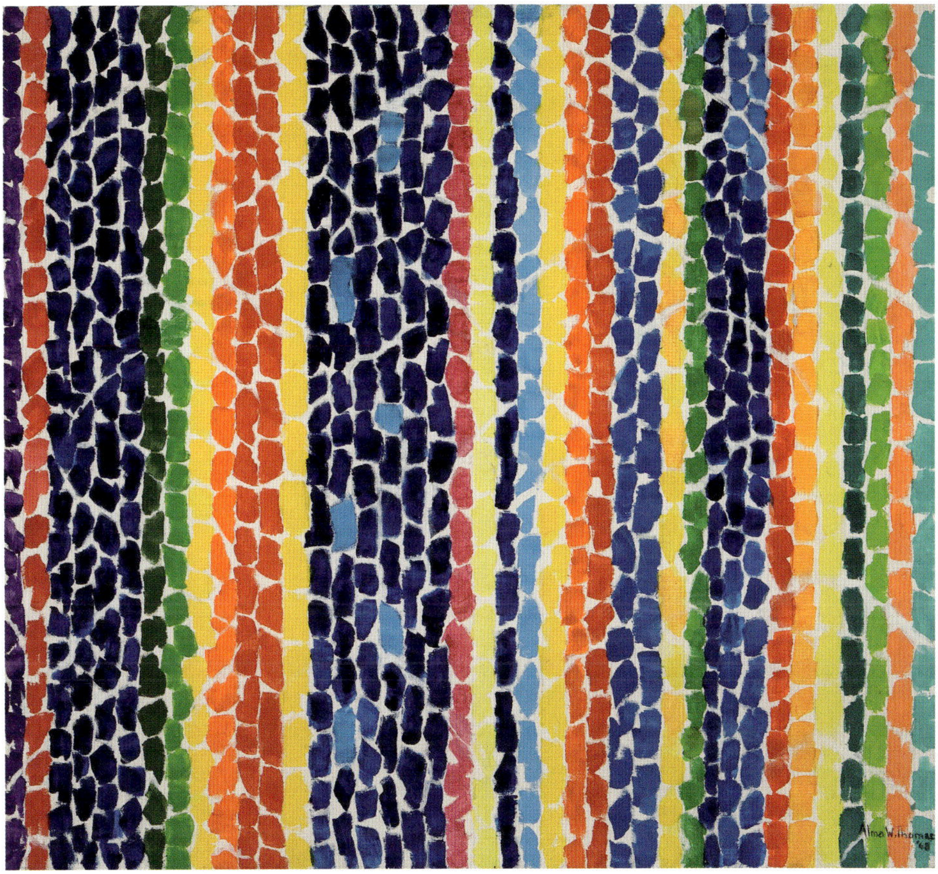

Alma Thomas, *Burst of Beauty*, 1968

addictive. I believe my greatest passion is for sculpture, and above all for wood. That is why I identify so much with Martin Puryear. We recently saw an exhibition of his work in Richmond in which he installed a wonderful staircase. I like the look, feel and aroma of his work, it touches me very deeply,' says Sylvia Brown. Her husband adds, taking over from her: 'Regardless of the artist's fame, we have to like the work in order for us to buy. We feel great passion, and we either like it or we don't, but I couldn't explain why. And although we do not always agree on who to choose, there are fewer times we do not agree than those in which we do.'

Amid praise for the art and character of Sam Gilliam, one of the jewels in their collection, he concludes: 'There has been a boom in African-American art for some years now. It really is a fabulous feeling, because for a long time the works of African-American artists were not taken into account. So this change in trend is exciting. But I believe that the boom, which is growing and will continue to grow, will one day explode.'

Estrellita Brodsky

'In a perfect world, there would be no need for museums to have a special department for Latin-American art'

Sarah Grilo, *Homenaje a mi idioma, letra Ñ,* 1965

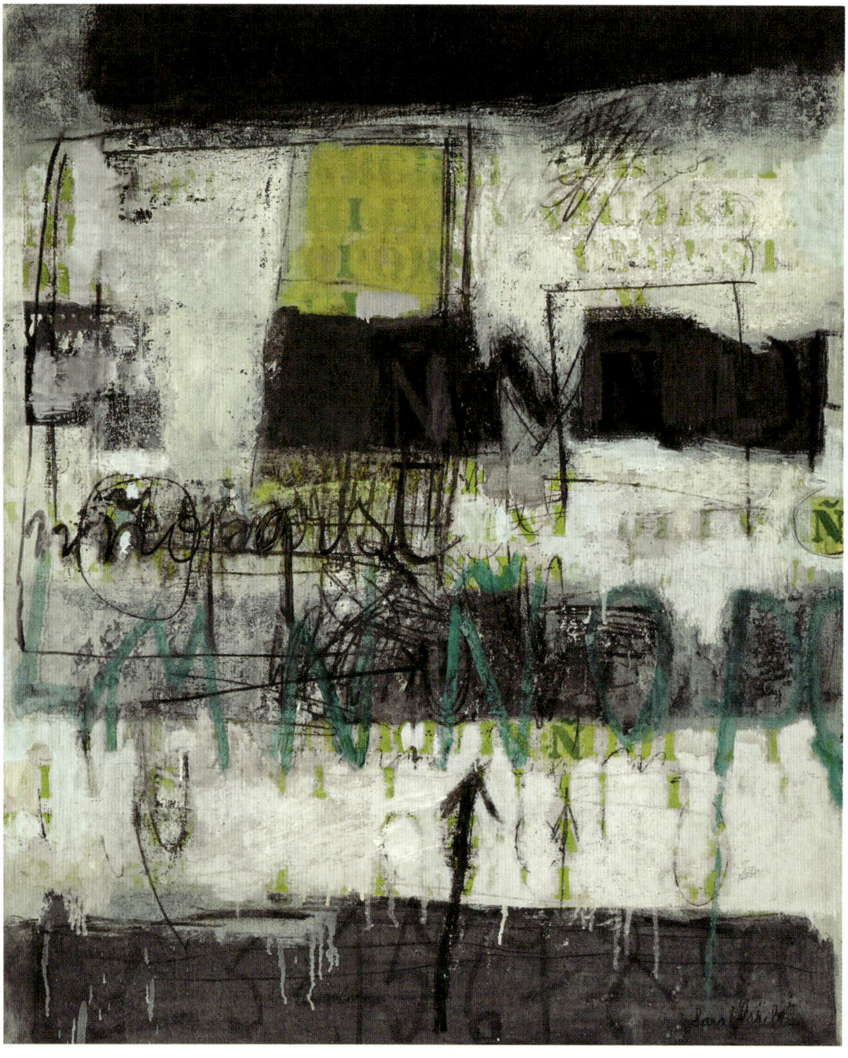

Mentor of extraordinary exhibitions in museums as prestigious as the Tate Modern, the Metropolitan, the Pompidou, the Museo del Barrio or the MoMA, right from the beginning Estrellita Brodsky lets drop a sentence that defines her essence: 'In a perfect world, there would be no need for the great art centers to have a special department for Latin-American art, because it would be seamlessly integrated into the whole.'

Clarity, pragmatism, good taste and character define her work as a collector, patron, curator, art historian and philanthropist, both on her own and with her partner, Daniel Brodsky, former president of the Metropolitan Board of Trustees, collector and real estate developer. Together they won the 2019 Ibero-American Patronage Award. While in conversation, it is clearly no coincidence that great artists such as Julio Le Parc (her doctorate at NYU was based on the work of Le Parc and Jesús Soto), and Artur Lescher have gifted her works directly inspired by herself.

She is American, although her family comes from Venezuela and Uruguay in a genealogy that goes back to the Uruguayan President Juan Idiarte Borda (1844-1897). 'My love for art started when I was little, because my father always liked it,' she explains. 'And I grew up seeing great works by Venezuelan artists in the public sphere, from Soto to Otero and Cruz-Diez. I loved that. I even tried to be an artist, although I didn't get too far. Later I began to collect in the United States, but always conscious of the widespread idea that Latin Americans were savages who grew up in the jungle, when, for instance, Uruguay was known as the Switzerland of the Americas and had a remarkable level of culture. I was interested in showing the interconnectedness that exists in Latin-American art. I am the product of different cultures, and even when I speak you don't know if I am Uruguayan, North American, Central American or South American. Because by understanding other cultures, one can not only respect them, but even understand oneself better.'

Brodsky adds that one of her great achievements has been to get the MoMA to agree to create the Estrellita Brodsky Curator of Latin-American Art, a key element in promoting her passion for investigating brilliant, heterogeneous and, until recently, marginalized Latin-American art. 'I am still fascinated by Russian Constructivism and Impressionism, especially Caillebotte. When I began studying for my MA at Hunter College, Latin-American art, unlike literature, was not part of the academic programs at the best universities. It was not until I began my doctorate that it became more common. Later I was able to focus my studies on the passion I always had for kinetic artists, a movement that in my view is still underrated,' she claims.

'Private collections are fine, and for that we have a personal space, Another Space, dedicated to Latin-American art and Latinx artists within a global

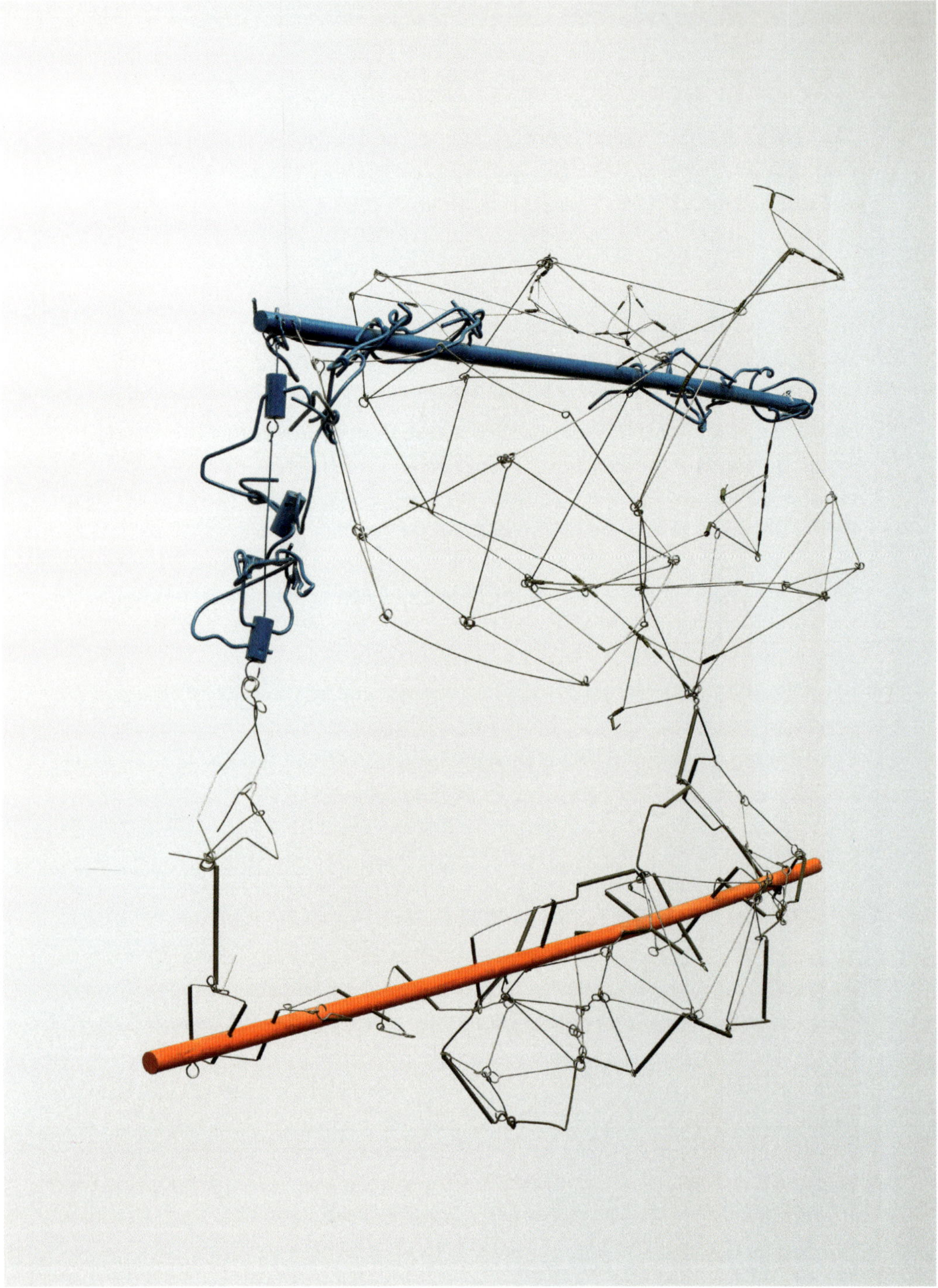

Gego (Gertrud Goldschmidt), *Untitled*, 1987

non-profit context so that people can come to see it. It is important that the public be exposed to art, as it is a human manifestation that makes us more sensitive,' advocates a woman who not only spreads her infectious passion in words and in the exhibitions she promotes and in her true championing of Latin-American art, but in her concrete support of scholarships for young people who otherwise would not have access to good education. And she adds: 'Anyway, I really like dialogues in shades of gray and the possibility of opening conversations, instead of simply saying "it is this way and no other" or things like that.'

The co-founder of the Daniel and Estrellita Brodsky Foundation explains how their private collection has evolved. 'At the beginning it was open and included quite predictable works, like the European ones. As my studies and trips to Latin America deepened, the search became more specialized, ranging from the great Brazil artists to the kinetics, the constructivism of Torres García or perhaps more inaccessible political artists, or those whose works are less suitable to have in a private home, like those by Marta Minujín or the great Argentinean artist Tomás Saraceno. I even like hanging alongside one another works by artists who didn't get along in real life, like Soto and Le Parc. And you know what? On the wall they understand each other perfectly!'

'In an increasingly more digitized world' Brodsky continues, 'I particularly appreciate the role of galleries, which are the agents who somehow support artists and select their best works. Encouraging and empowering young artists is something that small galleries can do better than anyone else. Although, of course, the problem is that later the big galleries come along and snatch them up. And then everything becomes monolithic and homogeneous, and you lose individualism. I don't like that.'

What will happen to her collection when she is gone? 'I have donated major works to museums when they have shown an interest and have really wanted them and I will continue to donate if the museum guarantees it will exhibit the work. But my children have loved art ever since they were little, and they collect too. So, we'll see.'

Armando Martins

‘Having artworks stored away in a warehouse is utter nonsense’

Vik Muniz, *Tackle (American Football)*, from the series *Pictures of Chocolate*, 2001

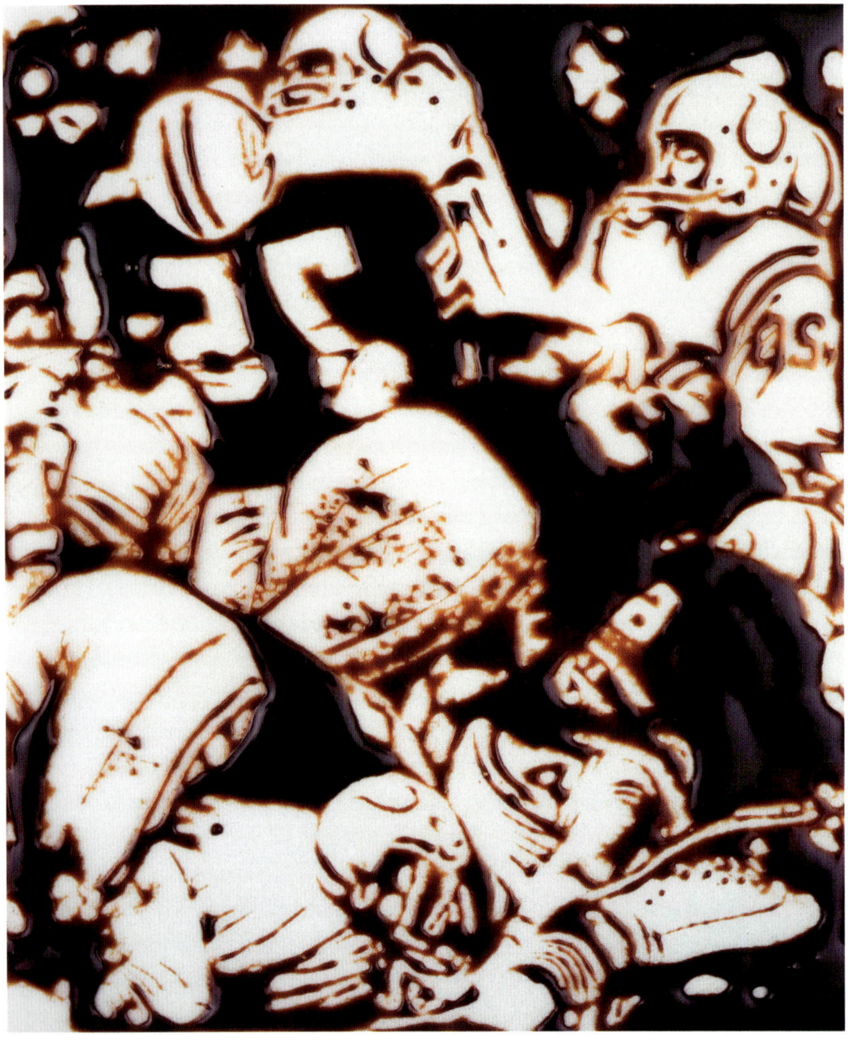

Don't be fooled by what many people might perceive at first sight in Armando Martins, because behind his shyness you will find not only the renowned Portuguese real estate developer, owner of the Fibeira group, but also a unique collector whose vision of universal art, and particularly the art of his home country, is of utmost interest for anyone with a minimum of curiosity. Martins is the owner of a collection of more than 400 Portuguese and international artworks, some of which have been on view in museums of the stature of Reina Sofía in Madrid and Soares dos Reis in Porto. Taken together, they make up a powerful, coherent and exceptional collection for which he was recognized with ARCO Foundation's prestigious A Award in 2018.

Well-earned then is the dream of his own museum, which will be fulfilled in the form of the Armando Martins Contemporary Art Museum (MACAM), if one takes a careful look at the works with which he has surrounded himself. In addition to being unique, they are enhanced by the rewarding dialogue which Martins, like a puppeteer, has set up between them. Works by artists as dissimilar and brilliant as Vik Muniz, Jorge Macchi, Antoni Tàpies, Santiago Ydáñez, Ernesto Neto, Eduardo Viana, Albert Oehlen, José Damasceno and Liam Gillick.

This is the result of an effort that took decades, causalities, aesthetic sense and the odd coincidence. 'When I was 18, an older friend who worked at a bank who comes from the same town as I do, told me: "I have a client who wants to sell me 35 serigraphs but I don't have enough money myself, do you want to go 50-50?" and, of course, I said yes. That's how I begun. Later when my friend retired he opened an art gallery, and the truth is that during many years he was a very peculiar dealer, and his love for collecting rubbed off on me. In 1974, I decided to buy my first original painting and it is naturally by a Portuguese artist. With what I was making at the time, I had to pay for it over six months! And then in 1985 I started buying in earnest, particularly twentieth-century Portuguese art,' Martins adds with a tone that combines shyness and a pleasant demeanor lacking in all solemnity.

Immediately, he adds: 'In the mid-nineties I broadened my scope to international art, and today I have no less than 100 major works in that category. But the collection, contrary to what it may seem, progressed little by little and with some difficulty until the early 2000s, when I seriously started thinking about opening a museum of contemporary art in Lisbon. For different reasons, I think that everything I do should be on my own, without depending on anyone else, especially public companies. So I bought a three-story eighteenth-century palace that belonged to a very important family, specifically to house the museum. And it will open in a few months after some architectural work but with the original facade, although I think it is important to clarify that it will be funded exclusively with my own capital.'

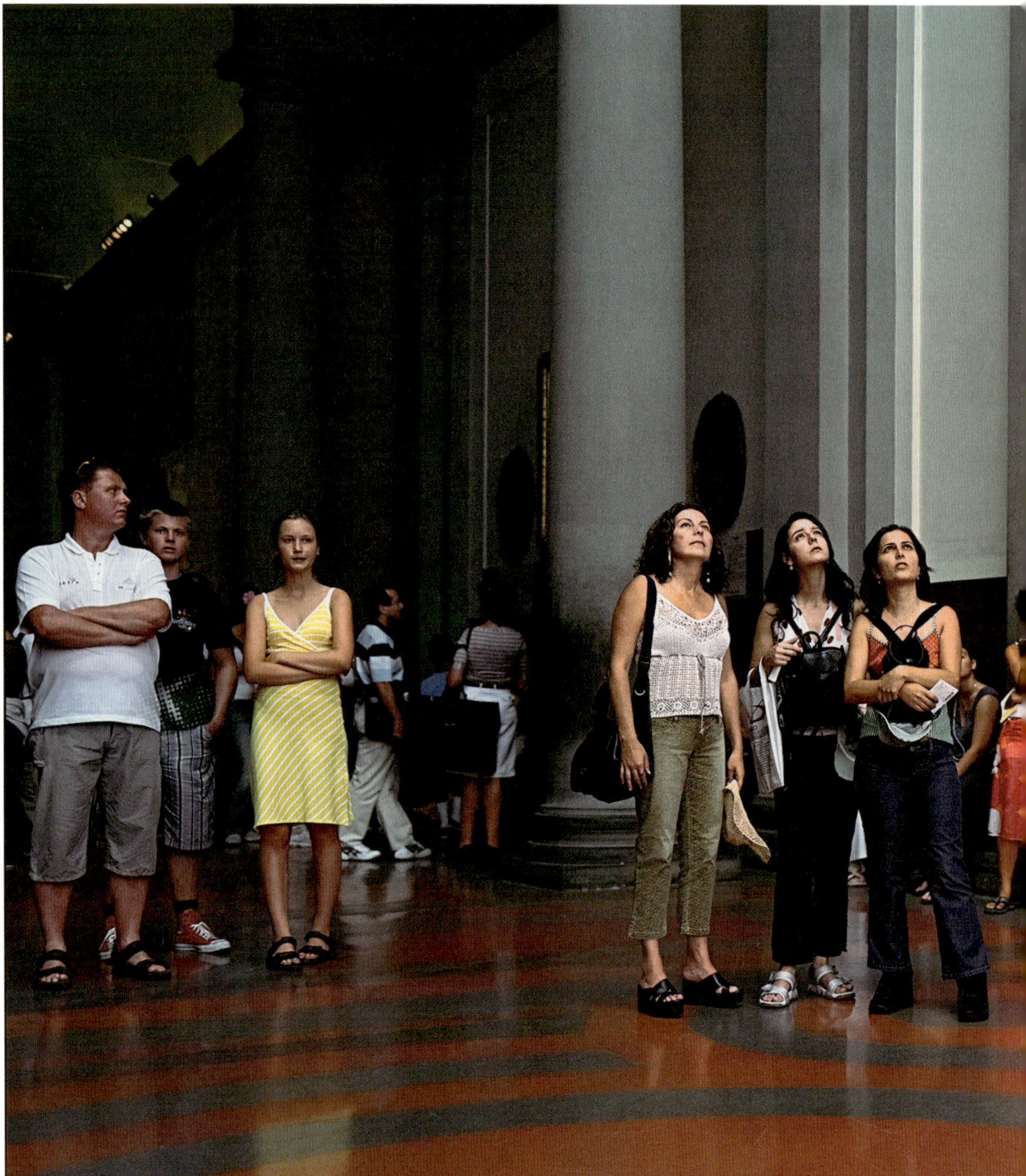

Thomas Struth, *Audience 4*, 2004

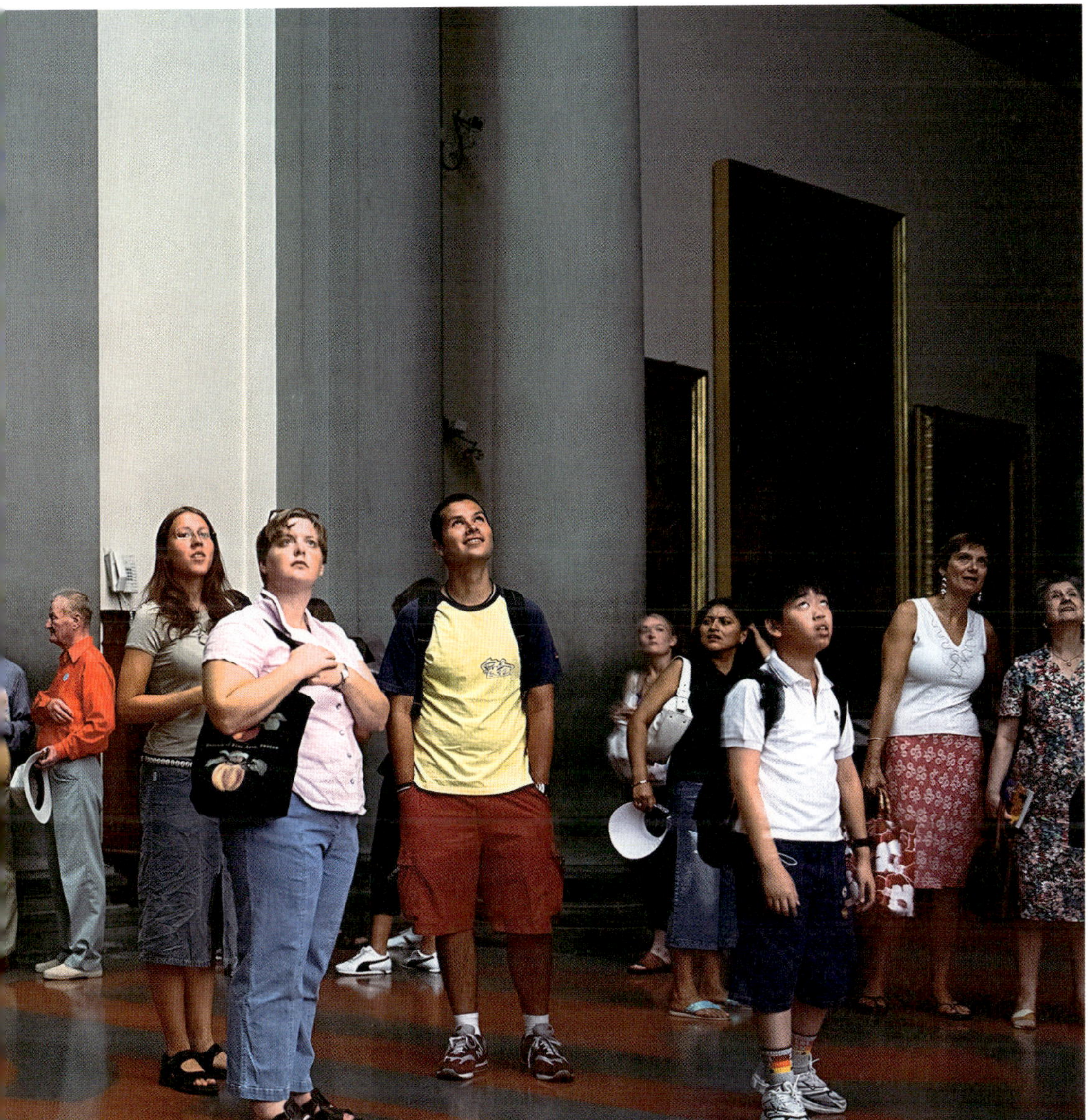

More than 4,500 square meters will be dedicated exclusively to house Armando's dream. As the conversation progresses, he gradually reveals a youthful enthusiasm that, like his passion for collecting, is equally contagious. In the meantime, we learn that, in addition to a one-of-a-kind museum, the former palace of the Counts of Ribeira Grande will have a 64-room hotel of rare sophistication.

But that sophistication is no accident. 'While I began to buy works by Portuguese artists based on my instinct and my taste, for the acquisition of international art I received professional advice from very serious galleries, such as Cristina Guerra, Filomena Soares and, above all, Pedro Cera, who has sold me about 70% of the international pieces I have. Not all the works come from the same place, and there are works by Belgian, Danish, Italian, British, Canadian, Cuban, Mexican, Slovenian, Israeli and, particularly, American and Spanish artists,' explains this man of Portuguese blood and character.

'It is difficult to explain what it is that moves me in a work. Without a doubt I have to like it but even more I have also to fall in love with it, which is not the same thing. Before, whenever I bought a work, I would hang it at home and look at it every day to see how we would get along together. That is, until I had to rent a warehouse, with all the necessary services to store artworks, because there was no longer room in my house, so now I don't look at them anymore. And yet recently, when I saw some works that had been stored away years ago, I reconnected with them,' he adds.

This coexistence has evolved, because by internationalizing his collection, his gaze has also evolved, he comments, while evoking the figure of the writer Fernando Pessoa, another Portuguese capable of moving any European with a minimum of sensitivity. And he immediately moves on to a more specific topic, which also offers a guarantee of future success: how the collaboration with a curator with a notable career such as Adelaide Ginga naturally led to her appointment as director of MACAM.

'Since the collection started to take on a certain dimension, many pieces are in storage and having artworks stored away in a warehouse is utter nonsense. So being able to present them to the public, especially young people and children, providing transport, food and accommodation is an incentive for me. Promoting culture by giving children the opportunity to enjoy works of art from a young age is something that I love. Making this collection known and bringing it to people without resources is fundamental for me. I was born in a very poor town, close to Spain, and I came to Lisbon when I was 13 years old. Of course, this collection is not the best in existence, because my resources are not infinite, but it is the best I could do, and

I want people to really enjoy it. Perhaps this means leaving behind a different legacy than the one I had outlined all my life, which was closely linked to the construction of buildings, offices, warehouses and hotels. But the truth is that the museum, where there will be a hotel with a restaurant, a bar, a merchandising store and an auditorium for music concerts and poetry recitals, where we can stimulate interdisciplinary dialogue, will be one of my last works. So I want to have fun with this palace,' says Armando frankly and poignantly.

Like all good collectors, Martins is first and foremost a humanist concerned about his own community. 'The prices of established international artists are very high, they go up every day and are no longer reasonable. But, apart from that problem in the market, there are very promising young artists, whose prices increase because of their authenticity,' Martins states.

And he openly confesses: 'When I started buying art, I also started investing in the stock market. But I no longer put a penny on stocks. For me, investment today is in property and in art. I have no other activity. At the moment collecting blue-chip artworks is very high profile and synonymous with status. That is why having a Picasso is something many people aspire to. And that is why available capital around the world is seeking refuge in art, at a time when oil and banking are no longer what they were, and when there are few alternatives for investment. Besides, the pandemic has altered everything and sown a lot of doubts, particularly in art fairs, not to mention the dramatic effects it has had on health and the economy, which in some countries has been closed way too much to my way of thinking.'

It seems that, now, with the buildings of Fibeira and the fantasy of a museum, Armando Martins, an engineer after all, has finally found a way to materialize his dreams.

Alain Servais

‘The art world is pure theater’

Nan Goldin, *Smoky car, New Hampshire*, 1979

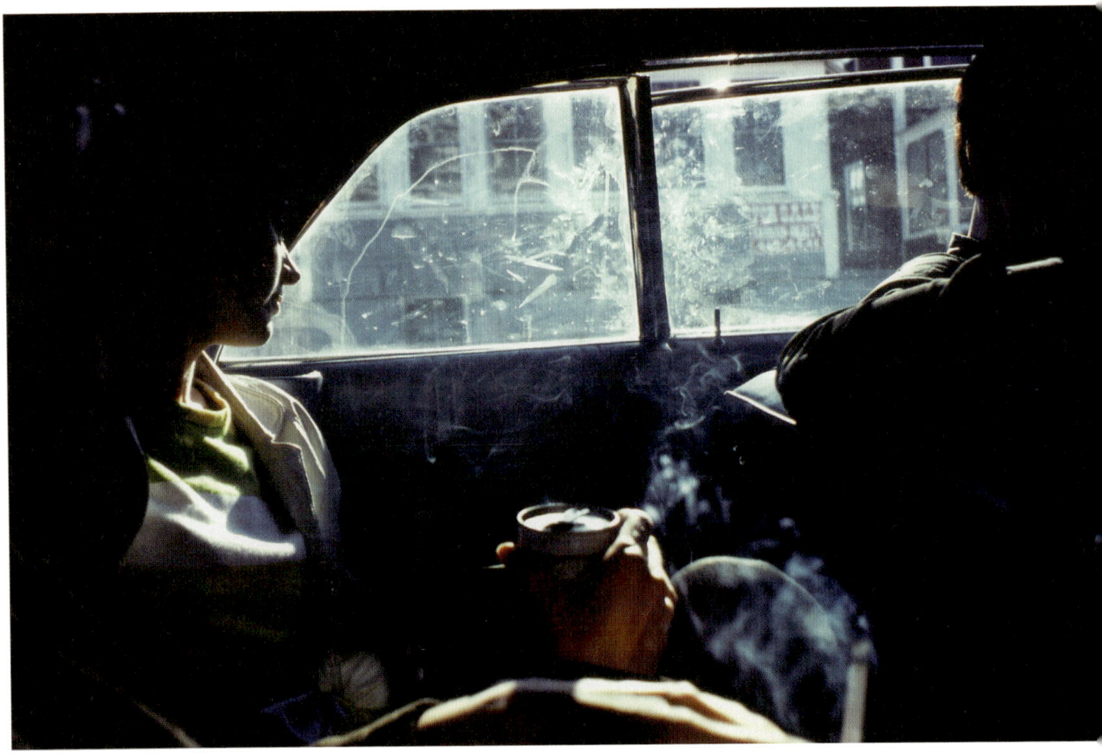

If you want to know about Alain Servais's talent, critical sense, mental acuity and corrosiveness it suffices to read his résumé, his statements or the artworks he has gathered and which, in short, are his own work. But there is nothing that defines him better than the views on reality he offers face-to-face. 'Sooner or later, most collectors realize that sharing art is an inseparable part of owning it,' says Servais to throw light on a probably unsuspected aspect of most of those who put order on the art market from a private perspective. So it is no surprise to learn that he shares his exceptional collection with the public. Despite the fact that he makes a point of clarifying that his intention is 'not to offend anyone,' his personal vision of the art world as being 'infected by money' can ruffle some feathers. Born in Brussels and specialized in investment banking, Servais does not shy away from controversy and avoids political correctness like a mantra. And he does so right from the starting point of a collection that has no place for drawing or for painting.

'There was no previous interest or connection with art in my family. I myself am a Wall Street man, a man of finance, with a different type of background. I first got interested in art as a distraction, and little by little I started visiting museums more and more. So the attraction grew and, thanks to a friend, I got to know the great artists of our time, for example Frank Stella, before I started collecting. This helped me to realize something in which I truly believe, and that is that the art world is pure theater. It looks real, but it is a performance. And since I am very analytical, I began to ask myself what is art and what it means, a question that still bugs me. The definition according to which art is what each artist says it is was not enough for me. So I delved into this question before putting together my collection. And with my salary and the confidence that I had gained, I thought that I could acquire about two pieces per year, the first of which were two photographs by Nan Goldin and Andrés Serrano.' And then he adds: 'For me, originality was never a problem. I am more interested in ideas than the fact that the work I have is exclusive.'

His view of the world is unique. 'The dealer Timothy Baum lived in the same building as a friend of mine, and I remember that in a Surrealism show at the Metropolitan Museum in New York I saw a stunning photograph by Hans Bellmer that Baum was selling for $10,000, which I ended up buying. With time, you begin to understand that there is no difference between an exhibit in a museum, a fair or a gallery. I evolved and grew thanks to the guidance of my mentors and to a very sound piece of advice, namely "always buy the strongest work by the artist you like." And I learned fast. Art gave me introspection, because understanding it helped me to understand myself and to open doors to unknown dimensions and disciplines.'

As part of that evolution, Alain even took the risk of collecting things that made him uncomfortable, knowing that his collection could only be judged with the passing of time: 'Why are Caravaggio, El Greco, the Impressionists, and Robert Whitman important? In my opinion, because they recognized how to relate adequately and deeply with the time in which they produced their work. However, I was never tempted by the idea of buying things from the past or works by great masters, because I want to understand my own time. And for this, the dialogue that current artists establish with their here-and-now is fundamental.'

What is an investment banker's view of the art market? 'I process information and transform it into advice regarding financial decisions. And I don't see my job in investment banking, which I enjoy every day, as being so far apart from the art world, where, despite having learned a lot, I have never wanted to earn money. I reserve that for the world of finance, which in a way is more transparent,' he says provocatively amid laughter. In any case, Servais contends that art builds bridges between different worlds. Perhaps that is why he has such a passion for collecting it, for explaining it, for understanding it and, no less importantly, for sharing it.

When talking about sharing, he emphasizes that his collection, of which he considers himself a mere custodian, is not just a compilation of excellence but, above all, 'more global than any other.' He does not say it boastfully, but from the pride of someone who embraces heterogeneity, precisely to seek those bridges that help to heighten his sensibility. 'How can we get people to communicate in a world where the same events are portrayed in so many different ways on opposing TV channels? Establishing a civilized dialogue is key,' he concludes.

But, when Duchamp has already left such a strong mark, how does one decide when something is art or not? 'I have always believed that if one understands theories, it is not necessary to apply them to the practical world. That is why the question of what is art still haunts me. And I have thirty pages full of definitions I like. There is not just one single answer. But the one that says "art is a language that opens your heart to others" continues to satisfy me,' he says before insisting on the idealist and at once sensorial conception of the artwork. 'I don't see a Pollock piece as a painting, but rather the whole process involved, the geopolitical context in which it was conceived and the history around which it was painted. Without the Cold War, I think Pollock would be unintelligible. But I also believe in the sensibility and sensuality of art. I need to see and feel it.' Perhaps that is why his unorthodox and rational collection is so authentic. 'It is one thing to have a collection, and another is to gather luxury commodities on sale in the art market,' he says.

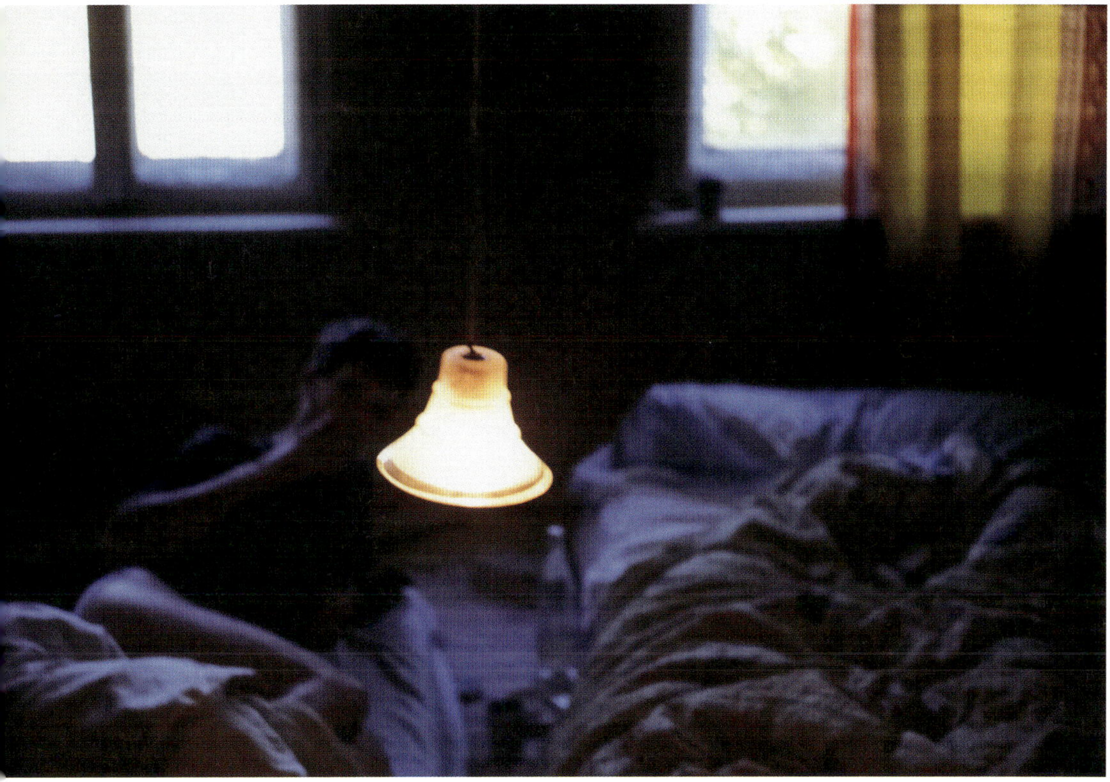

Nan Goldin, *David in bed, Leipzig, Germany*, 1992

However, and while commenting how he is struck by the contradiction of artists who 'need money to survive but want to destroy capitalism,' Servais has not yet answered one key question: what importance does he assigns to the market beyond his interest in money, and why painting is still not one of his passions. 'The market does not interest me nor does it have the least importance for me. And when I buy art, I try to have a look as close as possible to the local sensibility of the place where the artist belongs. I do not put myself in the place of the colonizer, not even when I acquire a piece that is important to a nation like Mexico. Painting is fading, and honestly it is worth more money than I am interested in,' he responds bluntly and with a hint of sarcasm on his face. However, while in Mexico—where he travels three times a year—he acquired the painting *La Revolución* by Fabian Chairez, a work that unleashed a storm of controversy due to the irreverent style in which the masculinity of the mythical revolutionary leader Emiliano Zapata is portrayed. But, as he explains, 'it is not a painting, it is an event.'

Javier Lumbreras

'Speculating with contemporary art can ruin an artist's career'

Pierre Huyghe, *Timekeeper*, 2002

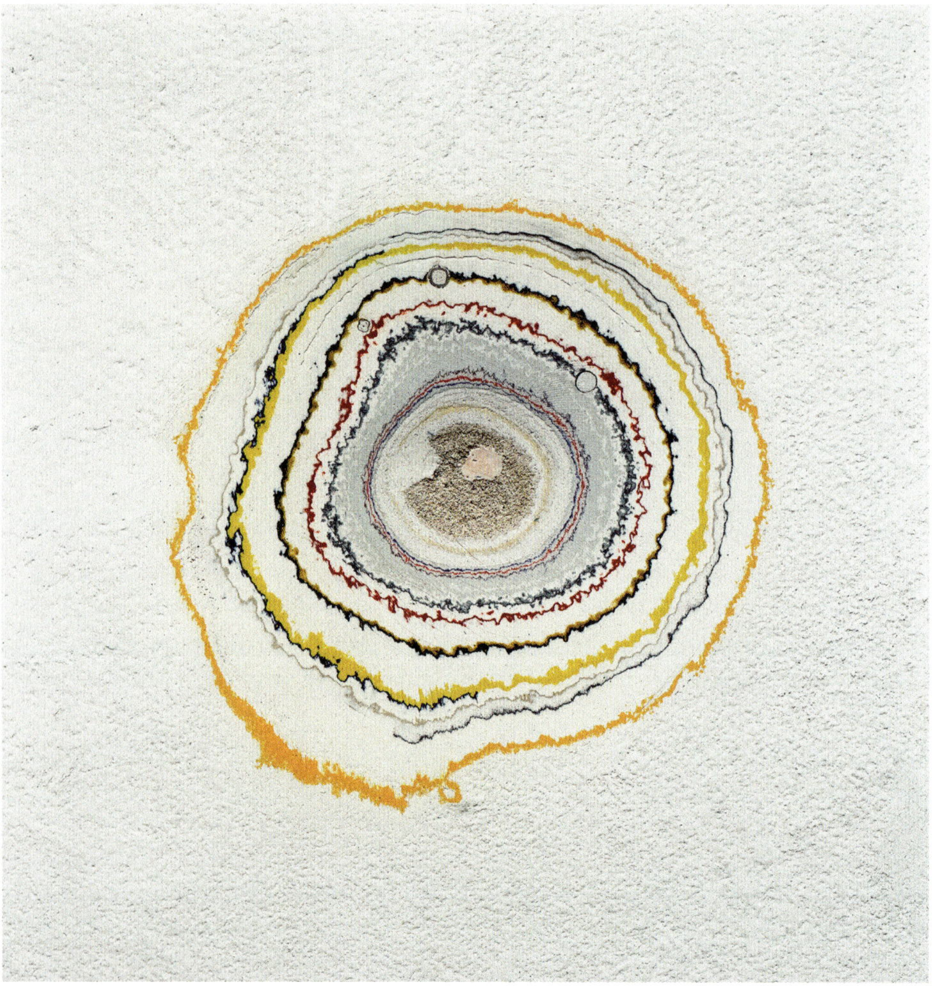

Javier Lumbreras, an elite Spanish collector, is not short on self-assurance, but he is never arrogant. Ambitious, modern and intellectually restless, he explains his latest project by videoconference from Miami. Collegium is a planned center for education, research and experimentation in contemporary art to be located in Arévalo, Ávila. It also aspires to be a space for the production and conservation of artworks.

The United States, the country where he built his career and where his children were born, means a lot in the life of this investor, collector, philanthropist, real estate developer and fund manager. He has played key roles in two New York institutions: the Hispanic Society of America and the Museo del Barrio. In Collegium he has been a member of the board of trustees that oversees a collection of almost one thousand works by more than 150 artists from 40 countries, some of whom truly essential for a proper understanding of what we mean when we talk about contemporary art.

'My first affinity with the world of art was through my grandmother on my mother's side, who had several nineteenth-century works and she introduced me to paintings by Zuloaga,' he recalls. 'Also, my mother painted, as did an aunt on my father's side. I used to go to the Prado Museum from a young age. Art has always been part of my life, first as something that intrigued me and now as a passion. I acquired my first work by exchanging a Zuloaga for a Tàpies. But it was when I graduated from college that I actively started to collect contemporary Latin-American art. I began in the late-1980s with a big attraction toward young artists of the time, such as Adriana Varejão, Vik Muniz and José Bedia, and I even organized exhibitions for some of them. Those artists particularly inspired me, but I didn't ask myself how far I wanted to go with it. Until the year 2000 when a divorce divided the collection into three: one part went up for auction at Sotheby's, and we divided the remainder in two.'

Lumbreras was able to take away a positive from that experience: 'After that disappointment, that setback, a time when I suffered a lot, Adrastus, my collection, was redefined because I got more into art and started buying, always for pleasure, historical works by masters such as Picasso, Warhol and Rubens. For me, art helps you me to understand yourself better and to build fascinating societies, but that is something that I only understood with time. My evolution as a collector has been more rational than passionate, because I reflect a lot on art as a instument for emotional learning.'

Javier, who studied in St. Louis, spent a good part of his career in New York and now spends more time in Madrid, chartered his own unique path. 'What Lorena, my wife and I wanted to create is a collection that would serve others. It is not by chance that Emerson, whom I greatly admire, says that the purpose of life is not to be happy, but to be useful. So we set out to collect twenty-first century works that are highly representative of this historical moment with a view to forming the basis for a museum project that cannot simply consist of building a permanent headquarters for the collection, but rather something that will touch the lives of all the people who enter it, and become a research and learning project that will generate social wellbeing. Collegium, which has been twelve years in the pipeline, is going to cover more than 15,000 square meters in a dozen different buildings. We are interested in managing the cultural space participatively, because a private museum runs the risk of becoming a mausoleum and, as I get older, I don't want to impose my personal taste. For this reason, we will establish a private non-profit board of trustees, in which the Junta de Castilla y León, the region's governing body, will participate. But I also hope that other patrons and collections will join, thus allowing us to build more cultural heritage. It will be a public-private collaboration.'

When asked what is the ultimate goal of his passion for collecting, Lumbreras answers: 'For me the act of collecting has nothing to do with accumulating material goods. Besides, when you only seek profit, you are inviting galleries to prostitute themselves. That being said, if I buy art as an investment, I basically buy the work of consecrated dead artists like Picasso, but not contemporary artists. Because when you speculate with contemporary art, you can ruin an artist's career, and that's not a nice thing. I'm not interested in the speculative angle. When I acquire contemporary works, I look at the emotional value. Over these years we have collected 900 works and we have never sold any,' explains Lumbreras for whom works of art are supranational. 'A museum can have an enormous economic and social impact, and, if it is conceived like we have, the collection becomes an instrument,' he adds.

Lumbreras has a deliberately international eye, that does not look at 'how many Latin Americans or how many women' there are in his collection, but rather prefers 'to judge each work by its merits.' He maintains that today, 'there is art for the rich, which is sold at high prices but may not necessarily transcend, and there is also art to enrich culture and knowledge. It is difficult for highly-priced artists with scant institutional recognition to leave a historical mark.' He prides himself on knowing the market like the back of his hand. 'For me, a great artist has to be in for the long haul. Today, Marcel Duchamp is relatively inexpensive, but he revolutionized the art world. As for my collection, I am not concerned with what the works are worth. Yes, it is true that some galleries have suggested that I should be sitting on the board of museums like MoMA, and it is no coincidence. Museums in Europe are still largely immune from the influence of major collectors, and I believe that, in the same way, there are galleries that have begun to create

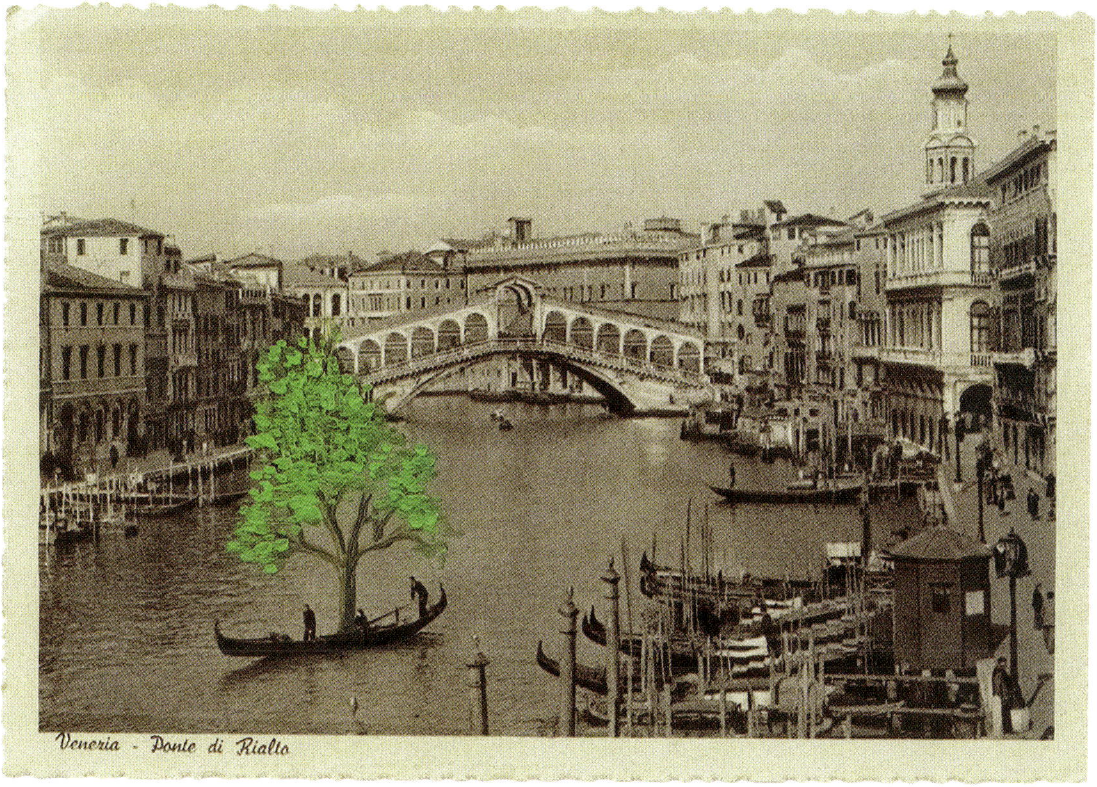

Roman Ondák, *Loop*, 2009

programs and notice certain difficulties in selling some wonderful artists who have a lot to contribute to the dialogue in contemporary art. So, because artists make difficult works and some rich people are mentally lazy, galleries are starting to compromise their exhibition programs and incorporate second-rate, higher-priced artists, who sell like hot cakes. These same galleries lobby to place their clients on the boards of museums in the United States in exchange for putting pressure for these artists to get exhibitions, which I believe is unethical. In Europe, with state-funded museums, we are freer from this kind of pressure and therefore we are less dependent on boards.'

Before concluding, Lumbreras, a big fan of the conceptual artist Roman Ondák, and author of the book *The Art of Collecting Art*, has time to remind us that his collection has lent some of its best works to such emblematic institutions as the Guggenheim in Bilbao, the New Museum in New York, the Palais de Tokyo in Paris, or the Museum of Contemporary Art in Chicago. It is his way, he says, of keeping art 'alive among the people.'

Martin Z. Margulies

‘Art taught me that the world is a more interesting place’

Anselm Kiefer, *Sprache der Vogel,* 1989

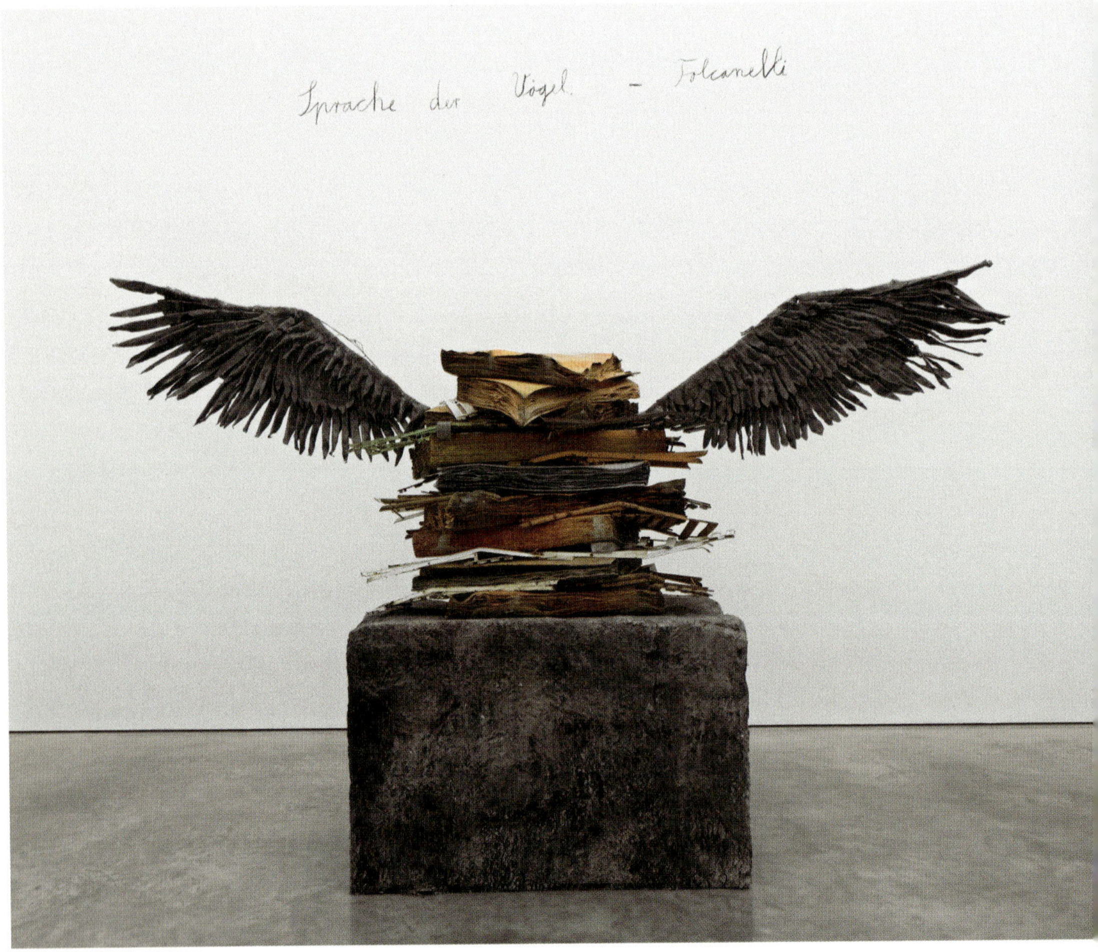

It is rare for a collector to be as interesting as his collection. Martin Z. Margulies, an American real estate developer, is. He is also a generous philanthropist and the owner of a set of wonders, a gallery of great names in art history ranging from Miró to Giacometti, from De Kooning to Pollock, from Mark Rothko to Andy Warhol, from Cy Twombly to Anselm Kiefer, and from Lichtenstein to Jasper Johns.

He welcomes us with elegance and humor in his magnificent apartment in Key Biscayne. Margulies is 83 years young, and explains that he manages to stay mentally active because he does not neglect his physical activity. And he sports a style far removed from any superficial temptation, as befits someone who grew up in Yonkers, New York, as a true descendant of European immigrants who, despite not having a higher education, managed with dedicated effort to build a food store business in the neighborhoods of Harlem and the Bronx.

In addition to his contribution to the world of culture, especially to the visual arts (museums such as the Metropolitan or the Whitney have benefited from his generosity), he has focused his efforts on combating inequality in the United States, Martin has been the key benefactor of Lotus House, a shelter in Miami created to house 500 Miami homeless women and children, to which he has donated $20 million. He also encourages a passion for art among students in the city where he lives. Although it is not always easy, he jokes, because it is a city that 'tends to be always partying.'

His collection is considered among the best in the world. It all started 'at an auction in New York with a friend' in the late-1970s. He recalls, 'I was struck by the amount of money that those who were there, truly intelligent people from the business world, invested in art. So I thought, "There must be something in it." And that's how I started, first I went to a dealer, and I was very frank. I explained that although I had a little money from the real estate business, I didn't really know what I was doing. As I became more exposed to the art world, things began to crystallize. Not wanting to be known as the mystery shopper who only bought sculptures, which is what I was doing in the beginning, I started collecting paintings. Eventually I acquired a warehouse, and from painting I moved to photography and video, again to sculpture and finally to younger artists, who I did not know at the time. The dealers I frequented, like Shaindy Fenton and Ivan Karp from OK Harris Gallery, helped me and taught me a lot, at a time when there were fewer collectors than there are now. In this way, I realized that the world was a more fascinating place than I previously thought, not only because I could acquire quality art, but because through this medium I could learn, which is fundamental, because when you learn from something, you see it much better. In this way, especially thanks to Shaindy, I also met fascinating people, such as the gallery owners Leo Castelli, André Emmerich and Arne Glimcher.'

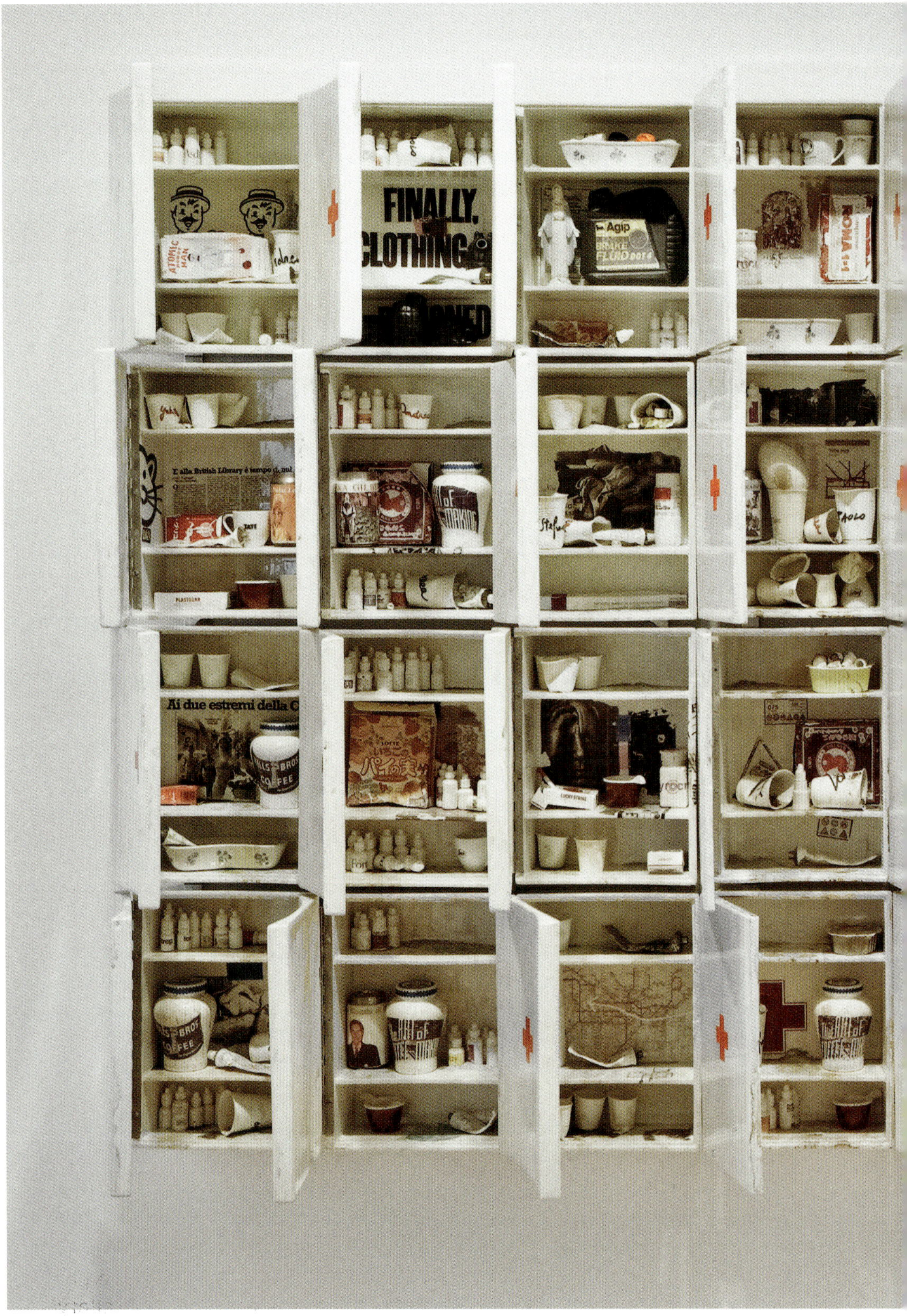
FINALLY,
CLOTHING
Agip
BRAKE FLUID DOT 4
Ai due estremi della
COFFEE
パイの実

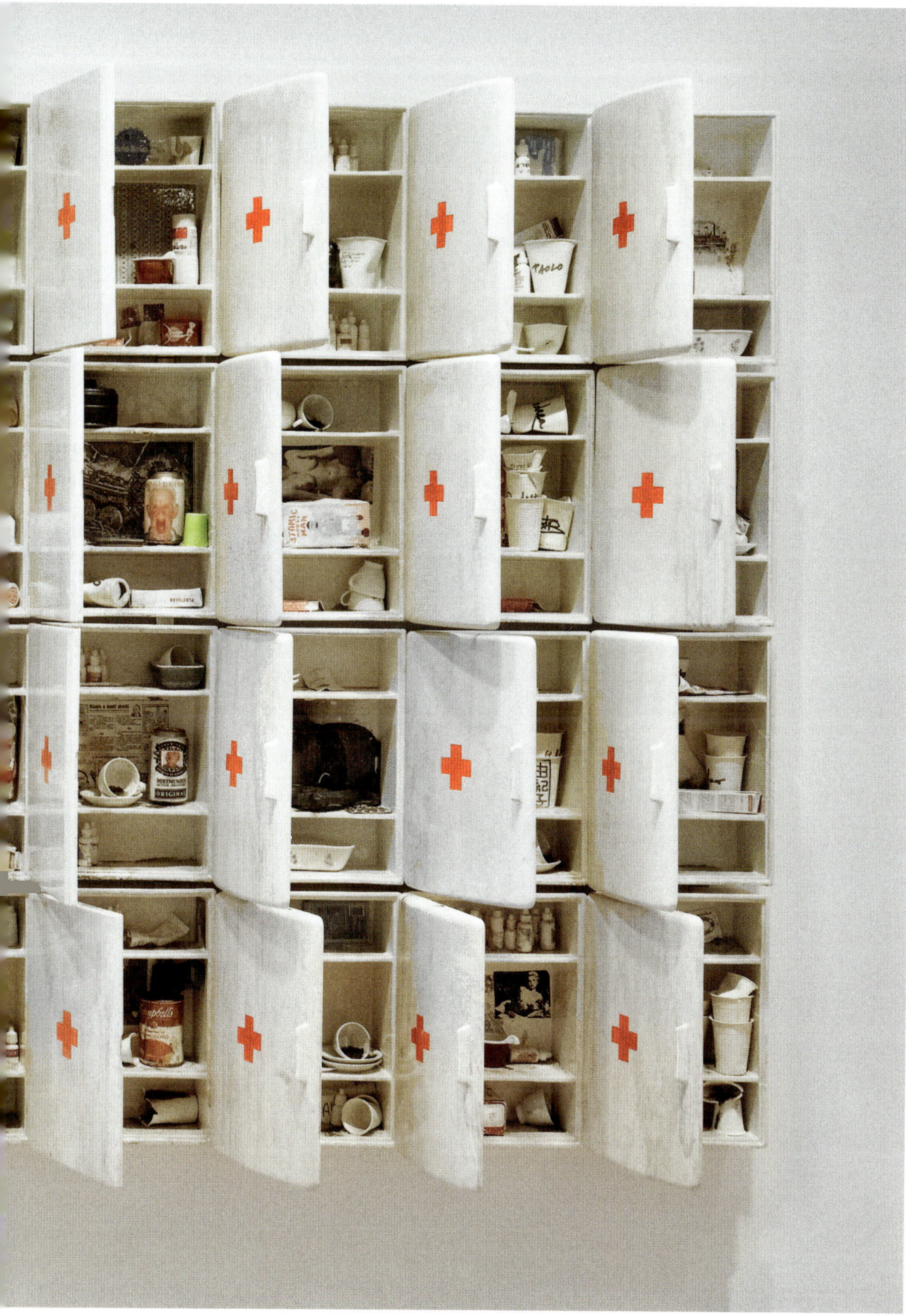

Bertozzi & Casoni, *Composizione no. 8,* 2005

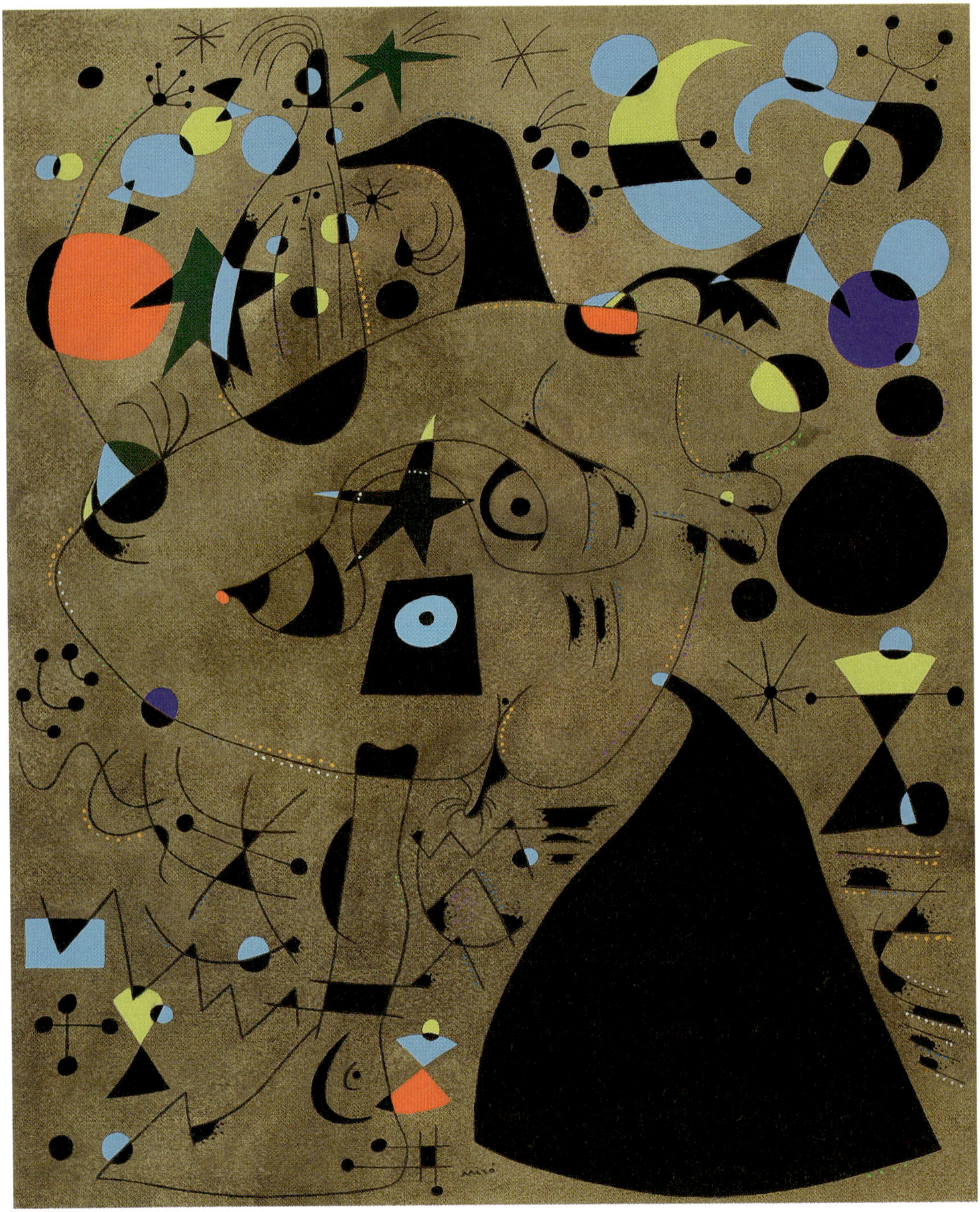

Joan Miró, *Femme dans la nuit,* 1940

Margulies, who can't disguise his New York accent, has a soft spot for the more refined face of the old continent. 'At first, I wanted to see absolutely everything and had no defined direction. But eventually the collection took shape and acquired its own rhythm and cohesion, with a special emphasis on Pop art and abstract art. So what I wanted was to have a collection that I could enjoy and, later, a space to share the collection so that the public could also appreciate it, as is now the case with my warehouse in Miami.' This is how he refers to the Margulies Collection At the Warehouse, a captivating 5,000-square-meter space in the vibrant neighborhood of Wynwood.

'Even today, when I see new artists, the works I buy excite me. That feeling hasn't changed,' he adds. But what makes him decide on an acquisition? The aesthetic and affective attraction for a work and the calculation of how it would fit into that greater cosmos that is the collection, he clarifies.

Asked about the fate of his collection, when Margulies, who is a personal friend of great living artists, such as Anselm Kiefer, or some already deceased, such as George Segal, is no longer here, he responds: 'I have a plan, and I think it is the right one for me and my children. Most of my legacy will go to a number of charities, from the homeless shelter that we founded to hundreds of schools we wish to establish so that education is not an obstacle in some of the most impoverished areas of the United States. To achieve these goals, the institutions that receive our works must sell them to fund themselves, so our collection as such will cease to exist. I believe that the great museums have excellent art and don't need more. Rather, I think, they need to connect with people and stop ignoring the extraordinary social disintegration that exists in a world where too little attention is paid to hunger, children and veterans. For me, what is important is to try to help improve the human condition.'

Grazyna Kulczyk

‘People are hungry for art, especially face-to-face’

Zofia Kulik, *Autoportret z pałacem* [Self-portrait with the Palace], 1990

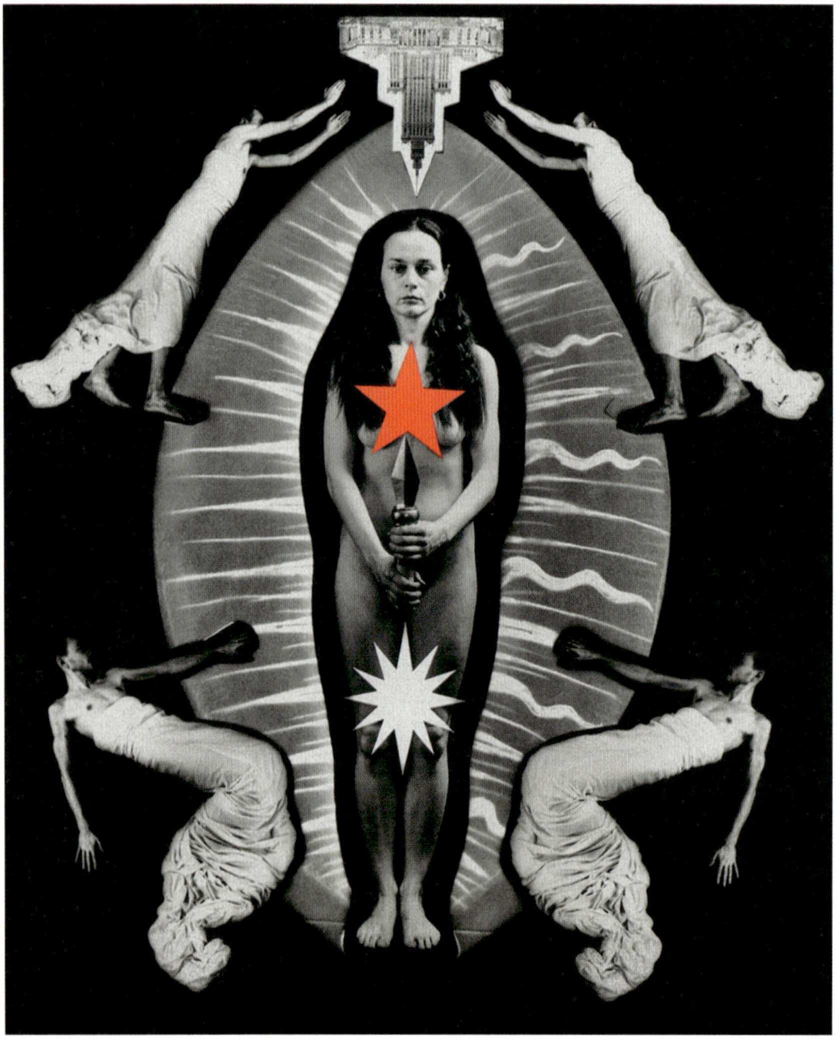

She turned a beautiful, peaceful valley in the Alps into a must-visit destination for anyone seriously interested in art. Grazyna Kulczyk, an elite collector who rarely talks to the press, was married to the successful businessman Jan Kulczyk, who died in 2015. She has excelled in finance and collecting on her own merits. It all started years ago, when she was a law student in her native Poland. Kulczyk is the soul of the Susch Museum, which, since 2019, houses her private collection in a charming Swiss village, located in the canton of Graubünden, not usually associated with these purposes. Thanks to her discerning eye, she has put together a singular collection—mainly contemporary conceptual and performance-based artworks made by women—with a highly personal and yet, nevertheless, universal stamp.

Her sensitivity comes to the surface when she talks about how the pandemic affected her. 'The time in lockdown due to COVID had a profound effect on my life, my feelings and my habits, but it also allowed me to focus on details that would have otherwise gone unnoticed during my daily routine. Like many other people, I rediscovered books, movies and music, and I have the enormous privilege of being able to enjoy art at home and in great depth. Collectors who publicly exhibit their art in institutions treat the works they have at home in a very personal way. And now I am able to discover countless hidden meanings and details.'

Kulczyk says that it might have seemed 'natural' to build the museum in Poland. 'That is my homeland and where I have developed most of my business. The museum was going to be designed by a big name in architecture and it was going to be donated to the Polish State. Unfortunately, none of my initiatives, neither in Poznan nor in Warsaw, were successful. Nobody showed any interest. I think they never understood the true role that art can play in a society,' she says with rare sincerity. 'We shouldn't forget that Poland is a post-socialist country, in which for many decades there was no contact with the type of contemporary art in which I have specialized.'

Asked about her beginnings, long before she ventured into fields as different as automobiles, energy and telecommunications, she recalls: 'I really started collecting as a Law student. Even then most of my time was spent with people who were engaged in creative activities. So whenever I was able I traveled around Europe to broaden my interests, but initially what I collected was exclusively Polish art. After the fall of communism in Poland, I started to work more naturally with other artists.'

A collector of such brilliant artists as Donald Judd, Eva Hesse, Jenny Holzer and Carol Rama, Kulczyk explains how her museum ended up where it is. 'Many wonderful projects come about by pure chance, without knowing why. I did not know Switzerland very well but as I got to know the Susch

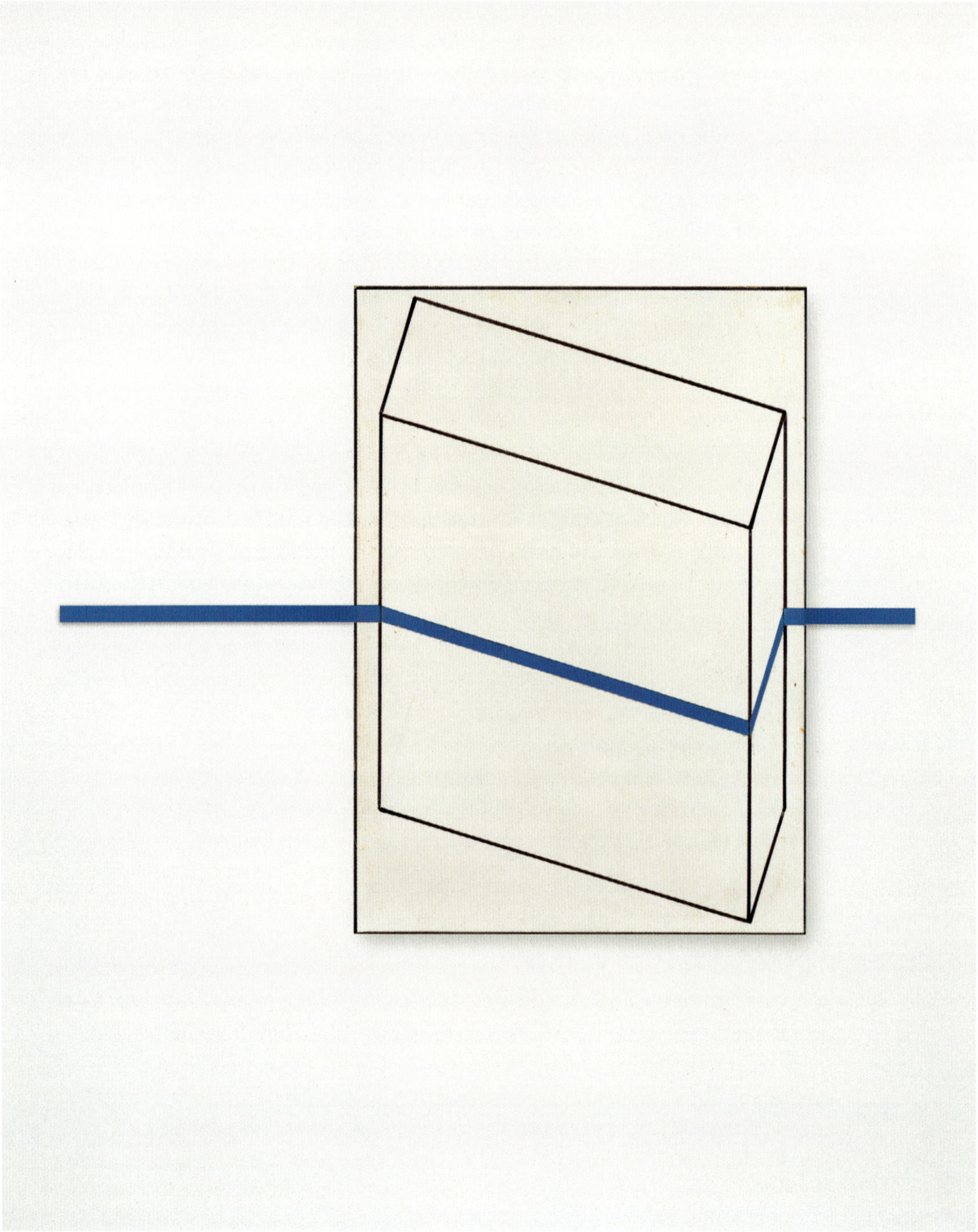

Edward Krasiński, *Interwencja* [Intervention], 1975

community I had a chance to see the country from a different perspective. And there was another attractive element: although the place is isolated, it is also in the heart of Europe. When I look for something I make sure I get it,' she laughs, before giving us an example of her tenacity in the way in which she became the biggest bicycle importer in Poland. And despite the coolness with which the idea for the museum was received, she has dedicated a 400-square-meter space in Poland to making high-quality artworks accessible to the wider public. As she says, 'education is one of the few words that I never tire of.'

What is the purpose of the Susch Museum beyond the inherent interest of its artworks? 'One of the pillars of the museum is our temporary exhibitions. And another, to which we dedicate an entire separate building, is our arts residency program. We also have a collaboration program with the Institut Kunst in Basel (FHNW), and another project dedicated specifically to performance art. I am really proud to be welcomed by so many museums and elite collectors around the world, especially if we consider that ours is such a young institution.'

Before finishing, Kulczyk has time to talk about the truly countercultural exhibition by Evelyne Axell on view in the museum, the effect of the pandemic on her life—'I have bought many works with this phone'—and the surplus of stimulus in the art market. 'The amount of information I receive every day makes it literally impossible to deal with. Messages that normally would interest me can become irrelevant.' And also about the future of her collection. 'I have thought a lot about it and every year I think about it more, especially since my children are not interested in art. I have seen how some world-class collections have been dispersed, with their major works being auctioned off. So, although for the moment I prefer not to say what decision I will make, it is something I take seriously. Despite the fact that there are much larger collections out there, I believe this one is essential for many reasons: because it reflects me, because it is very focused on the artists, because it has been personally curated, because it brings together things that move me and because, thanks to its style, it is atypical.'

Rafael Tous

'Things in life have to be spread around'

Eva Lootz, *A-B*, 1977

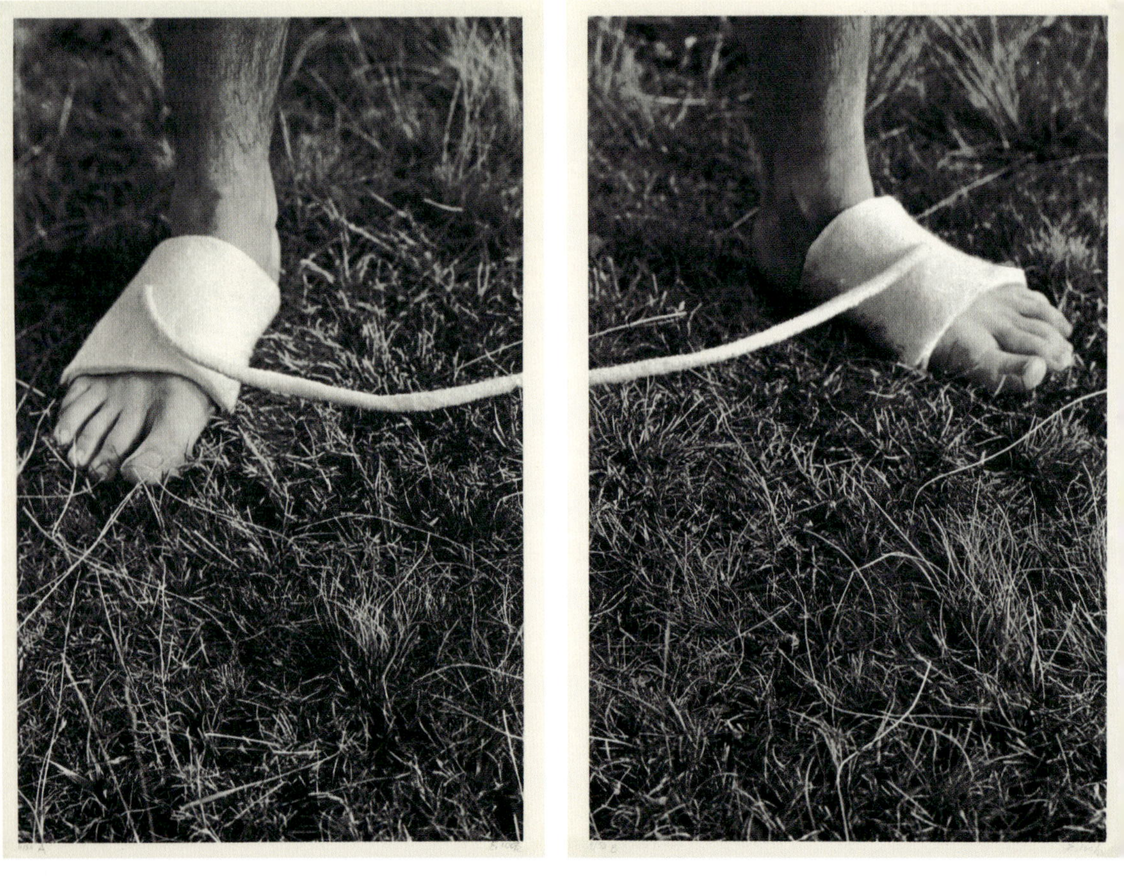

'Different' is a word bandied around a bit too lightly. But it fits to perfection with the personality of Rafael Tous (Barcelona, 1940), a man as fascinating as he is unorthodox. Tous has turned collecting into an art form in its own right, thanks to his ability to put together collections that are coherent in their difference, whether they be records, books or works of art. He made the headlines in May 2021 when he donated his legacy of conceptual art to MACBA (Barcelona Museum of Contemporary Art). The gift was so important that it forced the museum to rethink its permanent exhibition. It was the end of a path that the businessman, always linked with the textiles and fashion industry, began in 1965, at the age of 25, and which includes a brief period in which, more than contemporary art, he devoted himself to Catalan Impressionism. As a result of this donation to MACBA, an exhibition was organized with the appropriate title of *In Real Time.* Dressed in jeans, relaxed, talkative and with a still youthful spirit at 82 years old, Tous guided us through the exhibition before meeting us the next day at his imposing house, where books reign absolutely. This is not strange because as Tous says, he reads around 400 pages every day. From movie posters to travel books, cookbooks, English or Spanish literature, his library, which he classifies with patience and rigor, contains more than 150,000 titles and continues to grow at a dizzying pace.

He is also a collector of photographs and African primitive art. Tous was director of the fantastic Metrònom space (1980-2006), which presented the work of hitherto unknown artists to the Barcelona public. He won ARCO Foundation's 'A' Prize for Spanish Private Collection and the 2016 GAC Collecting Award. He is married to the artist Ana de Matos. And, in the time left over after all of the above, he runs an orphanage for 500 children in Burundi.

In this setting, surrounded by Venetian glass, postcards, toys, African wood sculptures, cassettes, CDs and LPs, art books and a huge variety of Buddhas from Tibet, our curiosity gets the conversation off to a start. Where do all these things, so much and so varied, come from? 'At the age of six I discovered a passion for collecting, through those beautiful stickers that the Jesuits at my school didn't like so much, and then through movie posters and comics. I became a collecting maniac,' he recalls with a laugh. 'My father, who was the eldest brother in his family, received a very large inheritance, but that was the source of many family squabbles. It was when I was married Carmen Godia, my first wife, that I began to collect paintings by artists such as Santiago Rusiñol. After a few years and, and after having three children together, we separated, to my father's great displeasure as he was a devout Catholic. Since I owed money to my father-in-law, Carmen kept all the works. And I was left empty-handed! So I started out on a new life and, with it, I set up my clothing business, manufacturing the garments basically in Catalonia. And then I began to earn real money: it was fantastic, because I could hardly keep up with demand.' After losing his *noucentisme* treasures in the separation, he made a decision: to collect contemporary art 'with a political and anti-Franco leaning, although not explicit', he specifies. 'When I realized that what was emerging internationally was conceptual art, I traveled the world, I engaged with that whole universe and I never left it since. I set out on the adventure of the Metrònom project with Isabel de Pedro, my wife at the time, and with whom I had a daughter.'

He dedicated himself whole-heartedly to promoting art. 'In one of the galleries I had, we organized 500 art and photography exhibitions, debates, roundtables, contemporary dance shows and concerts.' But what made him passionate about conceptual art, an often cryptic genre? 'Ignorance of its meaning, the message it contained, who made it, as well as the fact that no one wanted to exhibit it. Nobody had a clue about political and social conceptual art. But I did, and I looked out for its artists. How? By buying their works,' he explains. He also wittily recalls how, when he separated from Isabel de Pedro, she ended up with the more traditional work—by artists such as Tàpies—while he held onto his collection of conceptual art, which is now just as highly valued economically and critically esteemed. 'I have accumulated 1,100 works of this type. But parallel to that collection, especially from the mid-1970s, I became interested in contemporary photography, and collected up to some four thousand pieces with a strong leaning towards social photography—and there you will find gays fighting for their rights, political protests, mental asylums and prisons—coming from very diverse origins—from Central America to Japan, Canada, South Africa and Spain—and, in all cases, I would acquire entire series, because a single photograph by an artist tells you nothing'.

With the passing of the years, Tous decided 'to sell the collection at a very low price to a top museum, so that I could continue carrying out cultural activities. But since none of them accepted, and after thinking about it and talking to my children, who are very well-educated culturally but for whom the lack of space to house the collection became a problem, I decided to give it away. "Do whatever you want, because you collected it," they told me. So I donated the collection, which makes me happy, because it gives people a chance to see works by great artists. Of course, later I will have to decide what I will do with the many other kinds of work I have accumulated,' he confesses.

So, what will happen to his multiple collections when he is gone? 'I don't know exactly. Maybe I'll put a line in my will so that they can do whatever they want with it. My family knows that I have always been interested in social aspects and that as a young man I was very left-wing, despite the fact

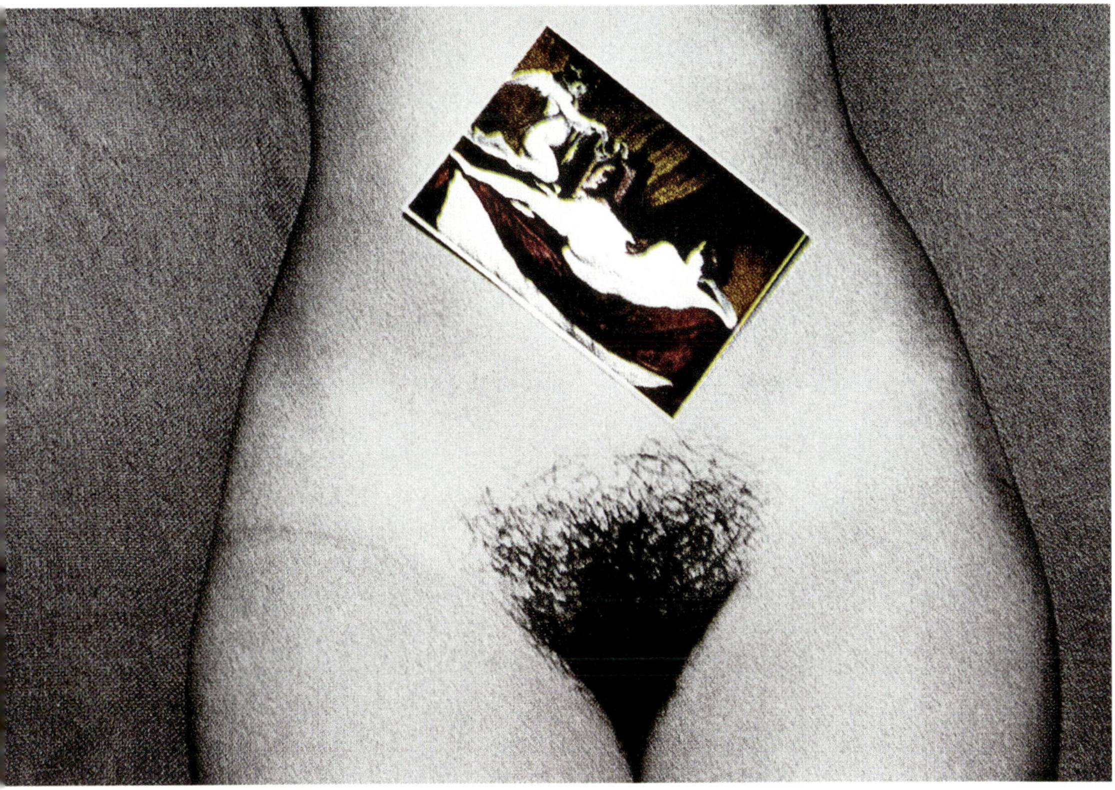

Jordi Cerdà, *Paral·lelisme Cos de dona dins l'art,* 1979

that my first wife was extremely conservative. What I mean is that I believe that things in life have to be spread around. And, so that all this work can be enjoyed by people and artists—who will be able to see the work in public places, as is already the case with MACBA—I still think the same. Although of course, it will not be easy, because between books and art magazines alone I have 250,000 copies.' And in African art, another four thousand pieces. But it all started with the trading cards. 'You start with that when you're little, you continue with more serious things and then you never stop. Why do I collect all those books you see? Well, because I read them. I catalog everything myself, because when I used to get help I would always end up not being able to find something or who was responsible. So I buy, order and classify everything myself,' he declares with a smile fixed on his face.

Harald Falckenberg

‘Political correctness is the end of freedom, the very essence of art’

Martin Kippenberger, *Self-portrait*, 1976

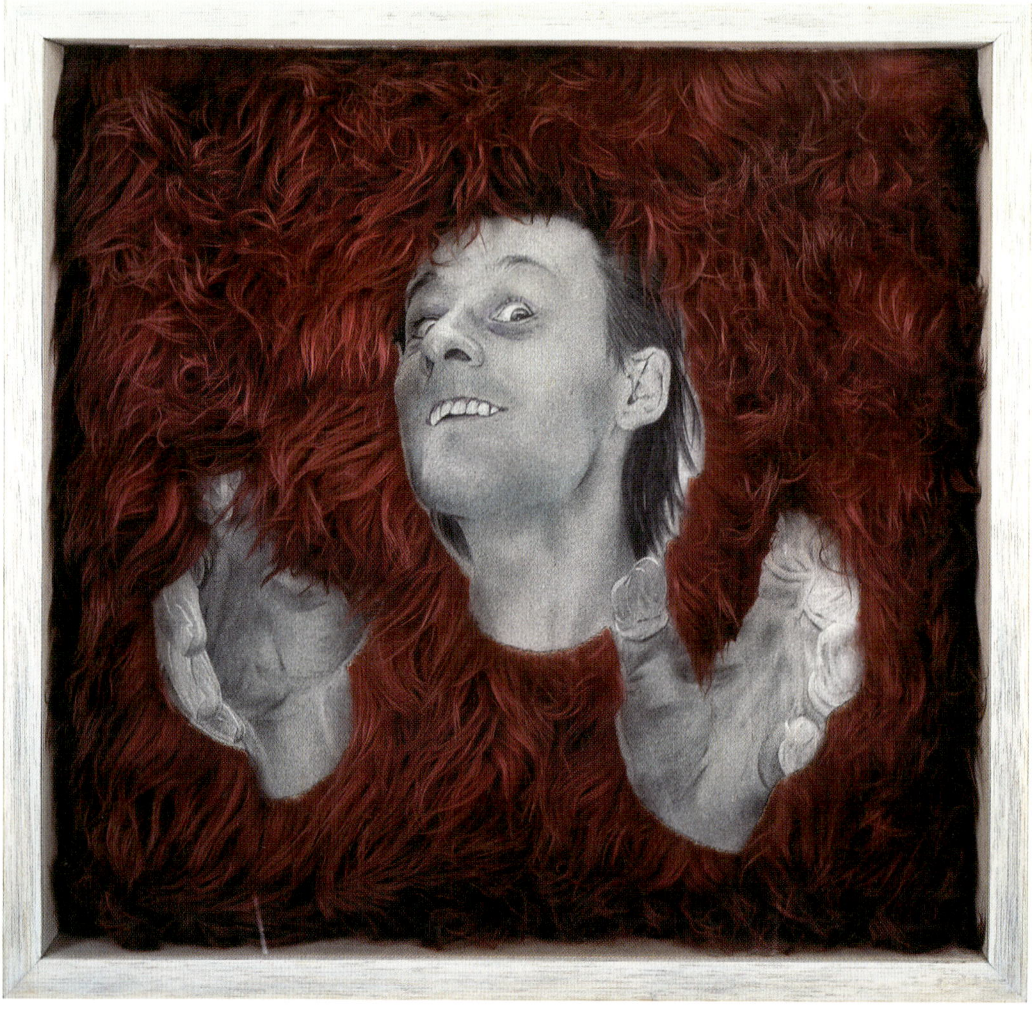

Harald Falckenberg's collection is built on both passion (which he feels for certain artists) and knowledge (which he has plenty of when it comes to art history). This apparently contradictory sum brings richness and complexity to his intellectual and aesthetic universe, and gives his tastes a strong, very particular and, above all, authentic character. Born in Germany in 1943, Falckenberg is an industrial entrepreneur, doctor of law and one of the most respected and influential collectors in the world, despite his unorthodox and scarcely commercial profile. The winner of multiple awards for his patronage work, he has chaired the Hamburg Kunstverein and has served as professor of Art Theory at Hamburg's Academy of Fine Arts, to which his soul humbly yet whole-heartedly belongs, and with whose tercentenary autonomous and non-conformist spirit he identifies so closely.

As Manuel Borja-Villel, director of the Reina Sofía museum in Madrid, explains, his collection combines 'history and emotion, the personal and the collective. A rare case at a time when it often seems that people collect brands more than artworks,' he adds of a collector who has collaborated with the museum he runs on some notable shows. And among the more than 2,400 works he treasures, names such as Albert Oehlen, Sigmar Polke, Dieter Roth, Georg Herold, Paul Thek and Mike Kelley stand out.

In addition to being on exhibit at the Deichtorhallen Art Center in Hamburg for more than a decade, this collection has another peculiarity: despite grouping works from different periods, everything is underpinned by a critical, contemporary and social sense that suggests that whoever has put it together is, more than a collector or a curator, an artist. Regularly included in the rankings of elite collectors since ARTnews first named him as one of the top 200 in the world in 1999, he is in a certain way a creator, as he demonstrated from the beginning of our meeting, which started with a tour of his beloved city. Then with a conversation of more than two hours the next day in his apartment in Hamburg, where time stood still. The German collector, accompanied by his wife, Larissa Hilbig, flitted from one theme to the next with the naturalness of a sorcerer, from the pressing urgency of contemporary art to the validity of Richard Wagner and his connection to Vladimir Putin.

Surrounded by that aura, by countless books, museum-quality works, and a strangely powerful energy for a man in his 80s, Falckenberg demonstrated, despite his success as a businessman and collector, a very definite taste removed from conventions and, on many occasions, against the mainstream.

'In May 1994 I bought my first work, *Running from Spots*, by Bill Beckley, an American conceptual artist. So, I was 51 years old and in the midst of a mid-life crisis that nonetheless turned out positive. And I began to reflect

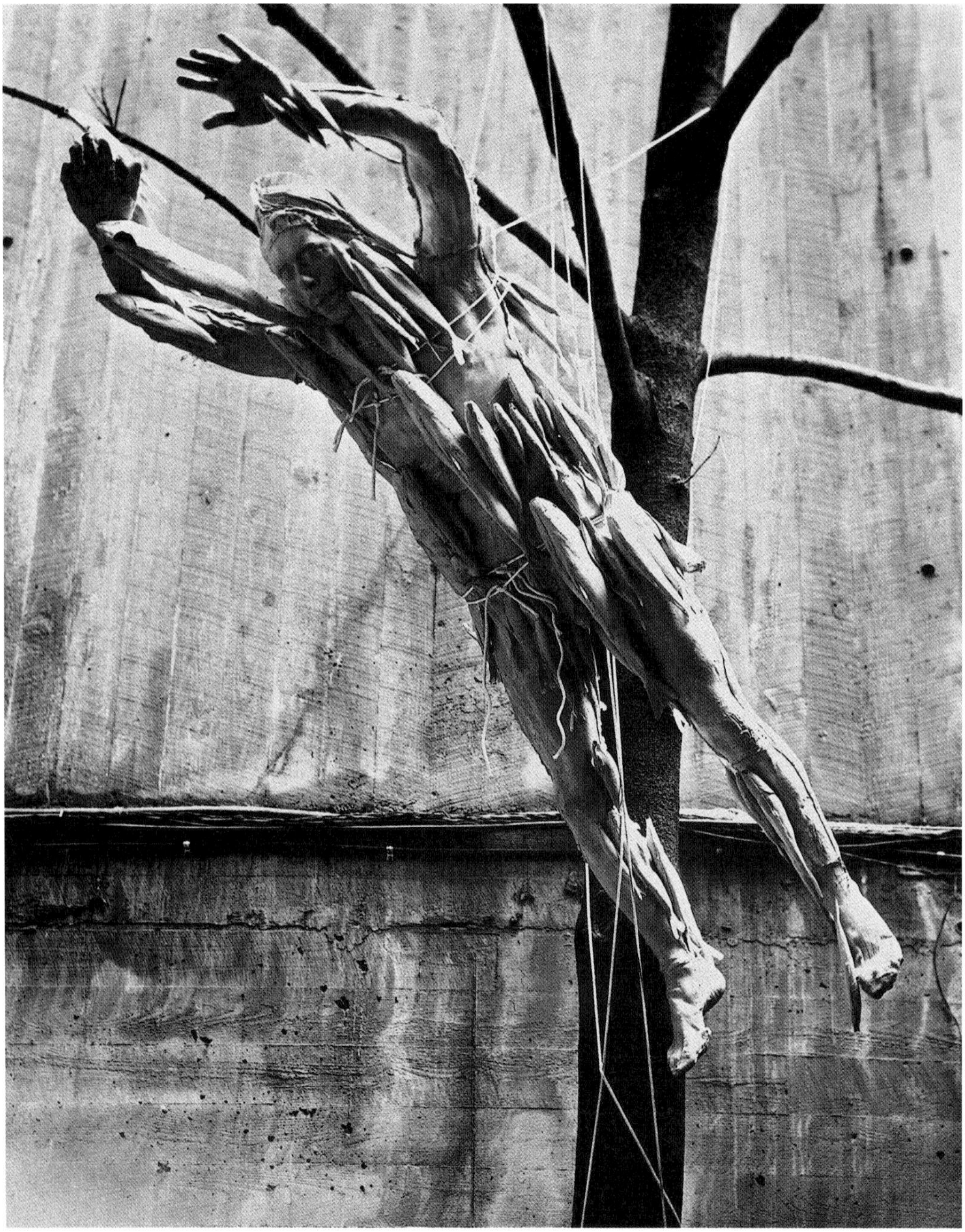

Paul Thek, *Fishman*, 1969

on what to do for the rest of my life, after having had a successful and conventional career. I retired as manager of a major company at the age of 65, and it became clearer to me that collecting art was a necessity. The process was progressive and also exponential, because I had very good influences, for example, from the gallery owner Hans Mayer, from Düsseldorf, who in the beginning was generous enough to lend me dozens of works, so that I could live with them for months and be able to decide which one to keep,' he declares, profoundly and rigorously, before moving on to more intimate memories, like when his first wife threw him out when she discovered he was being unfaithful, or when later he bought seventy works 'in one go' to get his collection off to a start once and for all.

That's how transparent Falckenberg is, whose intricate and musical pronunciation would surely have fascinated Borges. He recalls how a wise man told him, 'don't collect mainstream art. Everyone has it and it is not for you. You should never buy based on an artist's name, status or reputation.' And Falckenberg, who had studied Babylonian art, art history and the context in which his favorite contemporary artists created their works—especially the period between the wars—took that advice to heart.

'I don't look so much for beauty, authenticity or strict adherence to certain standards when I collect, but for something different. I was a law professor at university before dedicating myself to business, and perhaps that also explains my search, fueled by powerful, authentic, rebellious and free-spirited artists, with whose works I identified,' he explains while evoking the spirit of Willem de Kooning. He differentiates between culture, which in general he understands as longer-term, and art, one of his vital passions, 'which cannot come up with political solutions and in a certain way always resembles a kind of essay.'

Nor is it accidental then, the scientific conception that this essayist has about a literary genre that, he emphasizes, must always be open in its conclusions for the reader. 'Like art', he rounds it off. 'I don't look at it as an historian, but as a fundamental part of society, also because I don't like to be stuck in any tradition.'

The talk ranges from his interest in counterculture to the surprising freedom he gained through collecting, an unexpected destiny to which this individual with an orthodox past surrendered himself with a devotion not devoid of logic. 'Political correctness is the end of freedom, the very essence of art,' he continues, jumping from one subject to another: from the mysteries of non-fiction literature to the human psyche, pitching another frank and contentious opinion: that Sigmund Freud was a much better writer than he was a psychoanalyst.

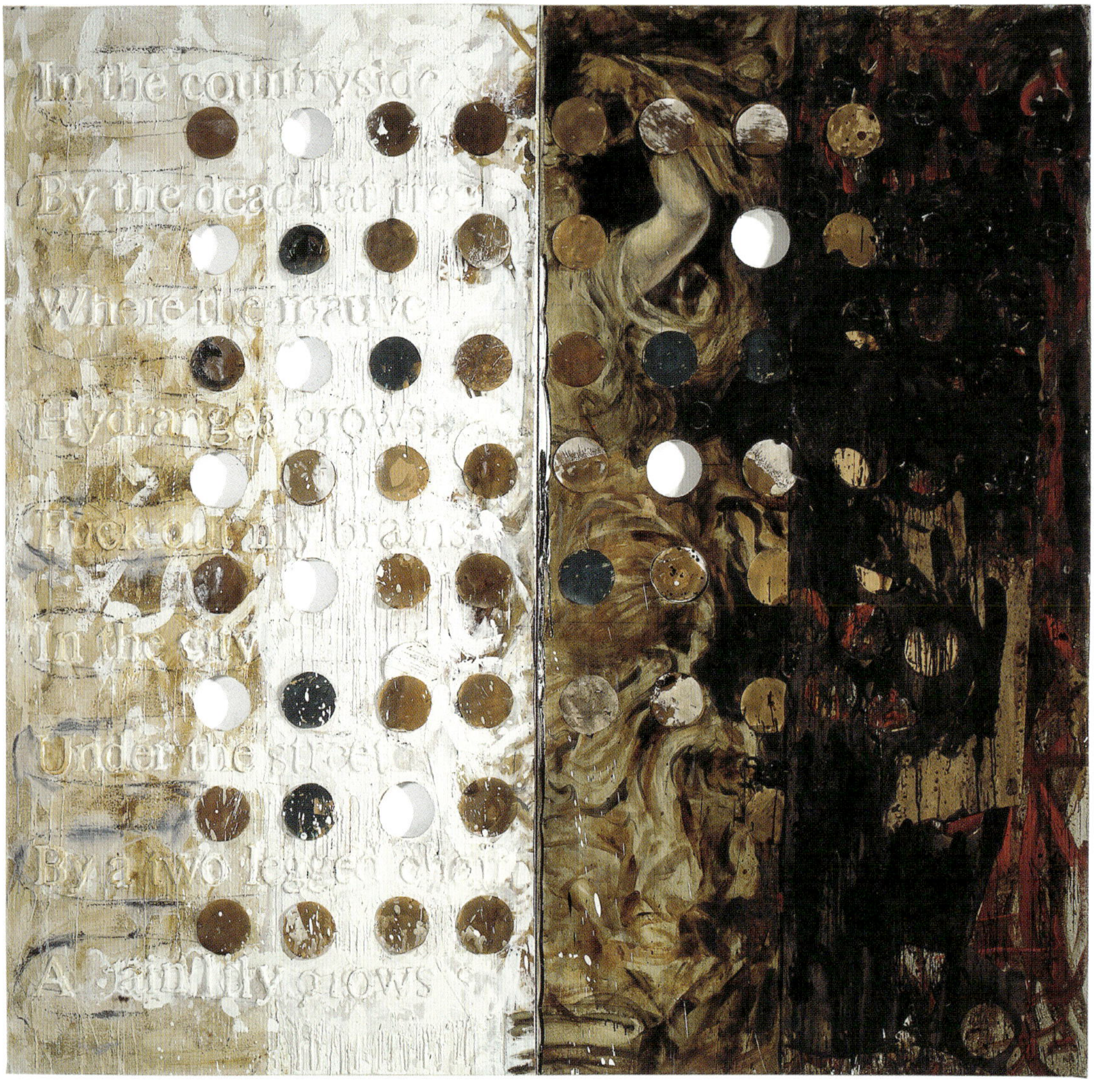

Bill Beckley, *Running from Spots*, 1982

From Henry David Thoreau to the roots of surrealism, how philosophical thought lost its primacy to sociology in the 21st century, and from materialism to politics in a broad sense as a fixed presence in contemporary art, different themes seem to emerge with the same versatility and rigor, more as a prompt for reflection than as a set of pre-digested answers. Once again, as if in a perpetual essay.

Before ending a conversation, which is as passionate as it is circular, and in which time seems to have stopped, Falckenberg has something else to say: 'I am interested in communicating with people who really express themselves in a personal way through their art, and who are always in search of freedom, whether they succeed or not, not just like De Kooning but also Mark Rothko.' Artistic expression most in tune with this intense way of feeling can be found in expressionism and figurative art more so than in abstract art, although he cannot find 'anything negative about Donald Judd and Lucio Fontana, who have another vision.'

Apart from temporary exhibitions, Harald offers not one but two entirely free spaces where anyone can see his permanent collection—one that belongs to him and another that he has developed in close contact with the city council. Near the end, he makes a confession consistent with his essays and with his generosity in sharing art: 'Everything I have collected has to do with my desire to communicate with others. That is why I would never conceive of a collection that was not public, that did not generate discussions and that did not leave my private walls. I am pleased to know that it is a collection that is up-to-date and alive, that it is rebellious and political in a broad sense—that is to say, aesthetic, but not explicit—and I am also pleased to know that true artists do not want to be used or be uncritical members of society, and that they appreciate the critical discourse and the way I collect their work, paying promptly and without asking for discounts, to the way I present their work in exhibits and not through catalogs but through first-class books. But I don't feel like the owner of what I have, rather a kind of patron, a temporary custodian of a legacy who arrived in time to discover them and who has been consistent in his work, without being distracted by the noise and nonsense of the art market'.

J. Tomilson Hill

‘I don’t collect. I look for artworks that challenge me and converse with one another’

Caravaggio, *Judith and Holofernes,* 1607

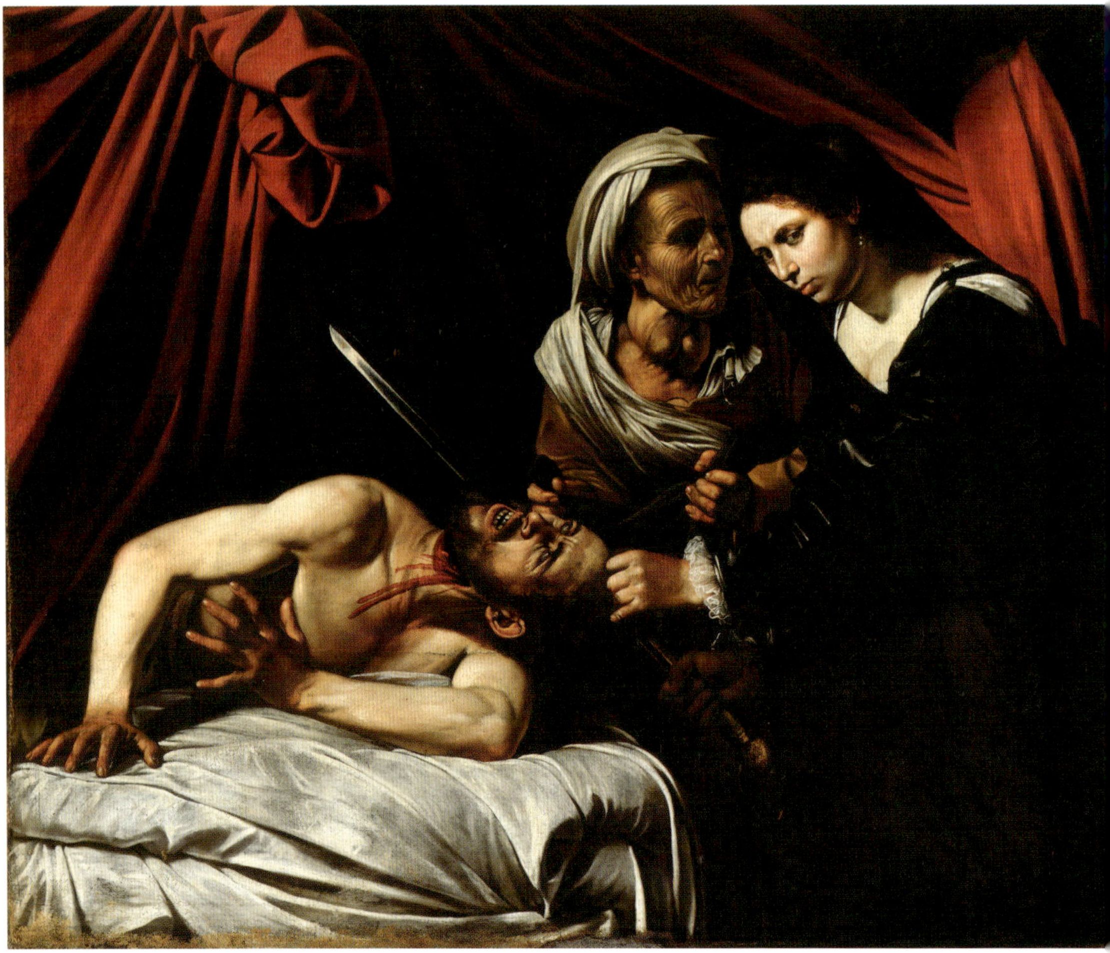

Caravaggio's *Judith and Holofernes*, 1607, an awe-inspiring canvas discovered in 2014 in an attic near the French city of Toulouse, and purchased in 2019 by a mystery buyer shortly before it went up for auction, is in J. Tomilson Hill's spectacular apartment overlooking Central Park and Fifth Avenue in New York. 'I don't confirm or deny the purchase,' explains the homeowner with a mischievous smile in front of one of the most sought-after paintings on the planet.

Hill, a man with an impeccable look and little given to conceding interviews, is one of the largest art collectors in the world, as the visitor to this exclusive place can confirm after a walk through the rooms of the house. He gives his permission to photograph his holdings. Well, almost all. The Caravaggio, that placed him at the center of all kinds of speculation three years ago, after a private sale valued somewhere between 100 and 150 million euros, was left out of the deal. The case, and the secrecy surrounding it, brings to mind the *Ecce Homo* from the same period by the quarrelsome genius from Milan which appeared last year in Madrid at the Ansorena auction house with an opening price of 1,500 euros. In both cases there were also doubts about authenticity.

A hedge fund manager and former vice president of the Blackstone investment company, Hill is a dedicated student of the history of painting, a member of the boards of several major museums and has his own private art gallery, the Hill Art Foundation, opened in Chelsea in 2019.

It is true that his apartment boasts many pieces that any museum would give their eyeteeth for. 'I wanted to buy the *Red Electric Chair*, but my wife, Janine, vetoed it,' he laughingly recalls in front of one of them. 'She said that she did not want our children, who were very young at the time, to have to live with that shocking image. But everything comes around, and once my daughters started in college, as I had agreed with her, I acquired that magnificent work by Andy Warhol, which today dialogues with another of the artist's emblematic works from his *Car Crash* series.'

Warhol is just one of the names on an extraordinary list that takes you by surprise in every corner of the apartment, designed by the influential interior designer Peter Marino, and includes Bacons, Rubens (with a work he painted over a Velázquez portrait of Philip IV's brother), Picassos, Twomblys ... Here, the old masters, more typical of museums than private homes, dialogue fluently with baroque bronzes and with post-war painters.

But Hill assures us during a profound and friendly conversation that he is not guided by the high-sounding names, but rather looks for works carefully selected for their importance in the history of art. And sometimes he does so by following curious rules: 'All my works dialogue with each other and make connections that at first sight do not appear obvious. We collect certain old masters

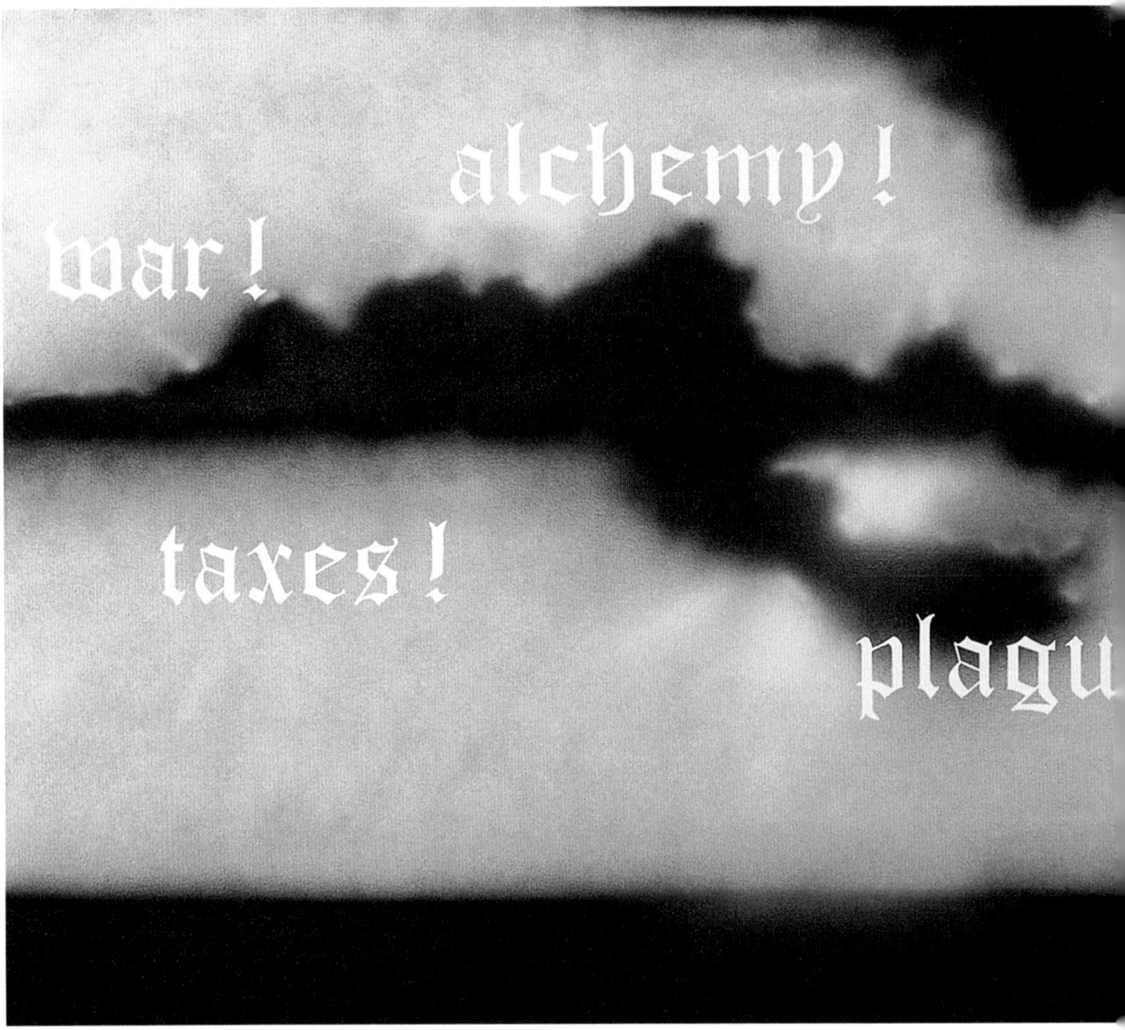

Ed Ruscha, *Seventeenth Century,* 1988

in depth, and we have at least four major works by each one of them. For instance, the wall over there is dedicated exclusively to De Kooning drawings. I should never have sold the Rothko I got rid of in 2007. I was wrong,' he confesses. 'But I did it because I couldn't find another three Rothkos to go with it, which made it impossible for me to comply with my "rule of four," which is fundamental because it strengthens the dialogue within the collection—for example, between abstraction and figuration—and thus avoids the logic by which a person can buy isolated paintings like someone who going to a shopping mall.'

On how he organizes the treasure in his cave of wonders, he explains: 'I have a hard time deciding where each piece goes, but once I decide, it never moves again.'

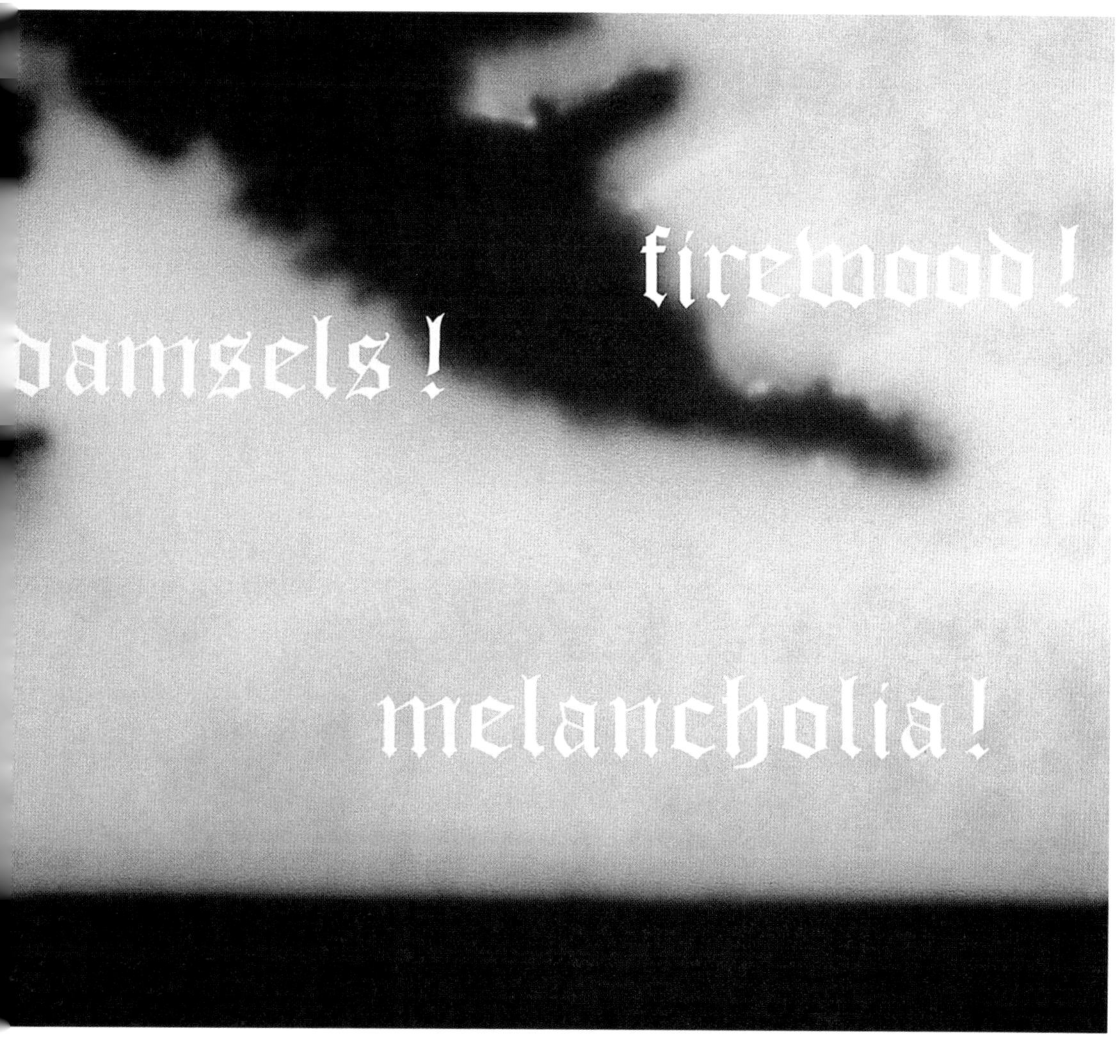

How does he conceive the art of collecting? 'I don't think too much about collecting in a conventional sense. I don't collect. Rather, I look for works of art that challenge me and that can converse with the other pieces I have. This is a vision that I largely owe to my mother, who, despite never having sold a single work, was an artist and worked fluently in painting, drawing, and sculpture in bronze and terracotta. She really loved art, she had a great eye and she took me to visit museums. And thanks to that inspiration, when I had no money, I was still able to acquire objects which I was interested in living with. From London to Saudi Arabia, I have lived surrounded by objects, which have always been an uplifting stimulus; they make me feel better. Because a collection, whether of paintings, stamps or pictures, is a declaration of principles. And for me, that declaration is in each object and in the way that it relates to the ones I collect. There are people who, instead of seeing works with their eyes, see them with their ears, based on what people say, or speculating about their future value. When I buy something I never think about its monetary worth. It doesn't bother me.'

When asked how he started his own collection, he replies: 'It was in the eighties, when I had little money, I collected still lifes, mostly Dutch, from the eighteenth century. I was drawn to them, and I still have them.' Also important in forging his taste was Jim Demetrion, the director who transformed the Hirshhorn Museum in Washington over many decades, and acted as a major influence by introducing him to artists such as De Kooning or Dubuffet.

Among his upcoming projects is, as president of the Guggenheim Board of Trustees, the construction of a new headquarters in Abu Dhabi, whose building he has entrusted to Frank Gehry. He is a privileged eyewitness to the relationship between the public and the private in art. On this issue, he warns: 'Currently it is very difficult for museums to put together competitive collections in a world in which private wellbeing has exploded, and in which the art market had gone through the roof. What is the answer to such an unsettling challenge? I believe it lies in private collectors donating. And another thing is clear to me: when my wife and I are no longer in this world, not only will our best works go to major museums, but our foundation will cease to exist. I believe that art fills a void, makes people interact, unite and feel better about themselves and their community. Some people now complain that museums are crowded, but they forget that in the sixties one used to see works by Pollock or Monet in empty museums. That is why I believe in the lines that underpin the history of art —because without Velázquez there would be no Bacon or Manet; without Manet there would be no Cézanne, and without Duchamp there would be no Warhol. I believe in museums, I believe in my country and I also believe a lot in New York, my city.'

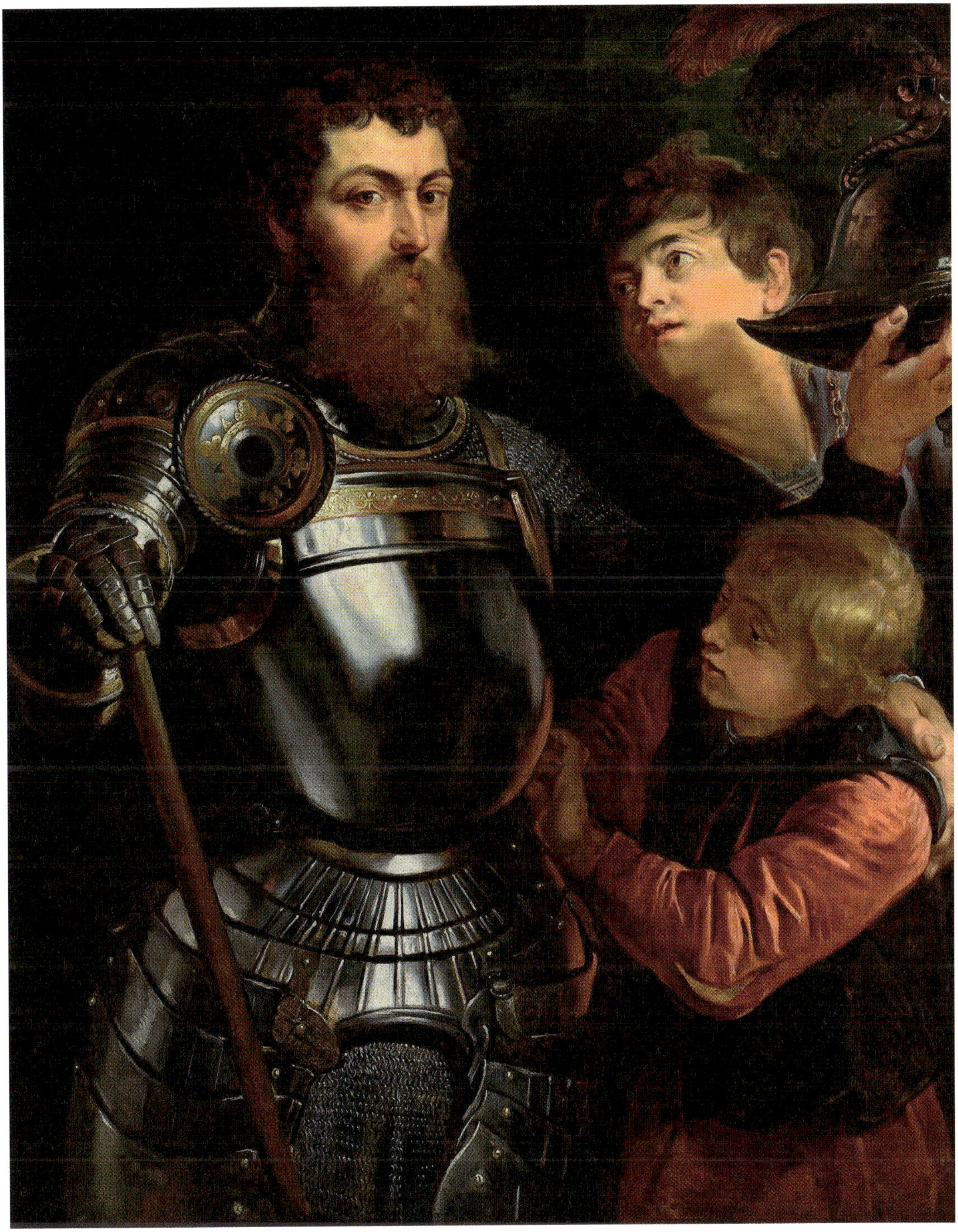

Peter Paul Rubens, *Portrait of a Commander Being Dressed for Battle,* ca. 1610

Han Nefkens

‘Producing a work is much more interesting than buying one already created’

Rinko Kawauchi, *Aila 95*, 2004

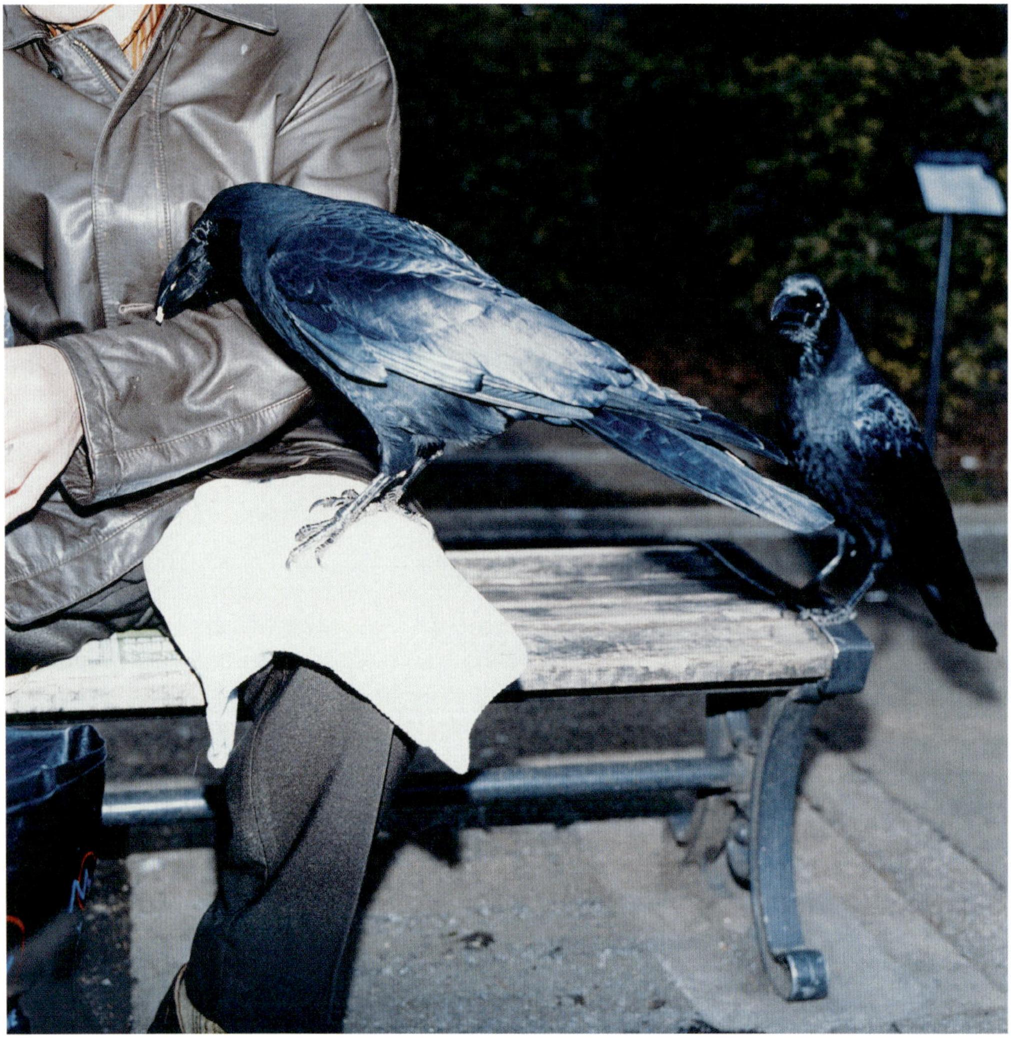

You don't have to spend long in Han Nefkens's company before you start to admire him. Born in Rotterdam in 1954, he studied Communication Sciences in France and the United States, worked for more than a decade as a correspondent in Mexico City, and then focused on writing once he discovered that he was HIV-positive. The most remarkable outcome of that decision was a semi-autobiographical novel about two brothers infected with the virus that wreaked havoc in the late-80s and ealry-90s, and which in one way or another marked the author's life and sensibility. Because Han did not become a collector and patron of contemporary art just because of his magical eye and his intelligence, but also because of his enormous capacity to fight and overcome.

But what led this entrepreneur with a great social conscious to leave the Netherlands? 'For me the country was very small and very gray, which is why I left it when I was 19 years old,' answers this globetrotter with a smile, who has now settled in Barcelona, the city in which he feels comfortable, even in question of scale. In 2001, many years after getting infected, Nefkens, who lived in Barcelona by this time, became seriously ill with a brain infection caused by HIV, which caused him aphasia. Learning to eat, talk, read and walk all over again was one of the biggest challenges in this incredible process, which he recounted in his exceptionally emotive book *This Bird Has Flown: Notes on a Recovered Life*. In it he said: 'What I like about visual art is its absolute ambiguity and confusion. You don't know what you are looking at, or believe that you don't know, which is something completely different.'

Nefkens, who gives signs of an enviable sense of humor during the interview, letting drop serious things with absolutely no inkling of solemnity, bought his first work in 2001, a video installation by Pipilotti Rist. That was the beginning of a collection that now contains more than 500 highly personal pieces, including photographs, videos, installations and paintings, by names such as Jeff Wall, Roni Horn, Bill Viola, Shirin Neshat and Félix González-Torres. Powerful, poetic and ambiguous, just as Nefkens defines them, these pieces speak of his good taste, as well as his sense of risk, although that doesn't prevent the unique, beautiful bright apartment in Barcelona in which he welcomes us from being all white and ordered, including lots of little sculptures from the many Asian countries he has visited.

'If you've heard good things about me they are true, but if they were bad, they are not,' is Han's opening repartee, adding not only a healthy pinch of humor to each word he pronounces, but also a strange sense of calm that impregnates everything.

The creator in the late-2000s of a foundation that bears his name, dedicated equally to social integration and the promotion of art, the collector is impeccable and casually dressed in beige chinos, royal blue shirt and black suede moccasins. He says in perfect Spanish: 'It seems that in any career there is always a strategy with steps to follow but in my case it was not like that. Everything flowed naturally, and I simply went from one thing to another. In 1999 I was in Paris, before I had started to collect, although I loved art and went to museums. And it never occurred to me that I would have a role to play in art. Everything changed during a visit to a Pipilotti Rist exhibition at Musée d'Art Moderne. Works were being screened everywhere, so that the viewer became part of the work, felt the moisture on his skin, smelled the grass, flowed with the music and immersed himself in the creation. I remember it was the month of May and I left saying to myself that I wanted to be part of this world, and I want to share this enriching experience with other people. The idea of collecting to possess works does not interest me. I collect experiences that take on very different forms and I like to share them.'

And he went on to add: 'Of course, this brought with it a challenge, because it is not easy for a private individual to turn such a desire into reality when he still didn't even have one single artwork. But I spoke with some very interesting people who really helped me, like the former director of Centraal Museum in Utrecht, Sjarel Ex, a very open person, especially when you take into account that in Europe, unlike the US, museums receive state funding, and don't like it when people from outside try to interfere in their line of work. So I started to collaborate with Sjarel, and we fed off the differences in each other's aesthetic sensibilities. We went to Art Basel together but in the two hours we spent at the fair, I didn't see a whole lot, because I became completely absorbed by a work by Pipilotti Rist. By pure chance, Sjarel said to me: "Come on, I want to show you a piece I am really interested in." And he took me to the work by Pipilotti. I left the work on deposit in the museum, and that was the beginning of my collecting, always thinking beforehand about a museum space, not a house: I could buy sculptures, installations or series, because they can be shown in a museum. I was delighted when Sjarel was appointed director of the Boijmans Van Beuningen from Rotterdam, my hometown, and so it was easier to continue working together.'

In 2005, they set in motion a project 'that consisted in following different artists for five years, buying not just existing works, but also giving them incentives to produce new ones. In fact, I gave the gift of a work by Olafur Eliasson to the museum, which helped me to decide on a criterion that would be the basis for the collaboration between the museum and myself. With the passing of time, I began to notice that many creators needed financial aid to be able to carry out their work. In this way I realized that producing a work is much more interesting than buying one already created.

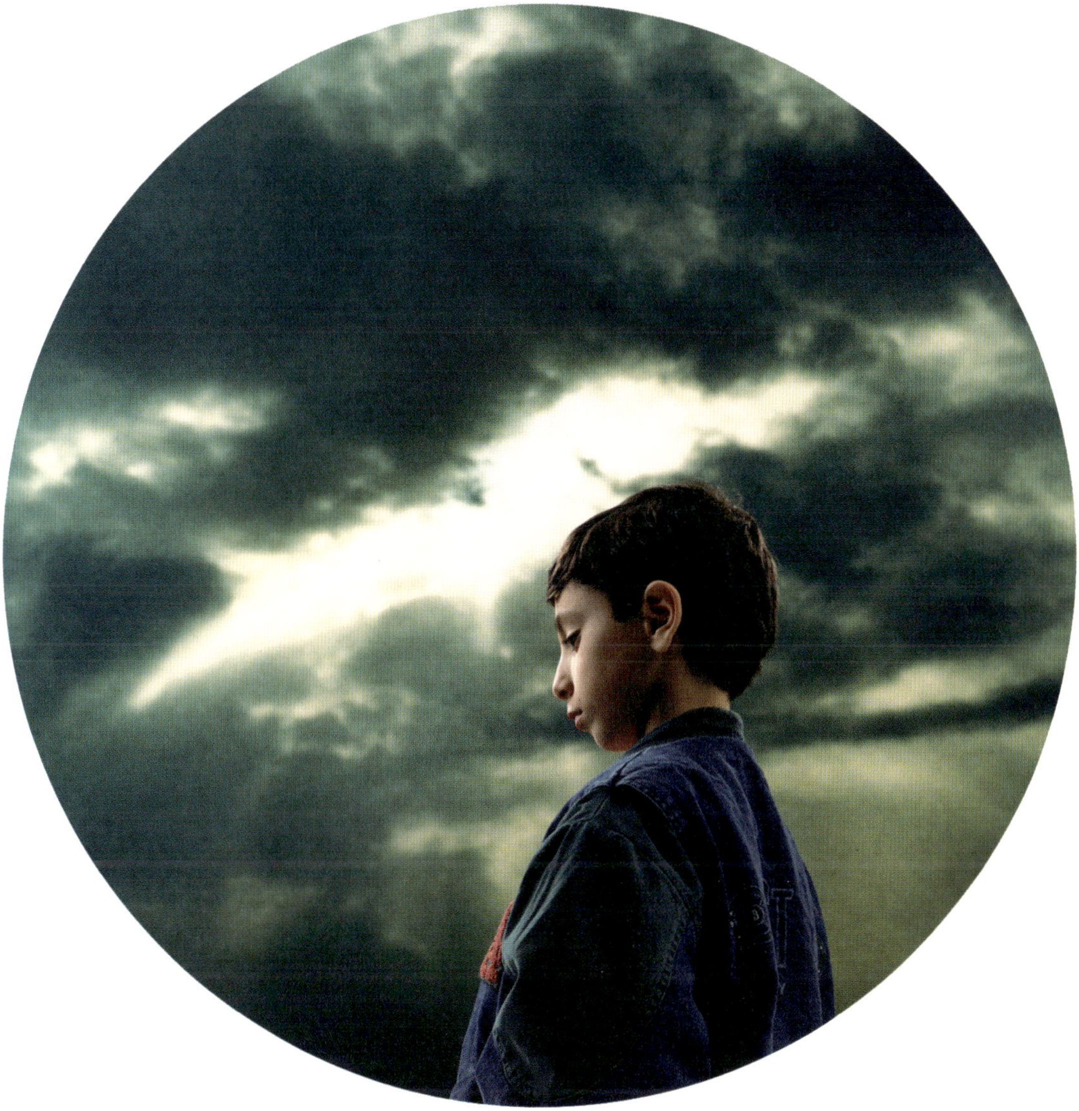

Jeff Wall, *Children*, 1998

Because it is an adventure that you set out on together with the artist, who tells you his doubts and his wishes, because you follow the whole process, because you are transmitting your confidence, and because the result can be surprising,' Nefkens explains.

Besides his active interest in the work of artists, the collaboration with the museum has led to paintings, installations, videos and 'even works related with fashion design, as we have organized major exhibitions of designers like Hussein Chalayan and Wouter van Beirendonck,' some of which have toured to China. Nonetheless, 'there came a moment when I was doing so many things with the foundation, from patronage with museums to health promotion on HIV, that it became difficult to explain, so I started to focus on what was my first love, which was video art. We didn't do it on our own but with other institutions, from Beijing, Dubai, Brussels and Kuala Lumpur to the Antoni Tàpies and Joan Miró foundations in Barcelona, and through scouts specialized in the art world who propose candidates. From the dynamics between them, us and the institutions that participate in the process, an exchange arises, until an agreement is reached in which each one offers generously, thinks of what is in our best joint interest and leaves egos to one side, so that, in the end, the artist is given money and a deadline to create, and then they can exhibit at top-tier institutions.'

There is still one key question to address before we finish: what kind of video art moves him today. 'The common denominator to everything I

Stephen Shore, *Room 115, Holiday Inn, Belle Glade, Florida, 11/14/1977*, 1977

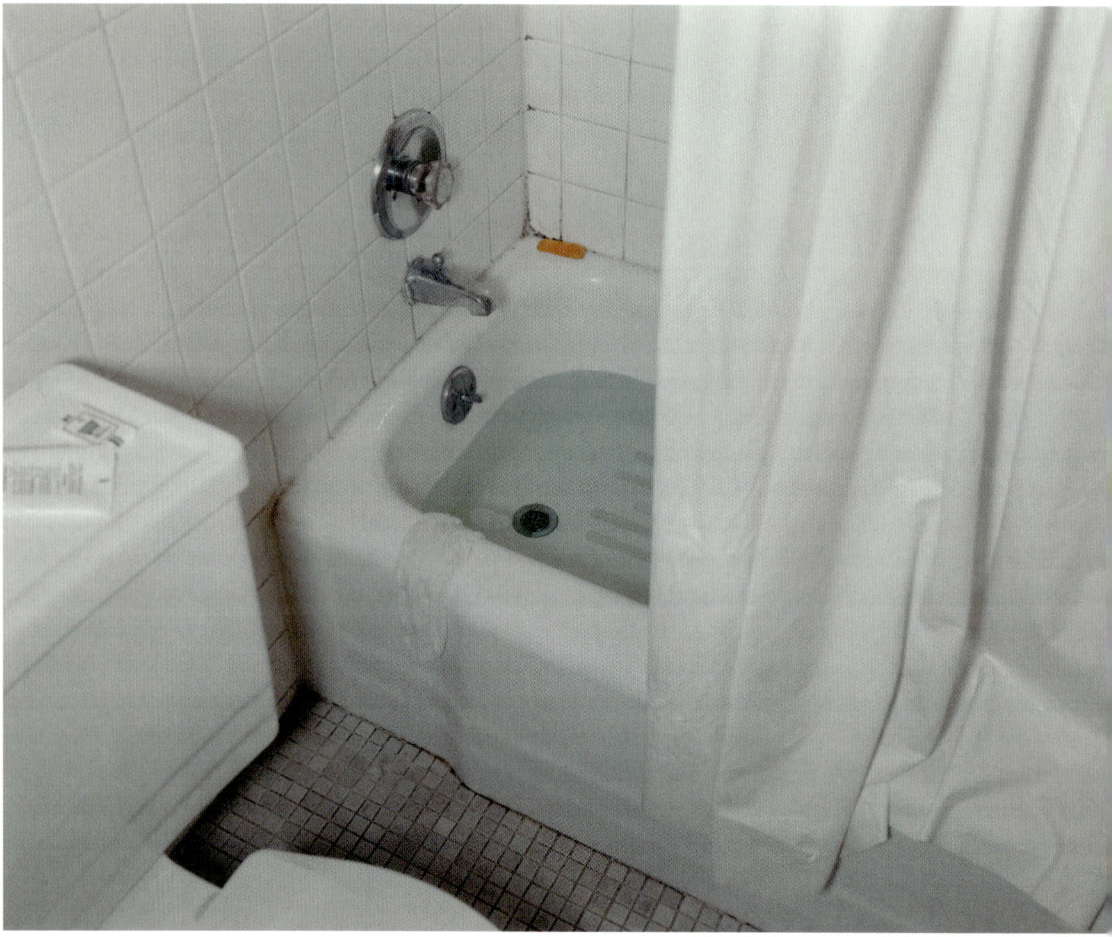

collect, above all to satisfy my more personal taste, is the aesthetic quality or, to put it another way, a certain restrained strength,' he replies, but not before reminding us that all his works belong or will belong in the future to elite museums.

However, the conclusion has to return to what has always been Han's passion, which is writing, now from his own blog. 'I started writing in Dutch but I've been abroad for almost fifty years and my readers are international, so now I write in English, always with autobiographical elements and with some literary license. That's what I do. It is a necessity for me. Because by writing I can explore my thoughts, so to know what I think, I have to write. And even if nobody reads me, I would write for myself, at the same slow pace, once every two weeks,' he says with an enviable peace and purity that recall the commitment to intimate devotion which Jorge Luis Borges famously spoke of.

There is still time for a fitting conclusion: 'When you have read a book that you like, you want your friends to read it and to share the feeling you have had. That's what moves me: connecting with people. Perhaps to compensate for the painful solitude I felt as a child. And if, in addition, I can fulfil an educational mission, then all the better. But the first thing is the need to connect with the world, for which there is no better way than through art. After all, artists precisely want people to see the world the way they see it. I don't want to bandy about the word "love" too lightly, though, at bottom, to come out of yourself and go to meet others is a form of love, especially if we agree with the thought that say the idea behind life, more than being happy, is to be useful.'

And what will the future of the foundation be like when he is no longer with us. 'Given the high degree of personal involvement that I have, although there will be money to continue with the task for ten to fifteen years, I think that it wouldn't be possible for any longer. In the meantime, I do this, among other things, because it gives me a lot of pleasure. The life of a writer is a very solitary one. And on the other hand, my life in particular, as well as the problems I have faced, has helped me to relativize the value of things and to revalue helping others. Because, apart from that, knowing that I have always been different has helped me to act in a different way than usual'.

These words should come as no surprise from a man who has made unpublicized charity his creed, who has said that 'giving is one of the most undervalued acts in society,' and who shrouds his every word with a halo of calm wisdom.

Biographies

Alain Dominique Perrin

The majority of the professional career of the businessman and collector Alain Dominique Perrin (Nantes, 1942) has been linked to Cartier. In the mid-1970s he led the rebirth and internationalization of the iconic French firm and in 1984 he created Fondation Cartier pour l'art contemporain, a pioneering institution and model for cultural patronage that has been replicated by the world's biggest luxury conglomerates.

Rosa de la Cruz

Cuban by birth, the collector Rosa de la Cruz is one of the driving forces behind the revitalization of Miami's art scene. In the 1980s, together with her husband, the businessman Carlos de la Cruz, she began to build a remarkable collection of contemporary art. Since 2009, the De la Cruz Collection, an independent non-profit cultural and educational institution, has its own museum.

Helga de Alvear

Helga de Alvear (Kirn, 1936) arrived in Spain in 1957 to learn the language. However, she ended up by staying, creating a family and became a pioneering gallery and collector in her adoptive country. After years working with Juana Mordó, in 1995 she opened her own gallery. Since 2006, her collection has its own contemporary art museum in the city of Caceres run by Fundación Helga de Alvear.

Aaron and Barbara Levine

Aaron and Barbara Levine shared their lives and their passion for art throughout 64 years of marriage. Born in Brooklyn, they settled in Washington DC where Aaron, who passed away in January 2023 at the age of eighty-eight, studied law and founded a successful law firm. Their passion for conceptual art led them to Duchamp, and they went on to possess one of the world's most important private collections of his works.

Thomas Kaplan

After making his fortune in the field of precious metals, Thomas Scott Kaplan (New York, 1961) discovered a passion for collecting after the age of forty. In 2003 he and his wife, Daphne Recanati, acquired the first piece of the present-day Leiden Collection, one of the biggest private collections of Dutch masters and the first in the world in the number of works by Rembrandt.

Giorgio Spanu

Born in Sardinia in 1954, Giorgio Spanu moved to the USA in the 1980s. There he met his wife, Nancy Olnick, and together they prospered and developed a shared passion for the most diverse forms of beauty, from Pop Art to Murano crystal. On one of their travels to Italy they discovered *Arte Povera* and began to put together a magnificent collection which they currently exhibit in their own museum, Magazzino Italian Art, in New York.

Jan Mulder

Born to a Swiss father and a Greek mother, Jan Mulder (Lima, 1949) was destined to follow in his family's pharmaceutical business—as was eventually the case to some extent—but photography introduced an unexpected twist in his path. He studied Photojournalism in Boston and exercised professionally for some time until devoting himself to business. He ended up by becoming a major collector, specializing in Peruvian photography, and a promoter of the arts in his home country.

Sheikha Al Mayassa

Since 2006, when she was appointed to the chair of Qatar Museums by her father, Sheikha Al Mayassa (Doha, 1983) has created an extraordinary cultural ecosystem in the small Persian Gulf emirate. Her acumen, coupled with the huge funds at her disposal, has turned the sister of the current Emir Al Thani into one of the most powerful women in the art world.

Luiz Augusto Teixeira de Freitas

Founding partner of one of Portugal's most important law firms, Luiz Augusto Teixeira de Freitas (São Paulo, 1962) has juggled his professional activity with his facet as a highly committed collector. Contemporary creation, emerging art and artists' books are the main lines of a collection that contains over three thousand works. Teixeira de Freitas is a board member of Fundación Museo Reina Sofía.

Jarl Mohn

An investor, businessman and media executive, Jarl Mohn (1951) relaunched MTV in the mid-to-late 1980s. More recently he injected new life into NPR, the US public radio. He currently dedicates his time to philanthropy and art, with commitments to many institutions and museums. He sponsors an important award for new artists granted through the Hammer Museum, affiliated with University of California.

Mitchell Rales and Emily Wei Rales

Mitchell Rales (Pittsburgh, 1956), co-founder of the powerful Danaher group together with his brother Steven, is one of the wealthiest individuals in the Washington area. But he also has a strong connection with the art world as a collector and philanthropist. In 2006 he opened Glenstone, an admission-free museum he set up together with his wife Emily Wei Rales to house their collection. He is also President of the National Gallery of Art.

Lekha Poddar

Lekha Poddar is a businesswoman and philanthropist who lives between London and New Delhi. In the 1970s she began to collect Indian modern and folk art. Thirty years later, her son Anupam, more interested in the production of artists from his generation, began his own collection. The joint result of their collecting activity, heedless of passing trends, is the Devi Art Foundation, which, with over seven thousand items, is one of the most important private art collections in India.

Susana Lloret

With a degree in Education and a PhD in Psychology, Susana Lloret gave up a university post in 2014 to devote herself exclusively to running Fundació Per Amor a l'Art. This private organization dedicated to art, research and social work, manages the collection of Lloret and her husband, José Luis Soler, and the Bombas Gens art center in Valencia, where it opened in 2017.

Don and Mera Rubell

With the scant funds of a young newly married couple, the New Yorkers Don and Mera Rubell began to collect in the 1960s. Making the best out of their situation, they started to acquire works by young emerging artists. Nearly six decades later, they now treasure one of the best private collections in the world, with their own museum in Miami and a campus in Washington opened in 2022.

Elena Rueda, Marcos and Rafael Martín

Marcos Martín Blanco (1929-2022) and Elena Rueda (1938) began, as a married couple, to collect artworks in the late-1970s under the guidance of the painter Gerardo Rueda. What started merely as purchases to decorate their new house in Segovia soon turned into a passion for collecting. The MER Collection, run by their son Rafael Martín, currently boasts more than eight hundred works by Spanish and international contemporary artists.

Eugenio López Alonso

Sole heir to Jumex, the major Mexican juice and nectar brand, Eugenio López Alonso (1967) has been instrumental in promoting greater knowledge of art practice and collecting in Mexico for three decades, through a variety of programs, grants and educational initiatives. In 2001 he created Fundación Jumex Arte Contemporáneo, custodian of the Jumex Collection, one of the most important holdings of art in the whole of Latin America, and responsible for Museo Jumex, opened in Mexico City in 2013.

José Darío Gutiérrez

Born in Medellín, in the department of Antioquia, José Darío Gutiérrez has lived in Bogotá since the age of thirteen. He studied law and was involved in a wide range of businesses before deciding to devote himself exclusively to the art world. Apart from a collector of Colombian modern and contemporary art, he is the promoter of the Bachué Project and of the Espacio El Dorado gallery, two initiatives conceived to instil new vitality into Colombia's art scene.

Ernesto Poma

Born in El Salvador into one of Central America's most important business dynasties, since the age of seventeen Ernesto Poma has lived in Miami. There he combines his business activities with collecting Latin-American art. Poma and his wife Cecilia are members of the Latin-American and Caribbean Fund at MoMA and of Art Basel's Global Patrons Council, which includes the world's leading private collectors.

Jonathan Ruffer

With a background in investment management, Jonathan Ruffer (London, 1951) dedicates a substantial part of his energy and resources to his philanthropic activity. It is estimated that he has invested a third of his fortune in revitalizing County Durham and the restoration of Auckland Castle, which now houses his extraordinary collection of Spanish art and the complete series of *Jacob and his Twelve Sons* by Zurbarán.

Dakis Joannou

The successful Greek-Cypriot industrialist Dakis Joannou (Nicosia, 1939) is internationally known for his activity as a bold and unconventional contemporary art collector. In 1983 he created the Deste Foundation, with exhibition venues in Athens and in the island of Hydra. Joannou has sat on the boards and councils of some of the world's most important museums.

Lia Rumma

The Italian collector Lia Rumma began collecting in the 1960s jointly with her husband, Marcello, who, among other exhibitions, organized the first *arte povera* show in 1968. One year after Marcello's early death in 1970, Lia Rumma founded the gallery that bears her name in Naples and where, for over fifty years, she has been a decisive force behind the careers of many consecrated Italian and international artists.

Juan Carlos Maldonado

Juan Carlos Maldonado is a Venezuelan businessman connected to banking and insurance. In 2005 he began to gather a collection that is defined by his passion for Latin-American geometric abstraction. In 2016 he set up the Juan Carlos Maldonado Art Collection (JCMAC) in Miami, with a strong educational leaning and a long-term project that includes exhibitions, publications and grants.

Anita Zabludowicz

Born in Newcastle in 1960, Anita Zabludowicz, together with her husband, the Finnish-born businessman Poju Zabludowicz, has put together a major art collection, centered, since the mid-1990s, on more experimental art. In 2007 they opened a center for the collection in a former Methodist church in north London, where they show selections of their holdings, organize exhibitions and develop a program to support emerging artists.

Eddie and Sylvia Brown

The philanthropy of an anonymous benefactor made it possible for Eddie Brown (Apopka, Florida, 1940) to study Electrical Engineering at the Howard University, where he met his wife Sylvia and laid the foundations of a successful career in the financial sector. This background is behind the Browns' commitment with countless social and educational projects in Baltimore, where they have been living for fifty years, through a foundation which is also the custodian of their extraordinary collection of Afro-American art.

Estrellita Brodsky

The art historian, curator and collector Estrellita Brodsky has played a key role in the promotion and popularization of Latin-American art in the USA and the rest of the world. She has done so through her initiatives and specific spaces in museums like the MoMA or Tate Modern. Together with her husband, Daniel Brodsky, she created Another Space, the headquarters of her collection in New York, and a program for the support and study of Latin-American art.

Armando Martins

Armando Martins (Penamacor, Castelo Branco, 1949), an entrepreneur dedicated to the real estate and hotel business, arrived in Lisbon as a teen-ager. He began to collect contemporary Portuguese graphic works and paintings at the early age of twenty-four. He is currently the owner of a collection of around five hundred works, with a significant representation of international artists, which he plans to exhibit at the Museu de Arte Contemporânea Armando Martins, due to open soon in Lisbon.

Alain Servais

Coming from the financial sector, Alain Servais (Belgium, 1963) began to collect art in the late-1990s, with a focus which is more intellectual than aesthetic, and one which he has further honed with the passing of the years. Interested in installation and in digital art, Servais occasionally shows his collection in his Brussels loft, a former factory located in Schaerbeek that also hosts a program of art residencies.

Javier Lumbreras

An investor, property developer and fund manager, Javier Lumbreras (Ávila, 1964) lives between United States and Spain. For ten years now, he has been working on the development of Collegium, a space for the creation, research and exhibition of contemporary art in a former Jesuit college that will also house the Adrastus collection, put together by Lumbreras and his wife Lorena Pérez-Jácome.

Martin Z. Margulies

This New Yorker, now based in Florida, where he made his fortune as a property developer, has been acquiring world-class artworks for more than fifty years. His collection is now one of the most important in the US and, since 1999, has its own headquarters, The Margulies Collection at the Warehouse, open to the public in the Miami neighborhood of Wynwood.

Grazyna Kulczyk

A successful entrepreneur and for decades the wife of the Polish tycoon Jan Kulczyk, Grazyna Kulczyk (Poznan, 1950) is one of Europe's most important collectors and patrons. She sits on the boards of institutions like MoMA and Tate Modern. Since 2019, the Muzeum Susch, in Switzerland, houses her collection specialized in conceptual and women's art, and organizes temporary exhibitions and artist's residencies.

Rafael Tous

A successful textile industrialist, Rafael Tous (Barcelona, 1940) has been collecting art since his youth. However, it was in the 1970s when his close relationship with artists from his generation led him to focus on contemporary art. In addition, between 1980 and 2006 he ran Sala Metrònom, a space of freedom and experimentation for artists working in all disciplines. In 2020 he donated his collection of conceptual art to MACBA.

Harald Falckenberg

Born in Hamburg in 1943, Harald Falckenberg is a businessman who also has a PhD in law. Although he entered in the art world later in life, he is currently one of Europe's most influential collectors, apart from a lecturer and essayist in Art Theory. Since 2011 his contemporary art collection is on exhibit at Deichtorhallen Hamburg, an art center in his hometown.

J. Tomilson Hill

James Tomilson Hill (New York, 1948) is one of the big names in Wall Street, where he has a long track record at firms like Lehman Brothers and Blackstone. However, he stands out from his peers in finance for his collection of artworks from all periods. Besides, in 2019 he opened the headquarters of the Hill Art Foundation, a non-profit institution devoted to education and patronage, in Chelsea, New York.

Han Nefkens

Born in Rotterdam in 1954, Han Nefkens studied journalism in France and the USA and worked as a correspondent in Mexico for over ten years. After being diagnosed with HIV, he dedicated himself to writing. In 2001 Nefkens began his art collection, centered on video-installation. The Han Nefkens Foundation, located in Barcelona, promotes art creation in collaboration with art fairs and institutions from all over the world.

Acknowledgments

To Mirella Levinas (Pelu), my editor and translator, the inspiration for my words and my life. Without her this book would not exist. I owe everything to her.

To my children Mariana, Diego and Pablo for believing in me.

To my siblings, Gaby and Salo, for not letting me forget who I am and where I come from.

To my childhood friends, Manuel Reich and Miguel Dictar, for always being so close despite living so far away.

To Pablo Cohen for helping me turning sounds into words.

To Joelle Levinas for her assistance with the translations and the logistics in organizing my conversations with the collectors.

To Moisés Naím for acting as my intellectual guide.

To Miguel Albero, Javier Monzón, Iker Seisdedos, José Manuel Calvo Roy and Manuel Borja-Villel for their expert advice and constant encouragement.

To Susana Naím for listening to my dreams.

And, finally, to the editor of this book, César Martínez-Useros, for putting my thoughts in order.

I am eternally grateful to them all,

Dani Levinas

Photo credits

p. 8 © RMN-Grand Palais / Daniel Boudinet. © Ministère de la Culture - Médiathèque du patrimoine et de la photographie, Dist. RMN-Grand Palais / Daniel Boudinet.

p. 11 © Guillermo Kuitca. Courtesy the artist and Hauser & Wirth.

p. 12 © The Estate of Ana Mendienta Collection, LLC, licensed by VEGAP, Madrid, 2023. Courtesy of the De la Cruz Collection and Galerie Lelong & Co.

p. 15 © Rob Pruitt. Courtesy of the De la Cruz Collection.

p. 16 © Rachel Whiteread / Photo: Mike Bruce. Courtesy of the Museo de Arte Contemporáneo Helga de Alvear, Cáceres, Spain.

p. 18 © Comissió Tàpies, VEGAP, Madrid, 2023 / Photo: Joaquín Cortés. Courtesy of the Museo de Arte Contemporáneo Helga de Alvear, Cáceres, Spain.

p. 20 © Juan Muñoz Estate, VEGAP, Madrid, 2023.

pp. 22-23 © Association Marcel Duchamp / ADAGP, Paris, 2023 / Photo: Joaquín Cortés.

p. 24 © Bruce Nauman, VEGAP, Madrid, 2023.

p. 32 © Michelangelo Pistoletto. Courtesy of Magazzino Italian Art.

p. 34 © Giulio Paolini. Courtesy of Magazzino Italian Art.

p. 35 © Alighiero Boetti, VEGAP, Madrid, 2023.

p. 36 © Javier Silva.

p. 39 © Edi Hirose.

p. 40 © Richard Serra, VEGAP, Madrid, 2023.

p. 42 © 1998 Kate Rothko Prizel and Christopher Rothko / VEGAP / Madrid, 2023.

p. 44 © Carlos Garaicoa Manso, VEGAP, Madrid, 2023 / Photo: Radilson Carlos Gomes y Luiz Roberto Moreira. Courtesy of Galería Elba Benítez, Madrid.

p. 46 © Damián Ortega.

p. 48 © Larry Clark. Courtesy of the artist and Luhring Augustine, New York. Courtesy of the International Center of Photography, Gift of Tom Wright, 1991 (400.1991).

p. 51 © John McCracken / Photo: Florian Folzherr, Jarl Mohn and Joshua White / JWPictures.com. Courtesy of Jarl Mohn.

p. 52 © The Easton Foundation / Authorized by VEGAP, Madrid, 2023.

p. 54 © Jasper Johns, VEGAP, Madrid, 2023.

p. 56 © Bharti Kher. Courtesy of Perrotin, Hauser & Wirth and Nature Morte.

p. 58 © André Kertész.

p. 61 © Aaron Siskind Foundation, New York. Courtesy of Bombas Gens Centre d'Art, Valencia.

p. 62 © 2022 Julian Schnabel / ARS, New York / VEGAP. Courtesy of Rubell Museum, Miami.

pp. 64-65 © The Estate of Jean-Michel Basquiat, VEGAP, Madrid, 2023. Courtesy of Rubell Museum, Miami.

p. 67 © The Keith Haring Foundation, 2023. Courtesy of Rubell Museum, Miami.

p. 68 © Eric Fischl, VEGAP, Madrid, 2023 / Photo: Eduardo Domenech Serrano.

p. 71 © Marilyn Minter. Coutesy of Andréhn Schiptjenko Gallery.

p. 72 © Gabriel Orozco. Courtesy of the artist and Marian Goodman Gallery, New York.

pp. 74-75 © Alighiero Boetti, VEGAP, Madrid, 2023. Courtesy of Colección Jumex, Mexico.

p. 76 © Meg Cranston. Courtesy of Colección Jumex, Mexico.

p. 78 © Antonio Caro.

p. 81 © Alejandro Obregón.

p. 82 © Fernando Pareja & Leidy Chavez. Courtesy of the artists.

p. 84 © Belkis Ayón. Courtesy of Belkis Ayón Estate & David Castillo.

p. 92 © Jakub Julian Ziolkowski.

p. 95 © Jeff Koons.

p. 96 © Michelangelo Pistoletto.

p. 98 © Mario Merz, VEGAP, Madrid, 2023 / Photo: Kevin Todora. Courtesy of Cardi Gallery.

p. 100 © Tomás Maldonado / Photo: Mariano Costa Peuser. Courtesy of Juan Carlos Maldonado Art Collection, Miami.

p. 103 © Ernesto Briel. Courtesy of Juan Carlos Maldonado Art Collection, Miami.

p. 104 © Gillian Wearing, VEGAP, Madrid, 2023. Courtesy of Maureen Paley, London.

p. 106 © Donna Huanca and Zabludowicz Collection / Photo: Thierry Bal.

p. 108 © Martin Puryear.

p. 111 © Alma Thomas, VEGAP, Madrid, 2023.

p. 112 © The Estate of Sarah Grilo. Courtesy of Estrellita B. Brodsky Collection, New York.

p. 114 © Gego (Gertrud Goldschmidt).

p. 116 © Vik Muniz, VEGAP, Madrid, 2023. Courtesy of Galería Elba Benítez, Madrid.

p. 118-119 © Thomas Struth.

p. 122 © Nan Goldin. Courtesy of the artist and Marian Goodman Gallery.

p. 125 © Nan Goldin. Courtesy of the artist and Marian Goodman Gallery.

p. 126 © Pierre Huyghe, VEGAP, Madrid, 2023.

p. 129 © Collegium / Colección Adrastus / Photo: Omar Luis Olguín, 2016.

p. 130 © Anselm Kiefer.

pp. 132-133 © Bertozzi & Casoni.

p. 134 © Succesió Miró, 2022.

p. 136 © Zofia Kulik. Courtesy of Parsons Projects.

p. 138 © Edward Krasiński.

p. 140 © Eva Lootz, VEGAP, Madrid, 2023.

p. 143 © Jordi Cerdà.

p. 144 © Martin Kippenberger / Photo: Egbert Haneke © Falckenberg Collection.

p. 146 © Paul Thek / Photo: John D. Schiff. Courtesy of the Estate of George Paul Thek and Leo Baeck Institute, New York.

p. 148 © Bill Beckley / Falckenberg Collection / Photo: Egbert Haneke.

pp. 152-153 © Ed Ruscha. Courtesy of the artist and Gagosian.

p. 156 © Rinko Kawauchi. Courtesy of Han Nefkens H+F Collection.

p. 159 © Jeff Wall. Courtesy of the artist.

p. 160 © Stephen Shore. Courtesy of Han Nefkens H+F Collection.

Author
Dani Levinas

Publisher
La Fábrica

Graphic Design
underbau

Graphic Editing
Estudio Larsen

Translations
Mirella Levinas
Lambe&Nieto

Production
Adriana Rodríguez

Pre-press
La Troupe

Printing
Macro Libros

The typeface used in this book is SangBleu Republic and it has been printed on 135-gram Magno Volume paper.

ISBN
978-84-18934-64-3

Legal Deposit
M-359-2023

Printed in Spain

LA FABRICA

President
Alberto Anaut

Publishing Director
César Martínez-Useros

Editorial Content Manager
Camino Brasa

Distribution Manager
Raúl Muñoz

La Fábrica
Verónica, 13
28014 Madrid
Tel. +34 91 360 13 20
edicion@lafabrica.com
www.lafabrica.com

The interviews in this book were originally published by the *El País* newspaper